JN323905

人物書誌大系 39

シュンペーター

米川紀生編

日外アソシエーツ

●制作担当●比良　雅治

ボン大学を去る前のシュンペーター
（1932年6月20日）

東畑夫人とシュンペーター
（1929 年頃）（東畑記念館所蔵）

鎌倉大仏前のシュンペーター
荒木夫妻・東畑と大仏前にて
（1931 年 1 月）（東畑記念館所蔵）

兼松講堂前のシュンペーター
（1931 年 1 月 28 日）（東畑記念館所蔵）

安田講堂前のシュンペーター
（1931 年 1 月 30 日）（東畑記念館所蔵）

まえがき

早熟の天才として知られたシュンペーター（1883年2月8日―1950年1月8日）は、経済学においてエレガントな所謂「シュンペーター体系」をうちたてた。だが、彼は「シュンペーター学派」を形成しはしなかった。何故か。にもかかわらず、多くの「シュンペーターリアン」を生み出した。何故か。こうした二つの疑問が成り立つ秘密は、どこにあるのか。その上、こうした設問自体が逆説的ですらある。彼の体系は、そもそも如何にして可能であり、体系形成にあたり如何なる生みの苦しみがあったのか、どのような体系内容なのであるのか。その解答は、他ならぬ人間シュンペーターその人にある。

1883年2月の木曜日のモラヴィアで生を得たこの天才は、わずか1歳の時に弟の死産に、そして3歳で父の死といううち続く悲惨の上に、いや増した母ヨハンナからの愛をひとり身に受けて成長した。青年にありがちな若気のいたりとも言うべき、時に女性との夜遊びに見られる、スキャンダラスな行動に対する母からの苦言を一つの例外として、彼は魅惑的な母の期待によく応えた。いや彼は生涯、母との愛の中に生き続けたと言っても過言ではないだろう。外面的には、貴族の出身でないことからくる似而非貴族的ともいえる立ち振るまい社交性、一見華やかな人的交流の中にあっても、彼は心奥では信頼し話し合える親友で心からの真友を、この母以外には見い出し得なかった。その結果、かつて私が叙述したごとく、彼は物事を否定的・逆説的に把握し、表現し、解釈する方法態度を身につけていった。「神聖なる二十代」ばかりか彼の全生涯は、この方法態度に規定された。多面的で逆説的な人間シュンペーターの生誕である。

このパラドクシカルな人間シュンペーターが、偶然にもはるか77年前にアメリカからボンへの帰国途中にわが国を初めて訪れ、日本で世界の経済学の現状と将来について、刺激的で勢力的な講述をしていった。そこでの経済学に対する彼の示唆は、その後のわが国の経済学の発展にどのように生かされてきたか、わが国でも「シュンペーター学派」は形成されなかった。が、少なからざる「シュンペーターリアン」は存在する。ところが、不思議なことに、このシュンペーターについてわが国で如何ように問題とされてきたのか、彼の体系がどのように受容されたかについて詳しい文献が不足している。第二次大戦後のわが国の経済政策の展開にあたって、ようやくケインズ経済学の有効性が疑問視され、あらためてわが国経済学の方向性が問われた。世界の経済学が、「シュンペーター・ルネッサンス」を迎えた時期と照応して、人間シュンペーターのヴェールにつつまれた厖大な手書き草稿類（速記を含む）も発見され解読された。

この期にいたり、過去60余年にわたるわが国でのシュンペーター体系の受容と理解をふり返り、今後のシュンペーター研究に資すべく、あわせてアイロニカルでパラドクシカルなシュンペーターの全体像にせまるために、わが国におけるシュンペーター関係文献目録を公表する。

2008年6月14日

米川 紀生

目　次

凡　例

Ⅰ．概　要

1．構　成

本書は、著作目録（洋書）、参考文献目録（和書）、付録、索引から成る。解説は、原則として付さない。

2．収録内容

著作目録は、著書・パンフレット、論文、書評、報告・報告書、講義、講演・演説、新聞記事、尋問、インタヴュー、政治的文書、書簡、アフォリズム、小説、自筆原稿を発表年月日順に通し番号を付してある。

参考文献目録は、著作の邦訳、論文・講演、関連著書・論文・書評・回想を発表年月日順に通し番号を付してある。日(週)刊紙、大学新聞、事典、卒論、博士論文等は省略する。

付録は、日本におけるシュンペーターの活動を、写真、記事、講演録で時系列的にたどる。

3．収録期間

著作目録は、アレン、スウェドベリー、アウゲロ、ヘドケの労作を参照して2007年までに発表された文献を収録した。

参考文献目録は、シュンペーター生誕110年の1993年末までを収録した。

Ⅱ．文献記載形式・排列

著作目録、参考文献目録とも

単行本は、書名、発行所、出版社名、出版年月日、刷数、頁数を記す。

論文・記事は、題名、誌(紙)名、巻号、発行年月日、頁数を記す。

I　著　作　目　録

I　著作目録

シュンペーター著作目録

シュンペーターは, 歴史を重視し, 深い歴史的知識と歴史的経験から過去をふり返ったが, 回想に耽って自らの来歴を詳しく語ることはなかった。 大学の講義で自説の典拠を明示したり, 内外での各種の講演で無謬の法王として君臨しふるまうこともなかった。それは, 彼が学派を形成しなかったからである。

彼は, 「群れを作る」のは「メダカの学校」のように魚であって, 科学には教義や学説があっても「スクール(学派)」が存在すべきでないと考えた。シュンペーターの体系は, 学派とはなじまない。彼には, ケインジアンがケインズ主義を唱えて行動するがごときことはなかった。ボン大学を去るに際しての感動的な訣別講演(1932年6月20日)でシュンペーターは, 「私に一つの役割があるとすれば, ドアを閉じることではなく, ドアを開けることであって, シュンペーターシューレ〔シュンペーター学派〕を実現させようとは決してしてこなかった」と学生達に語りかけた。従って彼の周りには, シュンペーターリアンとシュンペーターファンがいるのみであった。こうしたことのために彼の多面的な科学的仕事は, 統一的に記録に留められてこなかった。

彼の業績の簡単な内容は, ボン大学のシュンペーターお気に入りの女学徒で強制収容所で殺害されたCläre Tischによって, ようやくタイプ打ちされた(1)。その後, ウィーンに始まりボンを経てアメリカ時代の18年程の彼の全事蹟が, 彼の死後半年ばかりしてシュンペーターの俗事を世話した夫人エリザベスにより, 彼の遺稿類の整理中に公表された(2)。更にそれを補完し, 注釈付きのシュンペーター関連文献を含んだ本格的な著作目録が, オマハのネブラスカ大学のスティーブンソンによって編纂された(3)。わが国では既に第二次世界大戦前にシュンペーター学徒の中山伊知郎と東畑精一により, 恩師の著作目録や関連文献がシュンペーター著作の邦訳書に添えられた(4)。その後1970年代始めに佐瀬昌盛は、クレメンスやシュナイダーの文献を利用してシュンペーターの主要著作一覧をシュンペーターの三労作の邦訳書に付した(5)。マルクス没後100年, ケインズ・シュンペーター生誕100年が祝われた前後に金指基は, それらを補充し増補したシュンペーター著作目録を作成した(6)。これらを参考にしてアウゲロが, ついに世界のシュンペーター文献を網羅した詳しいシュンペーター文献目録を完成させた(7)。

それ以後にもシュンペーターの政治文書, アフォリズム, 書簡, 手書き草稿が, 相次いで発掘された(8)。ここでは, 以上の諸文献やアウゲロの目録やヘドケの一連の労作を参照して, シュンペーターの活動を資料的にたどる。日本語文献は後掲する。

なお, 著者としてのシュンペーターの筆名について。彼の本名は, Joseph Aloisius(短縮Alois) Julius Schumpeterである。彼は, 最初の論文をJosef Schumpeterとして書き, はじめてのイギリス滞在中やエジプトの生活ではJoseph Schumpeterと英語のスペルを使用し, 以後それを踏襲している。その他にSch. , Schumpeter, Joseph Alois Schumpeter, J. A. Schumpeter, Joseph A. Schumpeterと記しているが, 本目録では全て省略した。

注

(1) Verzeichnis der Schriften und Rezension von Joseph Schumpeter. Bonn, 1933. 26S.

(2) Elizabeth B. Schumpeter, Bibliography of the Writings of Joseph A. Schumpeter. *The Quarterly Journal of Economics,* Vol. LXIV, No. 3, August 1950. pp.373-384.

(3) Michael I. Stevenson, Joseph Alois Schumpeter. A Bibliography, 1905-1984. Westport, Greenwood Press, 1985. xv+137p.

(4) シュムペーター, 中山伊知郎, 東畑精一共訳『経済発展の理論』岩波書店, 1937年7月20日第1刷.pp.695-706. シュムペーター, 中山伊知郎, 東畑精一共訳『資本主義・社会主義・民主主義 第三版』下巻, 東洋経済新報社, 1952年12月15日.pp.1-22.

(5) 玉野井芳郎・監修『シュンペーター　社会科学の過去と未来』ダイヤモンド社, 1972年3月16日初版.pp.510-519.

(6) 金指基「シュンペーターの著作目録(資料)」「商学集志」第45巻第3号, 1976年1月30日.pp.83-100.『J・A・シュンペーターの経済学』新評論, 1979年5月10日初版第1刷.pp.247-264.『別冊 経済セミナー　シュンペーター再発見』日本評論社, 1983年7月30日.pp.180-189. シュンペーター『景気循環分析への歴史的接近』金指基編訳, 八朔社, 1991年4月10日第1刷.pp.189-212.

(7) Massimo M. Augello, Joseph Alois Schumpeter. A Reference Guide. Berlin Heidelberg New York, Springer-Verlag, 1990. xiii+353p.及びその増補 Edited by Richard Swedberg, Joseph A. Schumpeter. The Economics and Sociology of Capitalism. Princeton, Princeton University Press, 1991. pp.445-481. Richard Swedberg, Joseph A. Schumpeter. His Life and Work. Polity Press, 1991. pp.239-250.

(8) 書簡類ばかりか全ゆるシュンペーター文献を勢力的に調査・収集しているベルリンのヘドトケの最近の労作も, 注目に値する。Herausgegeben von Ulrich Hedtke, Joseph Alois Schumpeter. Werke, Briefe, Bibliografien—Ein Schumpeter-Archiv. Ausgabe vom 20. Juli 2007. www. Schumpeter. info.

1. 著書, パンフレット

1908年

S.001　*Das Wesen und der Hauptinhalt der theoretischen Nationalökonomie.*München und Leipzig, Duncker & Humblot, 1908. xxxii+626S.(Frau Johanna von Kéler verw. Schumpeterへの献辞。序文。Kairo, 2 März, 1908).

2. Auflage. Berlin, Duncker & Humblot, 1970. xxxii+626S.

3. Auflage. Berlin, Duncker & Humblot, 1998. xxxiv+626S. Faksimile-Ausgabe. Düsseldorf, Verlag Wirtschaft und Finanzen GmbH, 1991. xxxii+626S. (1000部).

L'essenza e i principi dell'economia teorica. Ed. by G. Calzoni. Bari, Laterza, 1982. xxi+508p.

1910年

S.002 *Wie studiert man Sozialwissenschaft. Vortraege und Abhandlungen* herausgegeben von Sozialwissenschaftlichen akademischen Vereine in Czernowitz. Nr. 2. Czernowitz, Im Kommissionsverlag der k. k. Universitätsbuchhandlung H. Pardini, 1910. 28+xiS.

Wie studiert man Sozialwissenschaft? Zweite Auflage. Schriften des Sozialwissenschaftlichen Akademischen Vereins in Czernowitz. Heft 2. München und Leipzig, Verlag Duncker & Humblot, 1915. 54S.

How does one study social science? Translated by Jerry Z. Muller. *Society*. Vol. 40, No. 3, March/April 2003, whole No. 263. pp. 57-63.

1912年

S.003 *Theorie der wirtschaftlichen Entwicklung.*Leipzig, Duncker & Humblot, 1912. viii+548S.（題辞 "Hypotheses non fingo".第2版以降削除。序文。Wien, im Juli 1911）。[1]

Nachdruck der 1. Auflage von 1912. Berlin 2006.

Translated by Ursula Backhaus, The Economy as a Whole. Seventh Chapter of The Theory of Economic Development. Joseph A. Schumpeter. *Industry and Innovation*, Vol. 9, Nr. 1/2, April/August 2002. pp. 93-145.

Theorie der wirtschaftlichen Entwicklung. Eine Untersuchung über Unternehmergewinn, Kapital, Kredit, Zins und den Konjunkturzyklus. Zweite, neubearbeitete Auflage. München und Leipzig, Duncker & Humblot. 1926. xiv+369S.（Frau von Kéler verw. Schumpeter への献辞。序文. Bonn am Rhein, im Oktober 1926）. 第1版第7章削除。

3. Auflage. München, Leipzig, Duncker & Humblot, 1931. xiv+369S.

4. Auflage. München, Leipzig, Duncker & Humblot, 1935. xxi+369S.（序文。Cambridge, Mass. , Ende 1934）.

5. Auflage. Berlin, Duncker & Humblot, 1952. xxvi+369S.

6. Auflage. Berlin, Duncker & Humblot, 1964. xxvi+369S.

7. Auflage. Berlin, Duncker & Humblot, 1987. xxvi+369S.

8. Auflage. Berlin, Duncker & Humblot, 1993. xxvi+369S.

9. Auflage. Berlin, Duncker & Humblot, 1997. xxvi+369S.

Faksimile-Ausgabe. Düsseldorf, Verlag Wirtschaft und Finanzen GmbH, 1988. viii+548S.（1000部）.

La teoria dello sviluppo economico. Translated by G. Demaria and K. Mayer. Torino, Utet, 1932. 17+182pp.

Teoria dello sviluppo economico. Ricerca sul profitto, il capitale, il credito, l'interesse e il ciclo economico. Translated by L. Berti. Florence, Sansoni, 1971. xlix+298p. 1977.

The theory of economic development. an inquiry into profits, capital, credit, interest, and the business cycle. Translated by Redvers Opie. Cambridge, Mass. , Harvard University Press, 1934. xii+255p.

1936, 1949, 1962, 1968.

New Brunswick, NJ, Transaction Books, 1983. lxiv+255p.

London and New York, Oxford University Press, 1935. 1961. 1974. 1978.

The fundamental phenomenon of economic development. Edited by Peter Kilby, Entrepreneurship and economic development. New York, The Free Press, 1971. pp. 43-70.

Joseph A. Schumpeter. Development. Translated by Marcus C. Becker and Thorbjørn Knudsen. *The Journal of Economic Literature,* Vol. XLIII, Nr. 1, 2005. pp. 108-120.

Théorie de l'évolution économique. Recherches sur le profit, le crédit, I'ntéret et le cycle de la conjuncture. Translated by Jan Jaques Anstett. Paris, Librairie Dalloz, 1935. xi+589p.

1983.

Theorie der wirtschaftlichen Entwicklung, Schumpeter. 2. Auflage. 翻刻 江草四郎編纂『独逸語経済学教材〔シュンペーター〕』有斐閣, 1942年10月30日発行, (非売品). vlii+369p. (300部)。

Teoria del desenvolvimiento economico. Una inrestigacion sobre ganancias, capital, crédito, interés y ciclo economico. Translated by Jesús Prados Arrarte, México, Fonda de cultura económica, 1944. 363p.

1957. 255p.

1963. 1967. 1976.

Teoria rozwoje gospodarczego. Ed. by J. Grzywicka. Warszawa, Panstow Widawn Naukowe, 1960. xlvii+405p.

Teoria do desenrolvimento eonomico. Translated by L. Schlaepfer. Rio de Janeiro, Editora Fundo de Cultura, 1961. 330p.

Teoria do desenrolvimento eonomico. San Paulo. Abril Cultural, 1982. xv+160p.

Arthanaitik unmayan matabad. Translated by T. Husain. Dacca, Bangla Academy, 1974. 314p.

A gazdasagi fejlodes elmelete. Vizsgalodas a vallalkozoi profitrol, a tokerol, a hitelrol, a kamatrol es a konjunkturaciklusrol. Translated by T. Bauer. Budapest, Kozgazdasagi es Jogi Kiado, 1980. 320p.

Теория экономического развития. исследование предпринимательской прибыли, капитала, кредита, процента и цикла конъюнктуры. Translated by В. С. Автономова, М. С. Любского, А. Ю. Чепуренко. Москва, Прогресс, 1982. 453p.

Theoria ospodarskeho vyvoja. Analiza podnikatelskeho zisku, kapitalu, uveru a Kapitalistickeho cyklu. Translated by J. Erben. Bratislava, Pravda, 1987. 478p.

1914年

S.004 *Epochen der Dogmen - und Methodengeschichte.* Grundriss der Sozialökonomik. 1. Abteilung. Historische und theoretischen 1. Teil Wirtschaft und Wirtschaftswissenschaft. Tübingen, J. C. B. Mohr (Paul Siebeck), 1914. S.19-124.

Zweite, erweiterte Auflage. Tübingen, Verlag von J. C. B. Mohr (Paul Siebeck), 1924, S. 19-124.

Istoria oikonomikon theorion kai dogmaton. Translated by N. Giannoulatos. Athens, Argyris, Papazisis, 1939. 196p.

Die historische Schule und die Grenznutzentheorie(J. Schumpeter). Zusammengestellt von M. Kambe, S. Kawada und G. Ogawa, *Lesestücke für die Nationalökonomie.* Teil IV. Tokyo, Osaka, Kyoto, Nagoya, Yokohama, Fukuoka, und Sendai, Verlag von Maruzen Company, Ltd. , 1923. S. 1-52.

Epoche di Storia delle dottrine e dei metodi. Dieci grandi economisti. Ed. by G. Bruguier Pacini. Torino, Utet, 1953. xi+174p.

1971.

Economic doctrine and method. An historical sketch. Translated by R. Aris. London, George Allen & L'nwin Ltd. , 1954. 207p. Second impression 1957. London, Routledge, 2003. 207p.

New York, Oxford University Press. 1954. 1967.

De ekonomiska doktrinernas historia till sekelskiftet. Translated by A. Byttner. Stockholm, Natur och Kultur, 1957. 240p.

Esquisse d'une histoire de la science économiqne. Ed. by G. H. Bousquet. Paris, Dalloz, 1962. 222p.

1972. 235p.

Sintesis de la evolution de la ciencia economica y sus metodos. Translated by J. Petit Fontseré. Barcelona, Ediciones de Occidente, 1964. 216p. Barcelona, Oikos-tau, 1967. 212p.

Gyeongjehagsa. Translated by M. J. Kim. Seoul, Ilsinsa, 1965. 267p.

Fundamentos do pensamento economico. Rio de Janeiro, Zahar, 1968. 212p.

経済学説與方法. 歴史的概述. 閻子桂訳. 台北, 台湾銀行, 1972. 162p.

1915年

S.005 *Vergangenheit und Zukunft der Sozialwissenschaft.* Schriften des sozialwissenschaftlichen akademischen Vereins in Czernowitz, Heft VII. München und Leipzig, Duncker & Humblot, 1915. 140S.

1916年

S.006 *Grundlinien einer neuen juristischen Studienordnung.* mit Otto von Dungern, Armin Ehrenzweig, Max Layer. Graz und Leipzig, 1916.

1918年

S.007 *Die Krise des Steuerstaats.* Zeitfragen aus dem Gebiete der Soziologie. Herausgegeben von der Soziologischen Gesellschaft in Graz. In Verbindung mit Josef Schumpeter, Hugo Spitzer und Friedrich Tönnies geleitet von Julious Bunzel. 4. Heft, Graz und Leipzig, Verlag Leuschner & Lubensky k. k. Universitäts=Buchhandlung, 1918. 74+1S.

R. Goldscheid und J. A. Schumpeter, Die Finanzkrise des Steuerstaats. Beiträge zur politischen Ökonomie der Staatsfinanzen. Herausgegeben von Rudolf. Hickel. Frankfurt, Suhrkamp, 1976. S. 329 - 379.

The Crisis of the Tax State. Translated by W. F. Stolper and R. A. Musgrave. International Economic Papers. No. 4. London, Macmillan and Company Limited, New York, The Macmillan Company, 1954. pp. 5-38.

The Crisis of the Tax State. Edited by Richard Swedberg, Joseph A. Schumpeter. The Economics and Sociology of Capitalism. Princeton, New Jersey, Princeton University Press, 1991. pp. 98-140.

La crisis del estado fiscal. Hacienda Publica Espanola, 1970, No. 2, pp. 145-169.

La crisi dello stato fiscale. Translated by A. Marietti Solmi. Ed. by N. de Vecchi, J. A. Schumpeter. Stato e inflazione, Torino, Boringhieri, 1983. pp. 130-180. *Il debito pubblico.* Ed. by M. Matteuzzi and A. Simonazzi. Bologna, Il Mulino, 1988.

1919年

S.008 *Grundlinien der Finanzpolitik für jetzt und die nächsten drei Jahre.* Wien, Österreichische Staatsdruckerei, 1919. 27S.（序文.Wien, Oktober 17, 1919）.

Eduard März, *Österreichische Bankpolitik in der Zeit der großen Wende 1913-1923. Am Beispiel der Creditanstalt für Handel und Gewerbe.* München, R. Oldenbourg Verlag. Wien, Verlag für Geschichte und Politik, 1981. S. 552-569.

Joseph Schumpeter, The Basic Lines of Financial Policy for Now and the Next Three Years (Vienna, 1919). Slightly abbreviated version. Eduard März, *Austrian Banking and Financial Policy. Creditanstalt at a Turning Point, 1913-1923.* Translated by Charles Kessler. London, Weidenfeld and Nicolson, 1984. pp. 566-585.

Le linee fondamentali della politica finanziaria per ora e per i prossimi, tre anni. *Rivista Milanese di Economia*, No. 25, 1988. pp. 147-165.

S.009 *Zur Soziologie des Imperialismen.* Tübingen, Verlag von J. C. B. Mohr(Paul Siebeck), 1919. 76S.Sonderabdruck aus "*Archiv für Sozialwissenschaft und Sozial politik*" Bd. XLVI, Heft 1 und 2, 1919.

1928年

S.010 *Das deutsche Finanzporblem. Reich, Länder, Gemeinden.* Schritenreihe des deutschen Vokswirt. Bd. 2, Berlin, Der Deutsche Volkswirt, 1928. 27S.

1939年

S.011 *Business Cycles. A Theoretical, Historical and Statistical Analysis of the Capitalist Process.* 2 vols. New York and London, McGraw-Hill Book Co. , Inc. , 1939. Vol. I. 1939. xiv+448p.Vol. II. 1939. ix+pp.449-1095.

1955. 1961.

Philadelphia, Porcupine Press, 1982. 2 vols.

Abridged edition. Ed. by Rendigs Fels. New York, Toronto, London, McGraw-Hill Book co. , Inc. , 1964. xiii+461p.

Abridged edition. ED. by Rendigs Fiels. Philadelphia, Pa. , Porcupine Press, 1989. xiii+461p.

Monopolistic Competition. Edited by Arthur D. Gayer, C. Lowell Harriss, Milton H. Spencer, *Basic Economics. A Book of Readings.* New York, Prentice-Hall, Inc. , 1951. 1952. 19 pp.104-107.

Konjunkturzyklen. Eine theoretische, historische und statistische Analyse des kapitalistischen Prozesses. Übersetzt von Kalaus Dockhorn. Göttingen, Vandenhoeck & Ruprecht. Erster Band. 1961. xvi+459S. Zweiter Band, xvi+S. 461-1132.

Il processo capitalistico — Cicli economici. Translated by G. Ricoveri. Torino, Boringhieri, 1977. 526p.

1942年

S.012 *Capitalism, Socialism, and Democracy.* New York and London, Harper & Brothers Publishers, 1942. xt381p.

Second editon　1947. xiv+411p. "The Consequences of the Second World War" 付加.

Third edition　New York, 1950. xiv+431p. "Comments on Further Postwar Developments" 付加. 1962. 1970.

Fourth edition Harper & Row, 1975.

Fifth edition 1983. xiv+431p. 初版, 第2版, 第3版の各序文及び "March into Socialism" が, "Prefaces and Comments on Later Development"として掲載.

Sixth edition 1987. xxii+437p.

Reduced edition. *Can Capitalism Survive?* Ed. by Robert Lekachman, New York, Hagerstown, San Francisco, London, Harper & Row, Publishers, 1978. xvi+103p. Part II of Capitalism, Socialism, and Democracy.

The Self-Destruction of Capitalism. Edited by Arthur D. Gayet, C. Lowell Harriss, Milton H. Spencer, *Basic Economics. A Book of Readings.* New York, Prentice-Hall, Inc. , 1951. 1952. pp. 408-412.

Capitalism, Socialism, and Democracy. London, George Allen & Unwin LTD, 1943. x+381p. Second impression 1944.

Second edition. 1947. xii+412p. "The Consequences of the Second World War" 付加.

Third edition 1950. xviii+412p. 新たな序文及び "Comments on Further Postwar Development" 付加.

Fourth edition 1952. xviii+422p. "The March into Socialism" 付加.

1957. 1959. 1961. 1965. 1966. 1970. 1974.

Fifth edition 1976. xiv+437p. "Prefaces and Comments on Later Development" 付加.

1979. 1981.

Sixth edition Unwin Paperbacks 1987. xxii+437p.

Capitalismo, socialismo y democracia. Translated by A. Sanchez, Buenos Aires, Editorial Claridad, 1946. 431p.

Kapitalismus, Sozialismus und Demokratie. Übersetzt von Susanne Preiswerk. Bern, Verlag A. Francke AG, 1946. 488S.

Zwiete, erweiterte Auflage. Berlin, München, L. Lehnen, Bern, A. Francke AG Verlag, 1950. 498S.

Dritte Auflage. 1972.

Vierte Auflage. 1977.

Fünfte Auflage. 1980.

7. , erweiterte Auflage 1993. Tübingen und Basel, A Francke Verlag. ix+542S.

8. , unveränderte Auflage. 2005.

Capitalisme, socialisme et démocratie. Ed. by Gaël Fain. Paris, Payot, 1951. 462p.

Second edition 1963. 439p. 1969.

1972

1979. 417p.

Capitalismo, socialismo y democracia. Translated by J. Diaz Garcia. Mexico, Aguilar, 1952. 533p.

Second edition 1961.

Third edition 1963.

Capitalismo, socialismo e democrazia. Translated by E. Zuffi. Milano, Edizioni di Commenità, 1954. xii+392p.

Second edition 1964. xii+396p.

Third edition Milano, Etas kompass, 1967. xii+396p. 1970.

Fourth edition Milano, Universale Etas, 1973. 1977. 1984.

Capitalilsmo, socialismo e democracia. Ed. by R. Jungmann. Rio de Janeiro, Editora Fundo de Cultura, 1961. xvi+512p.

Second edition Rio de Janeiro, Zahar. 1984. 534p.

Al-ra' simaliyah wa-al-ishtirakiyah wa-al-dimuqratiyah, Translated by K. Hammad. Al-Qahirah, al-Dar al-Qawmiyah lil-tiba'ah wa-al-Nashr, 1963. 226p.

1964. 356p.

Kapitalisme, Socialisme en Democratie. Translated by C. de Boer. Hilversum, De Haag, 1963. 306p.

Second edition 1967-1968. 303p.

Third edition Harlem, De Haag, 1979. 412p.

Capitalisme, socialisme i democracia. Translated by A. Monteserrat and J. Casajuana. Barcelona, Edicions 62, 1966. 590p.

Kapitalizm, sosyalizm ve demokrasi. Translated by T. Akoglu and R. Tinaz. Istanbul, Varlik Yayinevi, 1966-1967. 212p.

Second edition 1968-1971. 284p.

Third edition 1974. 251p. 1977.

Fourth edition Istanbul, Eren Matbassi, 1981. 260p.

Capitalismo, socialismo y democracia. Translated by J. Diaz Garcia. Madrid, Aguilar, 1968. 512p. 1971.

Madrid, Orbis Ediciones, 1983. 2 vols.

Madrid, Folio Ediciones, 1984. 512p.

Punjivad, Samajavad aur Janatantra. Translated by Ramavinayakasimha, Lucknow, Hindi Samiti, Suchana vibhag, 1970. 680p.

Capitalisme, Socialisme, va Democratie. Translated by Hossein Mansour. Teheran, Danechgah Teheran, 1976.

Zibenzhuyi, Shehuizhuyi, yu Minzhu. Beijing, The Commercial Press, 1979. 資本主义, 社会主义与民主、重印版, 吴良健译. 北京, 商务印书館, 1999. 13+580p.

Kapitalizam, socijalizam idemokracija. Translated by A. Marusic. Zagreb. Delo OOUR Globo, 1981. 570p.

Jabonjui, Sahoejui, Minjujui. Translated by Lee Sang-Gu. Seoul, Ilsinsa, 1982. 1985. Translated by Lee Young-Jae. Seoul, 1985.

Капиталчзм, социализм и демократия. Translated by В. С. Автономов. Москва, Экономика, 1995. 539p.

1946年

S.013 *Rudimentary mathematics for economists and statisticians.* with W. L. Crum. New York, London, McGraw-Hill Book Company, Inc. , 1946. xi+183p.

Third edition　New York, McGraw-Hill, 1946. 179p.

Elementos de matematicas para economistas y estadigrafos. Translated by Cristobal Lara Beautell. Mexico City, Fondo de Cultura Economica, 1948. 180p.

Second edition 1959. 183p.

Elementos de matematica para economistas e estatisticos. Translated by M. do Prado Valladares. Rio de Janeiro, Fundo de Cultura, 1962. 221p.

Second edition Sao Paulo, Vertice, 1986. 219p.

1951年

S.014 *Ten great economists. From Marx to Keynes.* Ed. by E. Boody Schumpeter. New York, Oxford University Press, 1951. xiv+305p.

Second edition 1960.

1965. 1966. 1970. 1971. 1977.

Ten great economists. From Marx to Keynes. London, George Allen & Unwin Ltd. , 1951, 1952. xiv+305p. Second impression 1956. Third impression 1962.

1997. with a new introduction by Marx A. Perlman. London, Routledge, 1997. 1+305p.

Epoche di storia delle dottrine e dei metodi. Dieci grandi economisti. Ed. by G. Bruguier Pacini. Torino, Utet, 1953. pp. 177-454.

Stora Nationalekonomer. Translated by A. Byttner. Stockholm, Natur och Kultur, 1953. 353p.

Diez grandes economistas. De Marx a Keynes. Ed. by F. Estapé. Barcelona, José M. Bosch, 1955. xx+382p.

Translated by Angel de Lucas. Madrid, Alianza Editorial, 1967. 446p.

Second edition 1969.

Third edition 1971.

Fourth editon 1979.

Fifth edition 1983.

Dez grandes economistas. Translated by J. Freire. Rio de Janeiro, Editora Civilizacao Brasileira S. A. , 1958. 296p.

Teorias economicas de Marx a Keynes. Rio de Janeiro, Zahar, 1970. 290p.

Asharah min a'immat al-Iqtisad 'min markis ila kins. Al-qahirah, Maktabit al-Sharq bel-Fajjalah, 1959. 273p.

Sepuluh sardjana economi terkemuka, dari Marx sempai Keynes. Translated by O. Bian Hong. Ojakarta, Bhratara, 1963. 334p.

Cong Marx dao Keynes. Yilai de Shi Wei Zhuming Jingjixuejia. Beijing, The Commercial Press, 1965. 312p.

IO dae gyeongje hagja. Translated by D. Y. Chung. Seoul, Han-gilsa, 1982. 348p.

S.015 *Imperialism and Social Classes.*Translated by Heinz Norden. Ed. by Paul M. Sweezy. New York, Augustus M. Kelley, Inc. , Oxford, B. Blackwell, 1951. xxv+221p. "Zur Soziologie der Imperialimen" (1919) 及び "Die sozialen Klassen im ethnisch homogenen Milieu" (1927) の英訳.

Fairfield, N. J. , A. M. Kelley, 1989. xxv+221p.

On Imperialism. Ed. by Kenneth E. Boulding and Tapan Mukerjee, *Economic Imperialism. A Book of Reading.* Ann Arbor, The University of Michigan Press, 1972. pp.34-59.

Imperialism. Social Classes. Two Essays. Translated by Heinz Norden. Cleveland and New York, Meridian Books. The World Publishing Company, 1955. x+182p. 1960. 1965. 1968.

New York, New American Library, 1974. x+182p.

Imperialismo e classes sociais. Rio de Janeiro, Zahar, 1961. 195p.

Imperialismo, clases sociales. Translated by V. Girbau. Ed. by F. Estapé. Madrid, Editorial Tecnos, 1965. 331p.

Second edition 1983. 336p.

Third edition 1986. 208p.

2005.

Impérialisme et classes sociales. Translated by Suzanne de Segonzac, Pierre Bresson Paris, Editions de Minuit, 1972. 291p. Paris, Flammarion, 1984. 291p.

"Les conquetes musulmanes et l'imperialisme arabe. "Ed. by. G. H. Bousquet. *Revue Africain,*vol. 2, 1950. pp. 283-297.

Sociologia dell'imperialismo. Translated by G. Fantozzi. Bari, Laterza, 1972. viii+184p.

Second edition 1974. ix+190p.

S.016 *Essays of J. A. Schumpeter.*Ed. by Richard V. Clemence. Cambridge, Mass. , Addison-Wesley Press, Inc. , 1951. 4+327p.

Reissued. *Essays On Economic Topics of J. A. Schumpeter.* Edited by Richard V. Clemence. Port Washington, N. Y. , Kennikat Press, 1969. 4+327p.

Essays on Entrepreneurs, Innovations, Business Cycles, and the Evolution of Capitalism. New Brunswick (U. S. A.) and London (U. K.), Transaction Publishers, 1989. xxxix+341p. Fourth Printing 2000.

Ensayos. Translated by J. Silvestre, E. Lluch Martin, and J. Planas Campos. Barcelona, Oikos-tau, 1968. 349p.

1952年

S.017 *Aufsätze zur ökonomischen Theorie.*Hrsg. von Erich Schneider und Arthur Spiethoff. Tübingen, J. C. B. Mohr (Paul Siebeck), 1952. 4+608S.

1953年

S.018　*Aufsätze zur Soziologie.*Hrsg. von Erich Schneider und Arthur Spiethoff. Tübingen, J. C. B. Mohr (Paul Siebeck), 1953. 3+232S.

1954年

S.019　*Dogmenhistorische und biographische Aufsätze.*Tübingen, J. C. Mohr (Paul Siebeck), 1954. viii+383S.

Economic doctrine and method. An historical sketch. Translated by R. Aris. London, George Allen&Unwin Ltd. , 1954. 207p.

S.020　*History of Economic Analysis.*Edited from manuscript by Elizabeth Boody Schumpeter, London, Allen&Unwin. New York, Oxford University Press, 1954. xxv+1260p.Second printing 1955. 1959. 1961. 1963. 1966. 1968. 1972. 1976. Tenth printing 1981.

London, Routledge, 1994. xlviii+1260p.

Paperback edition.

New York, Oxford University Press, 1986. xxv+1260p. 1994. lv+1260p.

London, Allen&Unwin, 1987. xxv+1260p.

London, Routledge, 1994. xlviii+1260p.

Review of the troops. *Quarterly Journal of Economics,*Vol. 65, No. 2, May1951, pp. 149-180.

Some Questions of Principle. Edited by Loring Allen. *Research in the History of Economic Thought and Methodology,*Vol. 5, 1987. pp. 93-116. The typescript of the following altermotive version of Chapter 1 of Joseph Schumpeter's History of Economic Analysis (Oxford university Press, 1954) in the Schumpeter papers in the Harvard University Archives.

Storia dell'analisi economica. Edited by P. Sylos Labini and L. Occhinero. 3 vols. Torino, Borginghieri, 1959-1960. xxiii+1536p.

abridged. Edited by C. Napoleoni. Torino, Boringhieri, 1968. 684p. 1972. 1976.

Historia da analise economica. 3 vols. Rio de Janeiro, Fundo de Cultura, 1964.

Geschichte der ökonomischen Analyse. Übersetzt von Gottfried. Frenzel. Erster Teilband, Göttingen, Vandenhoeck&Ruprecht, 1965. vii+915S. Zweiter Teilband, Göttingen, vendenhoeck&Ruprecht, 1965. xix+S916-1520.

Historia del analisis economico. Translated by L. Mantilla. Mexico City, Fondo de Cultura Economico, 1971, 810p.

Historia del analisis economico. Translated by M. Sacristan-Luzon, J. A. Garcia Duran and N. Serra. Barcelona, Ediciones Ariel, 1971. 1371p.

Second edition 1982. 1377p.

1995.

Povijest ekonomske analize. Translated by Z. Baletic, M. Hanzekovic and S. Stampar. 2vols. Zagreb, Informator, 1975.

L'histoire de l'analyse économique. Translated by Jean-Claude Casanova. 3vols. Paris, Gallimard, 1983. 519, 495, 710pp.

経済分析史. 王作榮訳. 第1冊~第4冊. 台北, 台湾銀行, 1978.

経済分析史. 朱泱, 孙鸿敞, 李宏, 陈锡龄訳. 第1巻, 第2巻, 北京, 商务印书館, 1991, 1992. 第1巻~第3巻. 1994—2001.

1970年

S.021 *Das Wesen des Geldes.* Aus dem Nachlaß herausgegeben Fritz Karl Mann. Göttingen, Vandenhoeck&Ruprecht, 1970. xxvii+341S.

1983年

S.022 *Stato e inflazione.* Translated by P. Castellanza, G. Giocchetti and A. Marietti Solmi. Edited by N. De Vecchi. Torino, Böringhieri, 1983. 210p.

1984年

S.023 *Schumpeter. Antologia di scritti.* Edited by M. Messori. Bologna, Il Mulino, 1984. 392p.

1985年

S.024 *Aufsätze zur Wirtschaftspolitik.* Herausgegeben von Wolfgang F. Stolper und Christian Seidl. Tübingen, J. C. B. Mohr (Paul Siebeck), 1985. vi+378S.

1987年

S.025 *Beiträge zur Sozialökonomik.* Herausgegeben, übersetzt von Stephan Böhm. Wien · Köln · Graz, Böhlau Verlag, 1987. 375S.

1991年

S.026 *The Economics and Sociology of Capitalism.*Edited by Richard Swedberg. Princeton, New Jersey, Princeton University Press, 1991. viii+492p.

1992年

S.027 *Politische Reden.*Herausgegeben von Christian Seidl und Wolfgang F. Stolper. Tübingen, J. C. B. Mohr (Paul Siebeck), 1992. ix+390S.

1993年

S.028 *Aufsätze zur Tagespolitik.*Herausgegeben von Christian Seidl und Wolfgang F. Stolper. Tübingen, J. C. B. Mohr (Paul Siebeck), 1993. vii+280S.

1996年

S.029 L. Berti and Messori. Joseph Alois Schumpeter. Trattato della moneta. Capitoli inediti. Con altri scritti sulla moneta Neapel. 1996.

2. 論文・序文

1905年

S.030 Die Methode der Standard Population. *Statistische Monatschrift,*Jg. XXXI, Neue Folge. Jg. x, 1905. S.188-191.

S.031 Die Methode der Index-Zahlen. *Statistische Monatschrift,*Jg. XXXI. Neue Folge, Jg. X, 1905. S.191-197.

S.032 Die internationale Preisbildung. *Statistische Monatschrift,*Jg. XXXI. Neue Folge, Jg. X, 1905. S.923-928.

1906年

S.033 Über die mathematische Methode der theoretischen Ökonomie. *Zeitschrift für Volkswirtschaft, Sozialpolitik und Verwaltung,*Bd. XV, 1906. S.30-49.

S.034 Professor Clarks Verteilungstheorie. *Zeitschrift für Volkswirtschaft.*Sozialgolitik und verwaltung, Bd. XV, 1906. S.325-333.

S.035 Rudolph Auspitz. *Economic Journal,*Vol. XVI, June 1906. pp.309-311.

1907年

S.036 Das Renterprinzip in der Verteilungslehre. *Jahrbuch für Gesetzgebung, Verwaltung und Volkswirtschaft, in Deutschen Reich,*Bd. XXXI, 1907. S.31-65, 591-634.

1909年

S.037 Bemerkungen über das Zurechnungsproblem. *Zeitschrift für Volkswirtschaft, Sozialpolitik und Verwaltung,*Bd. XVIII, 1909. S79-132.

S.038 On the Concept of Social Value. *Quarterly Journal of Economics,*Vol. 23, February 1909. pp.213-232.

1910年

S.039 Über das Wesen der Wirtschaftskrisen. *Zeitschrift für Volkswirtschaft, Sozialpolitik und Verwaltung,*Bd. XIX, 1910. S271-325.

S.040 Marie Ésprit Léon Walras+.*Zeitschrift für Volkswirtschaft, Sozialpolitik und Verwaltung,*Bd. XIX, 1910. S.397-402.

S.041 Die neuere Wirtschaftstheorie in den Vereinigten Staaten. *Jahrbuch für Gesetzgebung, Verwaltung und Volkswirtschaft im Deutschen Reich,*Bd. XXXIV, 1910. S.913-963.

1911年

S.042 Gründungsgewinn in Recht und Wirtschaft. *Zeitschrift für Notaritat und freiwillige Gerichtsbarkeit in Österreich,*Nr. 4, 25. Jänner 1911, S31.

1913年

S.043 Zinsfuss und Geldverfassung. *Jahrbuch der Gesellschaft österreichischer Volkswirt,*1913. S38-63.

S.044 Entgegnung. *Archiv für Sozialwissenschaft und Sozialpolitik,*Bd. XXXVI, 1913. S.679.

S.045 Eine "dynamische"Theorie des Kapitalizimse. Eine Entgegnung. *Zeitschrift für Volkswirtschaft, Sozialpolitik und Verwaltung,*Bd. XXII, 1913. S.599-639.

S.046 Meinungsäusserung zur Frage des Werturteils. *Äusserungen zur Werturteilsdiskussion im Ausschuss des Vereins für Sozialwissenschaft.*Düsseldorf, 1913. S.49-50.

Heine Heirich Nau, Der werturteilsstreit. Die Äußerungen zur Werturteildiskussion im Ausschuß des Vereins für Sozialpolitik (1913). Marburg, Metropolis・Verlag, 1996. S. 111-112.

1914年

S.047 Die'positive'Methode in der Nationalökonomie. Deutsch

S.048 Das wissenschaftliche Lebenswerk Eugen von Böhm-Bawerks. *Zeitschrift für Volkswirtschaft, Sozialpolitik und Verwaltung,*Bd. XXIII, 1914. S.454-528.

S.049 Die Wellenbewegung des Wirtschaftslebens. *Archiv für Sozialwissenschaft und Sozialpolitik,*Bd. XXXIX, 1914. S.1-32.

S.050 Railway rate making. Discussion. *American Economic Review,*Supplement, vol. iv, No. 1, 1914. pp.81-100.

1916年

S.051 Das Grundprinzip der Verteilungstheorie. *Archiv für Sozialwissenschaft und Sozialpolitik,*Bd. XLII, 1916. S.1-88.

The Fundamental Principle of Distribution Theory. Edited by Michio Morishima, Power or pure Economics? Howndmills and London, Macmillan Press ltd. , 1998. PP. 1-86

1917年

S.052 Das Bodenmonopol. Entgegnung auf Dr. Oppenheimers Artikel. *Archiv für Sozialwissenschaft und Sozialpolitik,*Bd. XLIX, Heft 1, 1917. S.495-502.

S.053 Das Sozialprodukt und die Rechenpfennige. Glossen und Beiträge zur Geldtheorie von heute. *Archiv für Sozialwissenschaft und Sozialpolitik,*Bd. XLIV, Heft 3, 1917. S.627-715.

Money and the social product. Translated by A. W. Marget. International Economic Papers. No. 6. London, Macmillan and Company Limited. New York, The Macmillan Company, 1956. pp. 148-211.

1918年

S.054 Karl Marx, der Denker. *Arbeiterwille,*Graz. Bd. XXIX, Nr. 120, 5 Mai 1918. S.3.

1919年

S.055 Zur Soziologie der Imperialismen. *Archiv für Sozialwissenschaft und Sozialpolitik,*Bd. XLVI, 1918/1919. S.1-39, 275-310.

1920年

S.056 Sozialistische Möglichkeit von heute. *Archiv für Sozialwissenschaft und Sozialpolitik,*Bd. XLVIII, 1920. S305-360.

Les possibilités actuelles du socialisme. *L'Amnée Politiqueet Franccaise et Étrangère.* Vol. 6, 1931. pp. 385-418.

S.057 Max Webers Werk. *Der östereichische Volkswirt,*Jg. 12, Nr. 45, 7. August 1920. S.831-834.

S.058 Die (allgemeine) finanzpolitische Situation. *Die Börse,*Oktober 1920.

1921年

S.059 Weltwirtschaftskrise? *Die Börse,*2/3, 20 Jänner 1921. S.1.

S.060 Karl Menger, Neue Freie*Presse, 1*März. 1921.

S.061 Österreichische Kreditprobleme. *Die Börse,* 2/14, 7 April 1921. S.1. f.

S.062 Carl Menger. *Zeitschrift für Volkswirtschaft und Sozialpolitik.*Neue. Folge, Bd. I, 1921. S.197-206.

S.063 Friedrich Wieser. Neues Wiener Tagblatt, 10 Juli 1921.

S.064 Kronenanleihe oder Valutenanleihe? *Die Börse,*2/45, 10 November 1921. S.5.

S.065 Aktuelle Wirtschaftsprobleme. *Die Börse,* 2/50, 15 Dezember 1921. S.1f.

1922年

S.066 Die großen Fragezeichen. *Die Börse,* 3/18, 4 Mai 1922. S.1f.

S.067 Die finanzpolitische Situation. *Die Börse,* 3/27, 6 Juli 1922. S.1f.

S.068 Soll die Notenbank gegründet werden? Die Börse, 3/38, 21 September 1922. S.1.

1923年

S.069 Angebot. *Handwörterbuch der Staatswissenschaften.*Herausgegeben von Ludwig Elster, Adolf Weber, Friedrich Wieser. 4 Auflage. Erster Band. Jena, Verlag von Gustav Fischer, 1923. S.299-303.

S.070 Kapital. 6 Nachtrag. Der heutige Stand der Diskussion. *Handwörterbuch der Staatswissenschaften.*Herausgegeben von Ludwig Elster, Adolf Weber, Friedrich Wieser. 4 Auflage. Fünfter Band. Jena, Verlag von Gustav Fischer, 1923. S.582-584.

1924年

S.071 Der Weg zur stabilen Wirtschaft. *Die Börse*, 5/36, 28 August 1924. S.5f.

S.072 Verkehrserschwerungen verteuern das Bankgeschäft. *Die Börse,* 5/44, 23 Oktober 1924. S.7f.

S.073 Der Sozialismus in England und bei uns. I. *Der österreichische Volkswirt,*Jg. 17, Nr. 11, 13 Dezember, 1924. S.295-297. Der Sozialismes in England und bei uns. II. *Der östereichische Volkswirt,*Jg. 17, Nr. 12/13, 20 Dezember 1924. S.327-330.

1925年

S.074 Das "volkswirtschaftliche"Einkommen aus der Landwirtschaft. *Zeitschrift für schweizerische Statistik und Volkswirtschaft,*Jg. 61, Heft 1, 1925, S.16-19.

S.075 Japans währungspolitische Situation. *Die Börse,*14 Mai 1925.

S.076 Eugen von Böhm-Bawerk. *Neue Österreichische Biographie*1815-1918. Bd. II, Wien, 1925. S.63-80.

Schumpeter on Böhm-Bawerk. Translated in abridged form. Edited by Henry William Spiegel, The Development of Economic Thought. Great Economists in Perspective. New York, John Wiley&Sons Inc. , London, Chapman&Hall Limited, 1952, pp. 568-579.

S.077 Edgeworth und die neuere Wirtschaftstheorie. *Weltwirtschaftliches Archiv,*Bd. XXII, 1925. S.183-202.

S.078 Kreditkontrolle. *Archiv für Sozialwissenschaft und Sozialpolitik,*Bd. LIV, 1925. S.289-328.

S.079 Kreditpolitik und Wirtschaftslage. *Berliner Börsen-Courier,*58/603, 25 Dezember 1925.

S.080 Oudo en nieuwe bankpolitiek. I, II, III. *Economisch-statistische. Berichten,*Vol. 10, 1925. pp.552-554, 574-577, 600-601.

S.081 The Currency Situation in Austria. Edited by John Parke Young, *European Currency and Finance.*Commission of Gold and Silver Inquiry, United States Senate. Foreign Currency and Exchange Investigation. Serial 9 (Volume I) .Washington, Government Printing Office, 1925, pp.225-231.

1926年

S.082 Subventionspolitik. *Berliner Börsen-Courier*58/87, 3 Beilage, 21 Februar 1926.

S.083 Konjunkturforschung. Teil I und Teil II. feil I in *Berliner Börsen-Courier,*58/157, Morgen Ausgabe, 4 Beilage, 4 April 1926. S.17 und Teil II in 58/159, Morgen Ausgabe, 2 Beilage, 7 April 1926. S.9.

S.084 Gustav v. Schmoller und die Probleme von heute. *Schmollers Jahrbuch für Gesetzgebung, Verwaltung und Volkswirtschaft im Deutschen Reiche,*Jg. L, Heft 3, 1926. S.337-388.

Herausgegeben von Reimut Jochimsen und Helmut Knobel, *Gegenstand und Methoden der Nationalökonomie.* Köln, Kiepenheuer&Witsch, 1971. S. 118-132.

S.085 G. F. Knapp.*Economic Journal,*vol. XXXVI, No. 143, September 1926, pp.512-514.

S.086 Steuerkraft und nationale Zukunft. *Der deutsche Volkswirt,*Jg. 1, Nr. 1, 1 October 1926, S.13-16.

1927年

S.087 Cassels Theoretische Sozialökonomik. *Schmollers Jahrbuch für Gesetzgebung, Verwaltung und Volkswirtschaft im Deutschen Reiches,*Jg. 51, I Halbband, Heft 2, 1927. S.69-88.

S.088 Sombart dritter Band. *Schmollers Jahrbuch für Gesetzgebung, Verwaltung und Volkswirtschaft im Deutschen Reiche,*Jg. 51, I Halbband, Heft 3, 1927. S.1-21.

S.089 Zur Frage der Grenzproduktivität. Eine Entgegnung auf den vorstehenden Aufsatz von Wilhelm Valk. *Schmollers Jahrbuch für Gesetzgebung, Verwaltung und Volkswirtschaft im Deutschen Reiche,*Jg. 51, II Halbband, Heft 5, 1927. S.19-28.

S.090 Unternehmerfunktion und Arbeiterinteresse. *Der Arbeitgeber,*Jg. 17, Nr. 8, 1927. S.166-170.

S.091 Die Soziale Klassen in ethnischen homogenen Milieu. *Archiv für Sozialwissenschaft und Sozialpolitik,*Bd. LVII, 1927. S.1-67.

S.092 Zur Einführung der folgenden Arbeit Knut Wicksells. Mathematische Nationalökonomie. *Archiv für Sozialwissenschaft und Sozialpolitik,*Bd. LVIII, 1927/1928. S.238-251.

S.093 Die Arbeitslosigkeit. *Der deutsche Volkswirt.*Jg. 1, Nr. 24, 11 März 1927. S.729-732.

S.094 Finanzpolitik. *Der deutsche Volkswirt,*Jg. 1, Nr. 27, 1 April 1927. S.827-830.

S.095 Finanzpolitik und Kabinettsystem. *Der deutsche Volkswirtschaft,*Jg. 1, Nr. 28, 8 Apil 1928. S.865-869.

S.096 Geist und Technik der Finanzverwaltung. *Der deutsche Volkswirt.*Jg. 1, Nr. 33, 13 Mai 1927. S.1028-1031.

S.097 Finanzausgleich *Der deutsche Volkswirt,*Jg. 1, Nr. 36, 3 Juni 1927. S.1123-1126 und Nr. 37, 10 Jun 1927. S.1156-1159.

S.098 Obituary. Friedrich von Wieser. *Economic Journal,*vol. XXXVII, Nr. 146, June 1927. pp.328-330.

S.099 The Explanation of the Business Cycle. *Economica,*vol. VII, No. 21, December 1927. pp.286-311.

S.100 Deutschland. Herausgegeben von Hans Mayer, Frank A. Fetter und Richard Reisch, *Die Wirtschaftstheorie der Gegenwart.*Bd. 1, Wien, Verlag von Julius Springer, 1927. S.1-30.

S.101 Zur Einführung. Enrico Barone, *Grundzüge der theoretischen Nationalökonomie.*Übersetzt von Hans Staehle. Bonn, Kurt Schroeder Verlag. 1927. S.7-10. Zweite, durchgesehene Auflage. Berlin u. Bonn, Ferd. Dümmlers Verlag. 1935. S7-10.

1928年

S.102 Unternehmer. *Handwörterbuch der Staatswissenschaften.*4 Auflage. Bd. VIII. Jena, Verlag von G. Fischer, 1928. S.476-487.

S.103 Staatsreferendar und Staatsassessor. *Schmollers Jahrbuch für Gesetzgebung, Verwaltung und Volkswirtschaft im Deutschen Reiche,*Jg. 52, II Halbband, Heft 4, 1928. S.123-140.

S.104 The Instability of Capitalism. *Economic Journal,*Vol. XXXVIII, No. 151, September 1928. pp.361-386. Edited by Richard V. Clemence, *Readings in Economic Analysis.*Vol. 1. General Theory. Cambridge, Massachusetts, Addison-Wesley Press Inc. , 1950. pp.133-158. Edited by R. L. Smyth, *Essays in the Economics of Socialism and Capitalism.*London, Gerald Duckworth&Co. Ltd. 1964. pp.193-220. Joseph schumpeter, *The instability of capitalism.*The American Classical College Press. pp.17-67.

S.105 Erbschaftssteuer. *Der deutsche Volkswirt.*Jg. 3, Nr. 4, 26 Oktober 1928. S.110-114.

S.106 Wen trifft die Umsatzsteuer?*Der deutsche Volkswirt,*Jg. 3, Nr. 7, 16 November 1928, S.206-208.

S.107 International cartels and their relation to world trade. Edited by Parker Thomas Moon, *America as a creditor nation.*New York, 1928. The Academy of Political Science. Proceedings of the Academy of Political Science in the City of New York. Vol. XII, 1928. pp.908-913.

1929年

S.108 Das soziale Antlitz des deutschen Reiches. *Bonner Mitteilungen,*Nr. 1, 1929. S.3-14.

S.109 Die Wirtschaftslehre und die reformierte Referendarprüfung. *Schmollers Jahrbuch für Gesetzgebung, Verwaltung und Volkswirtschaft im Deutschen Reiche,*Jg. 53, II Halbband, Heft 4, 1929. S.101-114.

S.110 Lohnpolitik und Wissenschaft. *Der deutsche Volkswirt,*Jg. 3, Nr. 25, 22 März 1929. S.807-810.

S.111 Grenzen der Lohnpolitik. *Der deutsche Volkswirt,*Jg. 3, Nr. 26, 28 März 1929. S.847-851. Dazu Nachbemerkung. Nr. 31, 3 Mai 1929. S.1022-1023.

S.112 Was vermag eine Finanzreform? *Der deutsche Volkswirt,*Jg. 4, Nr. 3, 18 Oktober 1929. S.75-80.

S.113 Ökonomie und Soziologie der Einkommensteuer. *Der deutsche Volkswirt,*Jg. 4, Nr. 12/13. , 20 Dezember 1929. S380-385.

S.114 Le rôle économique et psychologique de l'employeur. *Informations Sociales,*Bureau International du Travail, Genf, Vol. 31, July-September 1929. pp.113-115.

1930年

S.115 Wenn die Finanzreform mißlingt…*Der deutsche Volkswirt,*Jg. 4, Nr. 22, 28 Februar 1930. S.695-699.

S.116 Wandlungen der Weltwirtschaft. *Der deutsche Volkswirt,*Jg. 4, 19 September 1930. S1729-1733.

S.117 Mitchell's business cycles. *Quarterly Journal of Economics,*Vol. XLV, November 1930. pp.150-172.

S.118 Auspitz, Rudolf(1837-1906).*Encyclopaedia of the Social Sciences.*Vol. 2, New York, The Macmillan Company. September 1930. p.317.

S.119 Boehm-Bawerk, Eugen von (1851-1914).*Encyclopaedia of the Social Sciences.*Vol. 2, New York, The Macmillan Company. September 1930. pp.618-619.

S.120 Preface. F. Zeuthen, *Problems of monopoly and economic warfare.*London, Routledge&Kegan Paul, 1930. pp.vii-xiii. New York, Augustus M. Kelley Publihsers, 1968. pp.vii-xiii.

1931年

S.121 The present world depression. A tentative diagnosis. *American Economic Review,*Supplement, vol. XXI, march 1931. pp.179-182.

S.122 Dauerkrise? *Der deutsche Volkswirt,*Jg. 6, 25 Dezember 1931. S.418-421.

S.123 Bemerkungen über die gegenwärtige Lage, Born 20. Juli 1931. Joseph Alois schumpeter, Kleine Schriften 1906-1934. universitätsbibliothek Mainz.

1932年

S.124 World depression and Franco-German economic relations. A German view. *Lloyds Bank Limited, Monthly Review,*March 1932, Supplementary Number, pp.14-35.

S.125 Weltkrise und Finanzpolitik. *Der deutsche Volkswirt,*Jg. 6, 4 März 1932. S.739-742.

S.126 Ladislaus von Bortkiewicz. *Economic Journal,*vol. XLII, June 1932. pp.338-340.

S.127 Kreditpolitische Krisentherapie in Amerika. *Der deutsche Volkswirt,*Jg. 6, 22 Juli 1932. S.1415-1418.

S.128 Zur Soziologie der Außenpolitik. Bonn, 1932.

S.129 Entwicklung. Festschrift zum 50. Geburtstag (am22 Juli 1932.)von Emil Lederer.

1933年

S.130 The common sense of econometrics. *Econometrica*, Vol. 1, No. 1, January 1933 pp.5-12.

S.131 Vorwort und Joseph Schumpeter (Harvard) .*Der Stand und die nächste Zukunft der Konjunkturforschung. Festschrift für Arthur Spiethoff.*München, Duncker&Humblot, 1933. S.v-vi und S.263-267. Nachdruck 1989. Frankfurt am Main, Antiquaritat und Verlag Keip GmbH.

1934年

S.132 Imperfect competition. (Round table. J. A. Schumpeter chairman) .*Americal Economic Review*, Supplement, Vol. XXIV, No. 1, March 1934. pp.21-32.

S.133 Depressions. Douglass V. Brown, Edward Chamberlin, Seymour E. Harris, Wassily W. Leontief, Edward S.Mason, Joseph A. Schumpeter, Overton H. Taylor, *The Economics of the Recovery Program.*New York and London, Whittlesey House, McGraw-Hill Book Co. , Inc. , 1934. pp.3-21. Edited by Stewart Morgan and William Thomas, Opinions and attitudes in the twentieth century. New York,

Thomas Nelson and Sons, 1936. pp.329-339.

1935年

S.134 A theorist's comment on the current business cycle. *Journal of the American Statistical Association*, Supplement, Vol. XXX, March 1935. pp.167-168.

S.135 The analysis of economic change. *Review of Economic Statistics*, Vol. XVII, No. 4, May 1935. pp.2-10. Selected by a Committee of The American Economic Association under the Chairman of Gottfried Haberler, *Readings in Business Cycle Theory.*Philadelphia. Toronto, The Blakiston Company, 1944. pp.1-19. Edited by John J. Clark&Morris Cohen, *Business fluctuations, growth, and economic stabilization. A reader.*New York, Random House Inc. , 1963. pp.46-59.

S.136 Young, Allen Abbott(1876-1929).*Encyclopaedia of the Social Sciences.*New York, The Macmillan Company, vol. 15, June 1935. pp.514-515.

S.137 Geleitwort. D. H. Robertson, *Das Geld.*new übersetzt von Karl Bode. Zweite, verbesserte Auflage nach dem achten englischen Auflage. Wien, Verlag von Julius Springer, 1935. S.iii-v.

1936年.

S.138 Professor Taussig on wages and capital. *Explorations in Economics. Notes and Essays. Contributed in Honor of F. W. Taussig.*New York, McGraw-Hill Book Co. , Inc. , 1936. pp.213-222. New York, Augustus M. Kelley Publishers, 1967. pp.213-222.

1939年

S.139 The pure theory of production. (Round table. J. A. Schumpeter chairman)*American Economic Review.*Supplement, vol. XXIX, No. 1, March 1939. pp.118-120.

1940年

S.140 The influence of protective tariffs on the industrial development of the United States. *Proceedings of the Academy of Political Science.*Vol. XIX, May 1940. pp.2-7.

1941年

S.141 Frank William Taussig. with A. H. Cole and E. S.Mason. *Quarterly Journal of Economics*, Vol. LV, May 1941. pp.337-363.

S.142 Alfred Marshall's principles. A semi-centennial appraisal. *American Economic Review*, Vol. XXXI, No. 2, June 1941. pp.236-248. Edited by John Cunningham Wood, *Alfred Marshall. Critical Assessments.*London and Canberra, Croom Helm, 1982. pp.100-113.

1942年

S.143 Cost and demand functions of the individual firm. (Round table. J. A. Schumpeter chairman).*American Economic Review*, Supplement, Vol. XXXII, No. 1, March 1942. pp.349-350.

1943年

S.144 Capitalism in the postwar world. Edited by Seymour E. Harris, *Postwar Economic Problems.*New York and London, McGraw-Hill Book Company, 1943. pp.113-126.

S.145 Introduction. Bernard W. Dempsey, *Interest and usury.*Washington, American Council of Public Affairs, 1943. pp.vii-x. Second edition London, Dennis Dobson Ltd. , 1948. pp.vii-x.

1946年

S.146 The decade of the twenties. *American Economic Review*, Proceedings, vol. XXXVI, No. 2, May 1946, pp.1-10.

Alvin H. Hansen and Richard V. Clemence, *Readings in Business Cycles and National Income.* New York, W. W. Norton&Company Inc. , 1953. pp.35-45. London, George Allen&Unwin Ltd. , 1953. pp.35-45.

S.147 John Maynard Keynes. 1883-1946. *American Economic Review*, Vol. XXXVI, No. 4, part 1, September 1946. pp.495-518.

Keynes, the Economist (2). Edited by Seymour E. Harris, *The New Economics. Keynes' Influence on Theory and Public Policy.* New York, A. A. Knopf. 1947. pp.73-101. New York, Augustus M. Kelley, 1965. pp.73-101.

John Meynard Keynes 1883-1946. Edited by John Cunningham Wood, *John Maynard Keynes. Critical Assessments.* Vol. 1, London&Canberra, Croom Helm, 1983. pp.51-72.

S.148 Keynes and Statistics. Keynes' contributions to economics——four views. *Review of Economic Statistics*, Vol. XXVIII, November 1946, pp.194-196.

Keynes and Statistics. Edited by John Cunningham Wood, *John Meynard Keynes. Critical Assessments.* Vol. 1, London&Canberra, Croom Helm, 1983. pp. 233-236.

S.149 L'avenir de l'entreprise privée devant les tendances socialistes modernes. *Comment sauvegarder l'entreprise privée.*Montreal, Editions Association Professionelle des Industriels, 1946. Translated by Michael G. Prime and David R. Henderson, Schumpeter on preserving private enterprise. *History of Political Economy.*Vol. VII, No. 3, Fall 1975. pp.293-298. Edited by Richard Swedberg, *The Economics and Sociology of Capitalism.*Princeton, New Jersey, Princeton University Press. 1991. pp.401-405.

S.150 Capitalism. *Encyclopaedia Britannica.*Chicago, London and Toronto. Vol. IV, 1946. pp.801-807.

1947年

S.151 Keynes, the Economist. Edited by Seymour E. Harris, *The New Economics. Keynes' Influence on Theory and Public Policy.*New York, A. A. knopf, 1947. pp.73-101. New York, Augustus M. Kelley, 1965. pp.73-101.

S.152 Theoretical problems of economic growth. *Journal of Economic History*, Supplement, Vol. VII, 1947, pp.1-9. Edited by Joseph T. Lambie and Richard V. Clemence, *Economic change in America. Readings in economic history of the United States.*Harrisburg, Pennsylvania, The Stackpole Company, 1954. pp.2-9.

S.153 The creative response in economic history. *Journal of Economic History*, Vol. VII, November 1947. pp.149-159. Edited by Joseph T. Lambie and Richard V Clemence, *Economic change in America. Readings in economic history of the United States.*Harrisburg, Pennsylvania, The Stackpole Company, 1954. pp.9-17.

S.154 Comments on a plan for the study of entrepreneurship.Cambridge, Mass. , Harvard University, Widener Library, HUH 775. 13 January, 1947.

1948年

S.155 Bröckelnde Mauern. *Die Umschau*, Bd. 3, Nr. 2, 1948. S.137-144.

S.156 Der Kapitalismus und die Intellektuellen. *Merkur*, Jg. 2, Heft 2, 1948. S.161-173.

S.157 There is Still Time to Stop Inflation. *Nation's Business*, Vol. 36, No. 6, June 1948. pp.33-35, 88-91.

S.158 Irving Fisher's econometrics. *Econometrica.*Vol. XVI, No. 3, July 1948. pp.219-231.

S.159 Statement on the choice of textbooks. *American Economic Reiew*, Vol. XXXVIII, 1948. p626.

1949年

S.160 Economic Theory and Entrepreneurial History. Prepared by the Research Center in Entrepreneurial History. Harvard University, *Change and the Entrepreneur. Postulates and patterns for entrepreneurial history.*Cambridge, Massachusetts, Harvard University Press, 1949. pp.63-84. Edited by Hugh G. J. Aitken, Explorations in Enterprise. Cambridge, Massachusetts, Harvard University Press. 1967. pp.45-64. Edited by Ross M. Robertson and James L. Pate, *Readings in United States Economics and Business History.*Boston, New York, Atlanta, Geneva, Illinois, Houghton Mifflin Company, 1966. pp.101-110.

S.161 Vilfred Pareto(1848-1920).*Quarterly Journal of Economics*, Vol. LXIII, No. 2, May 1949. pp.147-173.

S.162 The communist manifesto in sociology and economics. *Journal of Political Economy*, Vol. LVII, No. 3, June 1949. pp.199-212. Edited by Earl J. Hamilton, Albert Rees and Harry G. Johnson, *Landmarks in political economy. Selections from the Journal of Political Economy.*Chicago, The University of Chicago Press, 1962. pp.337-358.

S.163 English economists and the state-managed economy, *Journal of Political Economy.*Vol. LVII, No. 5, October 1949. pp.371-382.

S.164 Der demokratische Kurs. *Der Monat*, Jg. 1, Heft 5, 1949. S.22-28.

S.165 The historical approach to the analysis of business cycles. Universities——National Bureau Conference on Business Cycle Research, New York, 25-27 November 1949. *Conference on Business Cycles.*Held under the auspices of Universities-National Bureau Committee for Economic Research, New York, National Bureau of Economic Research, Inc. , 1951. pp.155-162.

1950年

S.166 Wesley Clair Mitchell(1874-1948).*Quarterly Journal of Economics*, Vol. LXIV, No. 1, February 1950. pp.139-155. with only minor changes. The General Economist. Edited by Arthur E. Burns, *Wesley Clair Mitchell. The Economic Scientist.*New York, National Bureau of Economic Research, Inc. , 1952. pp.321-340.

S.167 The march into socialism. *American Economic Review*, Vol. XL, No. 2, May1950. pp.446-456. Edited by Lowel C. Harriss, *Selected readings in economics.*Englewood Cliffs, N. J. , Prentice-Hall, Inc. , 1958. Tokyo, Japan, Maruzen Co. , Ltd. , 1959. pp.499-503. Der Marsch in den Sozialismus. *Johrbuch für Sozialwissenschaft*, Bd. 1/1950, Heft 2, 1950. S.101-112.

1975年

S.168 The future of private enterprise in the face of modern socialistic tendencies. *History of Political Economy*, Vol. 7, No. 3, 1975. pp.294-298.

1983年

S.169 American Institutions and Economic Progress. *Zeitschrift für die gesamte Staatswissenschaft. Journal of Institutional and Theoretical Economics*, Bd. 139, Heft 2, Juni 1983. S.191-196. Edited by Richard Swedberg, Joseph A. Schumpeter. The Economics and Sociology of Capitalism. Princeton, New Jersey, Princeton University Press, 1991. pp.438-444.

1984年

S.170 The Meaning of Rationality in the Social Sciences. *Zeitschrift für die gesamte Staatswissenschaft. Journal of Institutional and Technological Economics*, Bd. 140, Heft 4, Dezember 1984. S.577-593.

1991年

S.171 Money and Currency. Translated by Arthur W. Marget. *Social Research*, Vol. 58, No. 3 (Fall 1991).pp.499-543. “Geld und Währung”のマニュスクリプトの最初の2章の英訳.

3. 書評

1906年

S.172 Bernhard Rost, Über das Wesen und die Ursachen unserer heutigen Wirtschaftskrise und Otto Karmin, Zur Lehre von den Wirtschaftskrisen. *Zeitschrift für Volkswirtschat, Sozialpolitik und Verwaltung*, Bd. XV, 1906. S.95-97.

S.173 Dr. Arthur Salz, Beiträge zur Geschichte und Kritik der Lohnfondstheorie. *Zeitschrift für Volkswirtschaft, Sozialpolitik und Verwaltung*, Bd. XV, 1906. S.97-98.

S.174 H. Deutsch, Qualifizierte Arbeit und Kapitalismus. *Zeitschrift für Volkswirtschaft, Sozialpolitik und Verwaltung*, Bd. XV, 1906. S.98-99.

S.175 Johannes Leonhard, Neue Feststellung des Wertbegriffes und ihre Bedeutung für die Volkswirtschaft. *Jahrbuch für Gesetzgebung, Verwaltung und Volkswirtschaft im*

Deutschen Reich, Bd. XXX, 1906. S.1271.

1907年

S.176 J. W. Schiele, Über den natürlichen Ursprung der Kategorien Rente, Zins und Arbeitslohn. *Jahrbuch für Gesetzgebung, Verwaltung und Volkswirtschaft im Deutschen Reich*, Bd. XXXI, 1907. S.395-398.

S.177 M. E. Waxweiler, Esquisse d'une sociologie. *Economic Journal,*vol. XVII, March 1907. pp.109-111.

S.178 Übersetzung von John B. Clark, Über das Wesen des Kapitales. *Eine Entgegnung. Zeitschrift für Volkswirtschaft, Sozialpolitik und Verwaltung*, Bd. XVI, 1907. S.426-440.

1908年

S.179 Einige neuere Erscheinungen auf dem Gebiete der theoretischen Nationalökonomie. 1. E. R. A. Seligman. Principles of Economics. 2. W. Stanley Jevons. The Principles of Economics. 3. Léon Polier, L'idée du juste salaire. 4. L. Querton. L'augmentation du rendement de la machine humaine. 5. W. Hasbach. Güterverzehrung und Güterhervorbringung. 6. H. von Leesen, Frédéric Bastiat. 7. A. Rudiger. Miltenberg, Der gerechte Lohn. 8. Thomas Nixon Carver, The Distribution of Wealth. 9. Frank A. Fetter. The Principles of Economics, with applications to practical Problems. *Zeitschrift für Volkswirtschaft, Sozialpolitik und Verwaltung*, Bd. XVII, 1908. S.402-420.

S.180 John Bates Clark. Essentials of Economic Theory as applied to modern Problems of Industry and Public Policy. *Zeitschrift für Volkswirtschaft, Sozialpolitik und Verwaltung,*Bd. XVII, 1908. S.653-659.

1909年

S.181 Rudolf Kaulla, Die geschichtliche Entwicklung der modernen Werttheorien. *Jahrbuch für Gesetzgebung, Verwaltung und Volkswirtschaft im Deutschen Reich*, Bd. XXXIII, 1909. S.1261-1262.

S.182 Irving Fisher, The nature of Capital Income. *Zeitschrift für Volkswirtschaft, Sozialpolitik und Verwaltung*, Bd. XVIII, 1909. S.679-680.

S.183 Mannstaedt Heinrich, Dr. , Die kapitalistische Anendung der Maschinerie. *Zeitschrift für Volkswirtschaft, Sozialpolitik und Verwaltung*, Bd. XVIII, 1909. S.680-681.

S.184 G. de. Molinari, Question's Économiques à l'ordre du jour. *Zeitschrift für Volkswirtschaft, Sozialpolitik und Verwaltung*, Bd. XVIII, 1909. S.681-683.

S.185 1. Ira Ryner, "On the Crises of 1837, 1847and 1857 in England, France and the United States. "2. Minnie Throop England, "On Speculation in Relation to the World's Prosperity 1897-1902. "3. W. G. Longworthy Taylor, "The Kinetic Theory of Economic Crises. "*Zeitschrift für Volkswirtschaft, Sozialpolitik und Verwaltung*, Bd. XVIII, 1909. S.683-685.

1910年

S.186 Alfred Weber, Über den Standort der Industrien. *Jahrbuch für Gesetzgebung, Verwaltung und Volkswirtschaft im Deutschen Reich*, Bd. XXXIV, 1910. S.1356-1359.

S.187 Otto Conrad, Lohn und Rente. *Jahrbücher für Nationalökonomie und Statistik*, Bd. XCIV, III Folge, 1910. S.827-831.

S.188 J. Conrad, Leitfaden zum Studium der Nationalökonomie. Fünfte ergänzte Auflage und J. Conrad, Grundriß zum Studium der politischen Oekonomie. Vierter Teil. Statistik. Erster Teil. Die Geschichte und Theorie der Statistik. Die Bevölkerungsatatistik. Dritte ergänzte Auflage. *Archiv für Sozialwissenschaft und Sozialpolitik*, Bd. XXXI, 1910. S.256.

S.189 Otto Neurath und Anna Schapiro-Neurath, Lesebuch der Volkswirtschaftslehre. *Archiv für Sozialwissenschaft und Sozialpolitik*, Bd. XXXI, 1910. S.256-257.

S.190 Vilfred Pareto, Manuel d'économie politique, Traduit de l'édition italalienne par italienne par Alfred Bonnet, revue par l'auteur. *Archiv für Sozialwissenschaft und Sozialpolitik*, Bd. XXXI, 1910. S.257.

S.191 Gustav Schmoller, Grundriß der allgemeinen Volkswirtschaftslehre. I. Teil. Begriff, psychologische und sittliche Grundlage. Literatur und Methode. Land, Leute und Technik. Die gesellschaftliche Verfassung der Volkswirtschaft. *Archiv für Sozialwissenschaft und Sozialpolitik*, Bd. XXXI, 1910. S.257-258.

S.192 Adolf v. Wenckstern, Staatswissenschaftliche Probleme der Gegenwart. Vol. 1. *Archiv für Sozialwissenschaft und Sozialpolitik*, Bd. XXXI, 1910. S.258.

S.193 Eugen von Böhm-Bawerk, Kapital und Kapitalzins. Zweite Abteilung. Positive Theorie des Kapitales. Dritte Auflage. *Archiv für Sozialwissenschaft und Sozialpolitik*, Bd. XXXI, 1910. S271.

S.194 Eugenie Fabian-Segal, Albert Schäffle und seine theoretisch-nationalökonomischen Lehren. Eine nationalökonomische Studie. *Archiv für Sozialwissenschaft und Sozialpolitik*, Bd. XXXI, 1910. S.271-272.

S.195 Hermann Levy, Monopole, Kartelle und Trusts in ihrem Beziehungen zur Organisation der kapitalistischen Industrie. Dargestellt an der Entwicklung in Großbritannien. *Archiv für Sozialwissenschaft und Sozialpolitik*, Bd. XXXI, 1910. S.285-286.

S.196 Alfred Lansburgh, Depositen und Spargelder. Drei Aufsätze zur Bankenquete. *Archiv für Sozialwissenschaft und Sozialpolitik*, Bd. XXXI, 1910. S.297.

1911年

S.197 Wilhelm Lexis, Allgemeine Volkswirtschaftslehre. *Archiv für Sozialwissenschaft und Sozialpolitik*, Bd. XXXII, 1911. S.865-867.

S.198 Albion W. Small, The Meaning of Social Science. *Archiv für Sozialwissenschaft und Sozialpolitik*, Bd. XXXII, 1911. S868-870.

S.199 Heinrich Niehuus, Geschichte der englischen Bodenreformtheorien. *Archiv für Sozialwissenschaft und Sozialpolitik*, Bd. XXXII, 1911. S873-874.

S.200 Neuere Erscheinungen auf dem Gebiete der Nationalökonomie. Lifschitz F. , Dr. Untersuchungen über die Methodologie der Wirtschaftswissenschaft. Grunzel Josef. Allgemeine Volkswirtschaftslehre. Hohoff W. Die Bedeutung der Marxschen Kapitalkritik. Gide Charles. par. Cours d'économie politique. Ruhland G. , Dr. System der Politischen Ökonomie. Jacoby Walther, Dr. Der Streit um den Kapitalsbegriff. S.J. Pesch Heinrich, Lehrbuch der Nationalökonomie. Lifschitz F. , Dr. Zur Kritik der Böhm-Bawerkschen Werttheorie. Weber Adolf. Die Aufgaben der Volkswirtschaftslehre als Wissenschaft. Soda Kiichiro. Geld und Wert. Eine logische Studie. Fisher Irving. The Rate of Interest, its Nature, Determination and Relation to Economic Phenomena. Davenport Joseph Herbert. Value and Distribution, a Critical and Constructive Study. Schachner Robert, Dr. Australien in Politik, Wirtschaft und Kultur. Conant Charles A. .A History of Modern Banks of Issue. *Zeitschrift für Volkswirtschaft, Sozialpolitik und Verwaltung*, Bd. XX, 1911. S.240-252.

1912年

S.201 Neue nationalökonomische Lehrbücher und Lehrbehelfe. W. Lexis, Allgemeine Volkswirtschaftslehre. H. R. v. Schullern zu Schrattemhofen, Grundzüge der Volkswirtschaftslehre. E. Schwiedland, Einführung in die Volkswirtschaftslehre. F. W. Taussig, Principles of Economics. L. H. Haney, History of Economic Thought. O. Spann, Haupttheorien der Volkswirtschaftslehre. O. und A. Neurath, Lesebuch der Volkswirtschaftslehre. K. Diehl und P. Mombert, Ausgewählte Lesestücke zum Studium der politischen Ökonomie. *Zeitschrift für Volkswirtschaft, Sozialpolitik und Verwaltung*, Bd. XXI, 1912. S.281-292.

S.202 R. Stolzmann, Die soziale Kategorie in der Volkswirtschaftslehre. R. Stolzmann, Der Zweck in der Volkswirtschaft. *Jahrbuch für Gesetzgebung, Verwaltung und Volkswirtschaft im Deutschen Reich*, Bd. XXXVI, 1912. S.928-934.

1913年

S.203 A. Adler, Leitfaden der Volkswirtschaftslehre zum Gebrauche an höheren Fachschulen und zum Selbstunterricht. 6. verbesserte Aufl. Quaritsch, Kompendium der Nationalökonomie, 8. Aufl. *Archiv für Sozialwissenschaft und Sozialpolitik*, Bd. XXXVI, 1913, S.238-240.

S.204 Georg Mollat, Volkswirtschaftliches Quellenbuch. *Archiv für Sozialwissenschaft und Sozialpolitik*, Bd. XXXVI, 1913. S.240.

S.205 Sp.-C. Haret, Mécanique sociale. *Archiv für Sozialwissenschaft und Sozialpolitik*, Bd. XXXVI, 1913. S.240-241.

S.206 James Bonar, Disturbing Elements in the Study and Teaching of Political Economy. *Archiv für Sozialwissenschaft und Sozialpolitik*, Bd. XXXVI, 1913. S.243-244.

S.207 Ernst Bundsmann, Das Kapital, wirtschaftstheoretische Skizzen. *Archiv für Sozialwissenschaft und Sozialpolitik*, Bd. XXXVI, 1913. S.244-246.

S.208 Irving Fisher, De la nature du capital et du revenu. *Archiv für Sozialwissenschaft und Sozialpolitik*, Bd. XXXVI, 1913. S.246-248.

S.209 Bernard Lavergne, La Theorie des marchés économiques. *Archiv für Sozialwissenschaft und Sozialpolitik*, Bd. XXXVI, 1913. S.249-251.

S.210 T. Lloyd, The Theory of Distribution and Consumption. *Archiv für Sozialwissenschaft und Sozialpolitik*, Bd. XXXVI, 1913. S.251-252.

S.211 Achille Loria, La synthèse économique, étude sur les lois du revenu. *Archiv für Sozialwissenschaft und Sozialpolitik*, Bd. XXXVI, 1913. S.252-254.

S.212 René Maunier, L'origine et la fonction économique des villes. *Archiv für Sozialwissenschaft und Sozialpolitik*, Bd. XXXVI, 1913. S.254-256.

S.213 Henry L. Moore, Laws of Wages, An Essay in Statistical Economics. *Archiv für Sozialwissenschaft und Sozialpolitik*, Bd. XXXVI. 1913. S.256-258.

S.214 Franz Oppenheimer, Theorie der reinen und politischen Ökonomie. *Zeitschrift für Volkswirtschaft, Sozialpolitik und Verwaltung*, Bd. XXII, 1913. S.797-799.

1915年

S.215 Karl Schlesinger, Theorie der Geld-und Kreditwirtschaft. *Archiv für Sozialwissenschaft und Sozialpolitik*, Bd. XLI, 1915. S.239-242.

1927年

S.216 R. G. Hawtrey, The Economic Problem. *Weltwirtschaftliches Archiv*, Bd. XXVI, 1927. S.131-133.

S.217 Heinrich Dietzel, Die Bedeutung des'Nationalen Systems'für die Vergangenheit und die Gegenwart. *Archiv für Sozialwissenschaft und Sozialpolitik*, Bd. LVIII, 1927. S.415-416.

S.218 Friedrich B. W. Hermann, Staatswissenschaftliche Untersuchungen. *Archiv für Sozialwissenschaft und Sozialpolitik*, Bd. LVIII, 1927. S.416-417.

S.219 Edwin R. A. Seligman, Essays in Economics. *Archiv für Sozialwissenschaft und Sozialpolitik*, Bd. LVIII. 1927. S.417-418.

S.220 C. A. Macartney, The Social Revolution in Austria. *Economic Journal,*vol. XXXVII, June 1927. pp.290-292.

1928年

S.221 Carl Landauer, Grundproblem der funktionelle Verteilung des wirtschaftlichen Wertes. *Weltwirtschaftliches Archiv*, Bd. XXVII, 1928. S.24-27.

S.222 L. V. Brick, The Theory of Marginal Value. *Weltwirtschaftliches Archiv*, Bd. XXVII, 1928. S.24-26. Bonn und Palyi. Festausgabe für Lujo Brentano. Wirtschaftswissenschaft nach dem Kriege. *Zeitschrift für Völkerpsychologie*, Bd. IV, 1928. S101-102.

S.223 Carl Rodbertus. Neuere Briefe über Grundrente. *Zeitschrift für Völkerpsychologie*, Bd. IV, 1928. S.102-103.

1932年

S.224 G. H. Bousquet, Institutes de science économique. *Economic Journal*, Vol. XLII, September 1932. pp.449-451.

1933年

S.225 Wilhelm von Winkler, Grundzüge der Statistik. *Schmollers Jahrbuch für Gesetzgebung, Verwaltung und Volkswirtschaft im Deutschen Reiche*, Jg. LVII, 1933. S136-139.

S.226 J. M. Keynes. Essays in Biography. *Economic Journal*, Vol. XLIII, December 1933. pp.652-657.

1934年

S.227 Joan Roibnson, The Economics of Imperfect Competition. *Journal of Political Economy*, Vol. XLII, April 1934. pp.249-257.

1936年

S.228 J. M. Keynes. General Theory of Employment, Interest and Money. *Journal of the American Statistical Association*, Vol. XXXI. December 1936. pp.791-795. Edited by Richard V. Clemence, *Readings in Economic Analysis.*Vol. 1. General Theory. Cambridge, Massachusetts, Addison-Wesley Press Inc. , 1950. pp.227-231.

1942年

S.229 George J. Stigler, The Theory of Competitive Price. *American Economic Reivew*, Vol. XXXII, December 1942. pp.844-847.

1944年

S.230 Harold J. Laski, Reflections on Revolution of Our Time. *American Economic Review*, Vol. XXXIV, March 1944. pp.161-164.

1946年

S.231 F. A. Hayek. The Road to Serfdom. *Journal of Political Economy*, Vol. LIV, June 1946. pp.269-270.

1950年

S.232 Elmer Clark Bratt, Business Cycles and Forecasting. *Journal of the American Statistical Association*, Vol. XLV, No. 249, March 1950. pp.140-142.

4. 報告及び報告書

1917年

S.233 Universität Graz. Leitung. Professor Dr. Joseph Schumpeter, Volkswirtschaftliches Seminar. Emil Lederer, Die volkswirtschaftlichen Seminaren an den Hochschule Deutschlands und Österreich-Hungarns. Berichte über ihre Tätigkeit. Tübingen, Verlag von J. C. B. Mohr (Paul Siebeck), 1917. S79-86.

1919年

S.234 Öffentliche Sitzung am 24. Januar 1919. Verhandlungen der Sozialisierungs-Kommission über den Kohlenbergbau im Winter 1918/1919. Berlin, Verlag Hans Robert Engelmann, 1921. S.388, 389.

S.235 Vorläufiger Bericht der Sozialisierungskommission über die Frage der Sozialisierung des Kohlenbergbaues. Abgeschlossen am 15. Februar 1919. Zweite durchgesehene Auflage. Berlin, R. v. Decker's Verlag. G. Schencke, 1919. 40S.Zur Sozialisierung des Kohlenbergbaues. Vorläufiger Bericht der Sozialisierungs Kommission (15. Februar 1919). *Correspondenzblatt der Generalkommission der Gewerkschaften Deutschlands*, Jg. 29, Nr. 11, 15 März 1919. S.89-101.

S.236 Schreiben des Staatssekretärs Schumpeter an Staatskanzler Renner. Wien, Herbst 1919.

1927年

S.237 Referat über das volkswirtschaftliche Studium der Juristen. 29 April 1929.

1934年

S.238 The nature and necessity of a price system. Economic Reconstruction. Report of the Columbia University Commission. New York, Columbia University Press. 1934. pp.170-176. Edited by Richard V. Clemence, *Readings in Economic Analysis*.Vol. II. Price and Production. Cambridge, Massachusetts, Addison-Wesley Press Inc. , 1950. pp.1-7. Edited by Arthur D. Gayer, C. Lowell Harriss, Milton H. Spencer, *Basic Economics. A Book of Readings*.New York, Prentice-Hall, Inc. , 1951. pp.75-77. タイトル変更して,

S.239 Prices as Coefficients of Choice. Edited by Wayne A. Leeman, *Capitalism, Market Socialism and Central Planning. Readings in Comparative Economic Systems*.Boston・New York・Atlanta・Geneva, III・Dallas・Palo Alto, Houghton Mifflin Company, 1963. pp.130-134.

1937年

S.240 Suggestions for the Quantitative Study of the Business Cycle. Colorado Spring, Cowles Commission. 1937.

5. 講義, 講演, 新聞記事, インタヴュー

1913年

S.241 The Working Faith of the Social Reformer. *New York Times*, 5 December 1913. p.13.

1914年

S.242 The Balkan Situation from the Austrian Viewpoint. *The Washington Post*, 8 February 1914. p.18.

Suffrage coming, says economist, because of changing family life. *The Washington Post*, 22 March 1914. p.18.

1915年

S.243 Zum 75. Geburtstage von Karl Menger. *Neue Freie Presse,*Morgenblatt, 23 Februar 1915. S.9.

1916年

S.244 Das gegenwärtige Verhälrtnis der Völker nach dem Kriege *Para Pacem,*Heft 3 und 4, Mai 1916. S.22-24.

S.245 Nationalökonomie. Nach den Vorlesungen des. ö.Professors Dr. Josef Schumpeter. Graz, vor 1916. 134S.

S.246 Volkswirtschafts-Politik. Zusammengestellt nach den Vorlesungen des o. ö.Professors Dr. Josef Schumpeter. Graz. vor 1916. 164S.

S.247 Finanzwissenschaffliche Vorträge. Gehalten von Professor Dr. Josef Schumpeter an der k. k. Universität in Graz. Für das Studium bearbeitet. I. Teil. Graz, vor 1916. 120S.

1917-18年

S.248 Grundsätzliche Bemerkungen zur Valutafrage. Harasgegeben von Christian Seidl und Wolfgangh. Stalper, Joseph A. Schumpeter, Politishe Reden, Tübingen, J. T. B. Mohr (Paul Siebeck), 1992. S.81-87.

1919年

S.249 Programmatische Äußerungen des neuen Staatssekretärs für Finanzen. *Fremden-Blatt,*16 März 1919.

S.250 Das Programm des neuen Staatssekretärs der Finanzen. Einmalige größe Vermögensabgabe. *Neue Freie Press,*Morgenblatt, 16 März 1919. S.2.

S.251 Das Programm des Staatssekretärs Schumpeter. *Neue Freie Press,*Morgenblatt, 20 März 1919. S.10f. *Wiener Abendpost.*20 März 1919. S.2f.

S.252 Staatssekretär Schumpeter über die wirtschaftlichen Aufgaben der Zukunft. *Neue Freie Presse,*Morgenblatt, 21 März 1919. S.11f.

S.253 Staatssekretär Dr. Schumpeter über die Vermögensabgabe. *Neue Freie Presse,*Morgenblatt, 29 März 1919. S.11.

S.254 Rede in der 7. Sitzung der Konstituierenden Nationalversammlung für Deutschösterreich am 2. April 1919. Stenographische Protokolle über die Sitzungen der Konstituierenden Nationalversammlung der Republik Deutschösterreich, 1919. Bd. 1. Staatsdruckerei, Wien 1919. S.146-147.

S.255 Rede in der 9. Sitzung der Konstituierenden Nationalversammlung für Deutschösterreich am 4. April 1919. Stenographische Protokolle über die Sitzungen der Konstituierenden Nationalversammlung der Republik Deutschösterreich, 1919. Bd. 1. Staatsdruckerei, Wien 1919. S.220.

S.256 Die Erfüllung der finanziellen Verpflichtungen Ungarns gegen Deutschösterreich. *Neue Freie Press,*Morgenblatt, 6 April 1919. S.2.

S.257 Staatssekretär Dr. Schumpeter über aktuelle finanzwirtschaftliche Fragen. *Neue Freie Presse,*Morgenblatt. 15 April 1919. S.6. *Wiener Abendpost,*15 April 1919. S.1f.

S.258 Bemerkungen des Staatssekretär Dr. Schumpeter auf der Konferenz der Interessenten der Metallindustrie. *Wiener Zeitung.*17. April 1919. S.8.

S.259 Rede in der 11. Sitzung der Konstituierenden Nationalversammlung für Deutschösterreich am 25. April 1919. Stenographische Protokolle über die Sitzungen der Konstituierenden Nationalversammlung der Republik Deutschöster reich, 1919. Bd. 1, Staatsdruckerei, Wien 1919. S.299-300.

S.260 Staatssekretär Schumpeter über Freihandel und Dauerfrieden. *Neue Freie Presse.*Morgenblatt. 27. April 1919. S.5f. *Neues Wiener Journal,*27 April 1919.

S.261 Rede in der Sitzung der Konstituierenden Nationalversammlung für Deutschösterreich am 6 Mai 1919. Stenographische Protokolle über die Sitzungen der Konstituierenden Nationalversammlung der Republik Deutschösterreich, 1919. Bd. 1. Wien, Staatsdruckerei, 1919. S.311-312.

S.262 Staatssekretär Schumpeter über die Friedenskonferenzen. *Neues 8 Uhr Blatt,*10 Mai 1919.

S.263 Staatssekretär Schumpeter über Kriegsanleihe und Vermögensabgabe. *Neue Freie Presse.*Morgenblatt. 13 Mai 1919. S.11f. *Neues Wiener Journal,*13 Mai 1919. S.10.

S.264 Staatssekretär Schumpeter über die industrielle Zukunft Deutschösterreichs. *Neue Freie Presse,*Morgenblatt, 31 Mai 1919. S.10f. *Wiener Journal,*31 Mai 1919. S.10-11.

S.265 Gespräch mit Doktor Schumpeter. *Le Temps,*4 Juni 1919.

S.266 Finanzpolitische und wirtschaftliche Ausblicke. *Die Woche,*Nr. 21. 6 Juni 1919. S.679-680.

S.267 Staatssekretär Schumpeter über die Friedensbedinuengen und Vermögensabgabe. *Neue Freie Presse,*Morgenblatt, 25 Juni 1919. S.10f.

S.268 Staatssekretär Dr. Schumpeter über die wirtschaftlichen Friedensverhandlungen in Saint-Germain. *Neue Freie Presse,*Morgenblatt, 28 Juni 1919. S.11. *Wiener Zeitung.*28 Juni 1919. S.4f. *Neues Wiener Journal,*28 Juni 1919. S.2.

S.269 Staatssekretär Schumpeter über die Vermögensabgabe und den wirtschaftlichen Wiederaufbau. *Neue Freie Presse,*Morgenblatt, 1 Juli 1919. S.7. *Wiener Zeitung,*1 Juli 1919 S.8f.

S.270 Der Plan einer Sozialisierungsbank. Rede des Staatssekretärs Dr. Schumpeter in Budgetausschusse. *Neue Freie Presse,*Morgenblatt, 4 Juni 1919. S.11.

S.271 Die Debatte über das Budgetprovisorium. Ausführungen des Staatssekretärs Schumpeter. *Neue Freie Presse,*Morgenblatt, 4 Juli 1919. S.11f. *Wiener Zeitung,*4 Juli 1919. S.4.

S.272 Konstituierende Nationalversammlung. Erledigung der drei finanziellen Vortragen. *Neue Freie Presse,*Morgenblatt, 5 Juli 1919. S.5f.

S.273 Rede in der 24. Sitzung der Konstituierenden Nationalversammlung für Deutschösterreich am 4. Juli 1919. Stenographische Protokolle über die Sitzungen der Konstituierenden Nationalversammlung der Republik Deutschösterreich, 1919. Bd. 1. Wien, Staatsdruckerei, 1919. S612-615.

S.274 Debattenbemerkung in der 24. Sitzung der Konstituierenden Nationalversammlung für Deutschösterreich am 4. Juli 1919. Stenographische Protokolle über die Sitzungen der Konstituierenden Nationalversammlung der Republik Deutschösterreich, 1919. Bd. 1. Wien, Staatsdruckerei, 1919. S.639-640.

S.275 Debattenbeitrag in der 24. Sitzung der Konstituierenden Nationalversammlung für Deutschösterreich am 4. Juli 1919. Stenographische Protokolle über die Sitzungen der Konstituierenden Nationalversammlung der Republik Deutschösterreich, 1919. Bd. 1. Wien, Staatsdruckerei, 1919. S.651.

S.276 Die Arbeiterräte bei Staatssekretär Dr. Schumpeter. *Neue Freie Presse,*Morgenblatt. 5 Juli 1919. S.8. *Wiener Zeitung,*5 Juli 1919. S.8.

S.277 Bericht über die Vorbereitung der Finanzierung der Vermögensabgabe, der Sozialisierung und der Industrieförderung. Streng geheimer Anhang zum Kabinettsprotokoll Nr. 86 vom 8. Juli1918.

S.278 Empfang des Staatssekretärs Schumpeter für die Grazer Finanzwaltung am 9. Juli 1919. *Grazer Tagblatt,*10 Juli 1919.

S.279 Staatssekretär Dr. Schumpeter über den Wiederaufbau. *Neue Freie Presse,* Abendblatt, 10 Juli 1919. S.3f. *Wiener Abendpost,* 10 Juli 1919. S.1. f.

S.280 Deutschösterreichs Kreditpolitische Aussichten. Ein Wiener Vortrag Dr. Schumpeter. *Die Reichspost,*13 Juli 1919. S.4.

S.281 Erhöhung der Erbgebühren, Einführung eines staatlichen Noterb-und Pflichtteilsrechtes. Schreiben des Staatsamtes für Finanzenvom 21. Juli 1919 an den Herrn Staatssekretär Dr. Otto Bauer.

S.282 Zwei Referate Schumpeters betreffend die Umgestaltung des Credit-Institutes und die Alpinen-Hausse. Streng vertraulicher Anhang zum Kabinettsprotokoll Nr. 88 vom 15 Juli 1919.

S.283 Schumpeter zum Verbereitungsstand der Vermögensabgabe. Streng vertraulicher Anhang zum Kabinettsprotokoll Nr. 89 vom 16 Juli 1919.

S.284 Die Dollaranleihe. Zuschrift des Staatssekretärs Dr. Schumpeter an die "Neue Freie Press. "*Neue Freie Presse,*Morgenblatt, 19 Juli 1919. S.1.

S.285 Einbegleitung der Vorlage der Staatsregierung betreffend den Staatsvorschlag für 1919/20. Stenographische Protokolle der 26. Sitzung der Konstituierenden Nationalversammlung der Republik Österreich, 1919. Bd. I1. Wien, Staatsdruckerei, 1919. S.676-680.

S.286 Der Staatsvoranschlag in der Nationalversammlun. *Neue Freie Presse,*Morgenblatt, 29 Juli 1919. S.6f.

S.287 Protestversammlung gegen den Vernichtungsfrieden. Eine Rede des Staatssekretärs Dr. Schumpeter. *Neue Freie Presse,*Morgenblat, 2 August 1919. S.6f.

S.288 Erklärung vor dem Untersuchungskomitee in der Sitzung am 28 August 1919. Die Protokolle des Untersuchungskomitees. Sitzung des Komitees am 28 August 1919.

S.289 Die Praxis des Neuaufbaues. Ein Vortrag des Staatssekretärs Dr. Schumpeter. *Wiener Zeitung,*2 September 1919.

S.290 Erklärung vom 14 September 1919 gegenüber einer Delegation der Staatspensionisten. *Wiener Abendpost,*15 September 1919.

S.291 Erganzende Erklärung Schumpeters zur Befragung von Direktor Kux durch das Untersuchungskomitee. Protokolle des Untersuchungskomitee. Protokoll aufgenommen am 15 September 1919 im Staatsamtes der Finanzen.

S.292 Schumpeter zum Problem der Länderfinanzen. *Wiener Zeitung,*16 September 1919. S.4.

S.293 Staatssekretär Dr. Schumpeter über den Finanzplan. *Neue Freie Presse,*Morgenblatt, 16 September 1919. S.6.

S.294 Vermögensabgabe und Landwirtschaft—Staatssekreär Dr. Schumpeter über die Kriegsanleihe. *Die Reichspost,*17 September 1919.

S.295 Staatssekretär Dr. Schumpeter über Kriegsanleihe und Vermögensabgabe. *Neue Freie Presse,*Morgenblatt, 18 September 1919. S.4. *Grazer Abendblatt,*17 September 1919. S.2.

S.296 Die Forderung der Staatsangestellten. Erklärung des Staatssekretärs Dr. Schumpeter. *Neue Freie Presse,*Morgenblatt, 26 September 1919. S.6.

S.297 Schumpeters Kabinettsvortrag vom 29 September zum Finanzplan. Streng vertraulicher Anhang zum Kabinettsprotokoll Nr. 110 vom 29 September 1919. Finanzplan.

S.298 Diskussion über den Finanzplan. Streng vertraulicher Anhang zum Kabinettsprotokoll Nr. 112 vom 1 Oktober 1919.

S.299 Bemerkung des Staatssekretärs Schumpeter anläßlich des Empfanges der Staatspensionisten am 14 Oktober 1919. *Wiener Abendpost,*25 Oktober 1919. S.3f.

S.300 Staatssekretär Dr. Schumpeter über die Valutafrage. Maßnahmen zur Stützung der Krone. *Der Neue Tag,*Morgenblatt, 16 Oktober 1919. S.9. *Wiener Zeitung,*16 Oktober 1919. S.3. *Neue Freie Presse,*Morgenblatt, 16 Oktober 1919. S.4.

S.301 Der Finanzplan des Staatssekretärs a. D. Dr. Schumpeter. *Neue Freie Presse,*Morgenblatt, 18 Oktober 1919. S.11f. *Wiener Zeitung,*18 Oktober 1919. S.12.

S.302 Verabschiedung Dr. Schumpeters. *Wiener Zeitung,*19 Oktober 1919. S.5.

S.303 Die Vereinigten Staaten von Amerika in Politik und Kultur. *Neue Freie Presse,*Morgenblatt, 21 Oktober 1919. S.6. *Wiener Abendpost.*21 Oktober 1919. S.2.

1920年

S.304 Die Beschaffung ausländischen Kredits. *Neue Freie Presse*, Morgenblatt, 24 Januar 1920.

S.305 Unterredung mit Staatssekretär a. D. Dr. Schumpeter. *Die Börse*, 1/1, 11 November 1920. S.3f.

1922年

S.306 Finanzpolitik und Völkerbund. *Neue Freie Presse*, 23 März 1922.

S.307 Soll der Staat eine Politik der Geldknappheit betrieben? *Deutsches Volksblatt*, 14 Juni 1922.

1924年

S.308 Sanierungswerk und Geldwertpolitik. Rede des Staatssekretärs a. D. Präsident Dr. Schumpeter. *Neue Freie Presse*, 30 Januar 1924.

1926年

S.309 Kreditpolitische Wirtschaftstheorie. Neunte Hauptversammlung der Gesellschaft von Freunden und Förderern der Rheinischen Friedrich Wilhelms-Universität zu Bonn am 24. Juli 1926 in der Aula der Universität zu Bonn, Bonn 1926. S.32-36. Recherchiert und zusammengestellt von Ulrich Hedtke, Joseph A. Schumpeter. Reden in der Bonner Zeit. *Berliner Debatte Initial*, Jg. 8. Heft 3, 1997. S.61-64.

1927年

S.310 Die goldene Bremse an der Kreditmaschine(Die Goldwährung und der Bankkredit) .Kölner Vorträge. Veranstaltet von der Wirtschafts-und sozialwissenschaftlichen Fakultät der Universität Köln Winter-Semester 1926/27, Band 1. Die Kreditwirtschaft. Erster Teil. G. A. Gloeckner, Verlagsbuchhandlung in Leipzig, 1927. S.80-106.

S.311 The instability of our economic system. *The Manchester Guardian*, 3 September 1927. p.16.

1928年

S.312 Der Untenehmer in der Volkswirtschaft von heute. Herausgegeben von Bernhard Harms, Strukturwandlngen der Deutschen Volkswirtschaft. Erster Band. Berlin, Verlag von Reimar Hobbing in Berlin, 1928. S.295-312. Zweite, vervollständigte Auflage, 1929. S.303-326.

S.313 German economist speaks at Columbia. *The New York Times,*24 January 1928. p.42.

S.314 The Gold Standard and the Control of Credit, *Washington Post*, 25 January 1928. p.5.

S.315 The Problem of Europe. 20 February 1928.

S.316 The Responsibilities of Citizenship.*The New York Times,*28 February 1928. p.16.

S.317 Lectures by Josef Schumpeter at Harvard University. 1927-1928. Recordet by his student Joe Freedman. Copied by Harry Pelle Hartekemeier. Harvard University. February bis April 1928. 51p.

S.318 Lohngestaltung und Wirtschaftsentwicklung. *Deutsche Arbeitgeber Zeitung*, Nr. 27, Beiblatt. 1. Juli 1928. Recherchiert und zusammengestellt von Ulrich Hedtke, Joseph A. Schumpeter. Reden in der Bonner Zeit. *Berliner Debatte Initial*, Jg. 8. Heft 3, 1997. S.64-66. *Der Arbeitgeber*, Jg. 18, Nr. 19, 1 Oktober 1928. S.479-482.

S.319 Deutschlands staatsfinanzielle Zukunft. *Zement*, Jg. 17, 1928. S.1483-1488. Recherchiert und zusammengestellt von Ulrich Hedtke, Joseph A. Schumpeter. Reden in der Bonner Zeit. *Berliner Debatte Initial*, Jg. 8. Heft 3, 1997. S.66-74.

S.320 Individualismus und gebundene Wirtschaft. *Geschäfftliche Mitteilungen für die Mitglieder des Reichsverbandes des Deutschen Groß-und Überseehandels*, Jg. 13, Nr. 31/34, Oktober 1928. S.61-67. Recherchiert und zusammengestellt von Ulrich Hedtke, Joseph A. Schumpeter. Reden in der Bonner Zeit. *Berliner Debatte Initial*, Jg. 8. Heft 3, 1997. S.74-83.

S.321 Lohnniveau und nationale Zukunft. *Der Papier-Fabrikant*, Jg. XXVI, Nr. 4, 28 Oktober, 1928. S.881-883. Recherchiert und zusammengestellt von Ulrich Hedtke, Joseph A. Schumpeter. Reden in der Bonner Zeit. *Berliner Debatte Initial*, Jg. 8. Heft 3, 1997. S.83-85.

S.322 Schumpeter. Finanzwissenschaft. Wintersemester 1928/29 von Cläre Tisch. 79+ 3S.

S.323 Der neueste Stand des Konjunkturproblems. Vortrag von Professor Dr. J. Schumpeter, Bonn. Münster, Samstag, 24 November 1928.

S.324 Die Tendenzen unserer sozialen Struktur. Vortrag des Herrn Prof. Dr. Schumpeter, Bonn, auf der Hauptversammlung des Vereins zur Wahrung der Interessen der Chemischen Industrie Deutschlands E. V. am 8. Dezember 1928. 25S.*Die Chemische Industrie*, Jg. 51, Nr. 51/52, 24 Dezember 1928. S.1381-1387.

S.325 Kann eine Krise der deutschen Wirtschaft verhindert werden und wie? *Rauch und Staub*.Jg. XVIII, Nr. III, November 1928. S.119f. *Der Deutsche Leinen—Industrielle*.Jg. XXXXVI, Nr. 51, 20 Dezember 1928. Recherchiert und zusammengestellt von Ulrich Hedtke, Joseph A. Schumpeter. Reden in der Bonner Zeit. *Berliner Debatte Initial*, Jg. 8. Heft 3, 1997. S.86-87.

1929年

S.326 Zinsfuß und Rentabilität. *Dresdner Neueste Nachrichten*, 30 Januar 1929.

S.327 Wirtschaftspolitische Möglichkeiten. *Sprechsaal für Keramik, Glas und verwandte Industrien*.Coburg, Jg. 62. 21 Februar 1929. Recherchiert und zusammengestellt von Ulrich Hedtke, Joseph A. Schumpeter. Reden in der Bonner Zeit. *Berliner Debatte Initial*, Jg. 8. Heft 3, 1997. S.87-88.

S.328 Ökonomie und Psychologie des Unternehmers. Vortrag von Professor Dr. Schumpeter, Bonn, in der 10 Ordentlichen Mitgliederversammlung des Zentralverbandes der deutschen Metallwalzwerks=und Hütten=Industrie E. V. am 22. Mai 1929 in München. 15S.

S.329 Ökonomie und Psychologie des Unternehmers. *Industrie—und Handels-Zeitung,*Jg. 10, 23 Mai 1929. Recherchiert und zusammengestellt von Ulrich Hedtke, Joseph A. Schumpeter. Reden in der Bonner Zeit. *Berliner Debatte Initial*, Jg. 8. Heft 3, 1997. S.88-89.

S.330 Gesellschaftswissenschaftliche Seminar. 6 Juni, 20 Juni, 27 Juni, 4 Juli, 11 Juli, 18 Juli, 25 Juli 1929 in Bonn.

1930年

S.331 Vernehmung des Sachverständigen Schumpeter zur Kartellpolitik. Ausschuß zur Untersuchung der Erzeugungs- und Absatzbedingungen der deutschen Wirtschaft. Verhandlungen und Berichte des Unterausschusses für allgemeine Wirtschaftsstruktur.（I. Unterausschuß）.3. Arbeitsgruppe. Wandlungen in den wirtschaftlichen Organisationsformen. Vierter Teil. Kartellpolitik. Zweiter Abschnitt.（Vernehmungen. ）Berlin, Verlegt bei E. S.Mittler & Son. 1930. S.358-366.

S.332 Die Zukunft unserer Gesellschaftsordnung. *Bonner Zeitung*, 14 April 1930. *Deutsche Reichs-Zeitung*, 14 April 1930. Recherchiert und zusammengestellt von Ulrich Hedtke, Joseph A. Schumpeter. Reden in der Bonner Zeit. *Berliner Debatte Initial*, Jg. 8. Heft 3, 1997. S.90-91.

1931年

S.333 Das Kapital im wirtschaftlichen Kreislauf und in der wirtschaftlichen Entwicklung. Herausgegeben von Bernhard Harms, Kapital und Kapitalismus. Vorlesungen gehalten in der Deutschen Vereinigung für Staatswissenschaftliche Fortbildung. Erster Band. Berlin, Verlag von Reimar Hobbing in Berlin 1931. S.187-208.

S.334 The World Depression with Special Reference to the United States of America. Lecture delivered at Japan Industry Club. Tokyo. January 29, 1931. 「日本工業倶楽部会報」第16号.1931年5月25日.pp.11-19.

S.335 The Theory of the Business Cycle. 「経済学論集」第4巻新刊第1号, 1931年4月.pp.1-18.

S.336 The Present State of International Commercial Policy. Lecture delivered at the Kobe University of Commerce. 「国民経済雑誌」第50巻第4号, 1931年4月1日.pp.1-26.

S.337 The Present State of Economics or On Systems, Schools and Methods. 「国民経済雑誌」第50巻第5号, 1931年5月1日.pp.1-27.

S.338 Reparationen und Weltkrise. *Deutsche Reichs-Zeitung*, 12 November 1931. Recherchiert und zusammengestellt von Ulrich Hedtke, Joseph A. Schumpeter. Reden in der Bonner Zeit. *Berliner Debatte Initial*, Jg. 8. Heft 3, 1997. S.90.

1932年

S.339 Soziale und wirtschaftliche Entwicklung. Vortrag in der sozialphilosophischen Arbeitsgemeinschaft am 28. April 1932.

S.340 Das Woher und Wohin unserer Wissenschaft. Abschiedsrede gehalten vor der Bonner staatswissenschaftlichen Fachschaft am 20. Juni 1932.

S.341 Tendenz zum Sozialismus. Vortrag vor der Politisch-Akademische Vereinigung an der Universität Bonn. 18 Juli 1932. General-Anzeiger für Bonn und Umgebung, 19 Juli 1932. Recherchiert und zusammengestellt von Ulrich Hedtke, Joseph A. Schumpeter. Reden in der Bonner Zeit. *Berliner Debatte Initial*, Jg. 8. Heft 3, 1997. S.91.

1936年

S.342 Can Capitalism Survive? Edited by Richard Swedberg, Joseph A. Schumpeter. The Economics and Sociology of Capitalism. Princeton, New Jersey, Princeton University Press, 1991. pp.298-315.

1941年

S.343 An Economic Interpretation of Our Time. The Lowell Lectures. First Lecture given at the Lowell Institute in Boston, Massachusetts. March 4, 1941. The Economic and Political Structure of Modern Society. Second Lecture, March 7, 1941. Success and Failure in the Adjustments of 1919-1929. Third Lecture, March 11, 1941. The Impact of the World Crisis. Fourth Lecture, March 14, 1941. Investment, Unemployment, and Planning during the Thirties Fifth Lecture, March 18. 1941. The Role of Fiscal and Monetary Policies. Sixth Lecture, March 21, 1941. The Falling Birth Rate. Seventh Lecture, March 25, 1941. International Trade. Eighth Lecture, March 28, 1941. Possible Consequences for the United States. Edited by Richard Swedberg, Joseph A. Schumpeter. The Economics and Sociology of Capitalism. Princeton, New Jersey, Princeton University Press, 1991. pp.339-400.

S.344 The Future of Gold. Paper presented at the Economic Club of Detroit, Michigan. April 14, 1941. 19p.

1942年

S.345 Guest Speaker. *World Union.*Students International Union, 1942. p.6.

1944年

S.346 Professor Schumpeter, Austrian Minister, Now Teaching Economic Theory Here. *The Harvard Crimson*, 11 April 1944. p.1, 4.

1948年

S.347 Wage and Tax Policy in Transitional States of Society. Five lectures given from January 16 to 22, 1948, at the National School of Economics of the National Autonomous University of Mexico, Mexico City. Edited by Richard Swedberg, Joseph A. Schumpeter. The Economics and Sociology of Capitalism. Princeton, New Jersey, Princeton University Press. 1991 pp.429-437.

1949年

S.348 Science and ideology. *American Economic Review*, Vol. XXXIX, No. 2, March 1949. pp.345-359. Edited by Daniel M. Hausmann, *The philosophy of economics. An anthology.*Cambridge, London, New York, New Rochelle, Melbourne, Cambridge University Press, 1984. pp.260-275.

1982年

S.349 The 'Crisis' in Economics——Fifty Years Ago. Edited by Robert L. Allen. *Journal of Economic Literature*, Vol. 20, No. 3, September 1982, pp.1049-1059.

S.350 Present Developments of Political Economy. Note by Loring Allen. *Kobe University Economic Review*, Vol. 28, 1982, pp.1-15. Edited by Richard Swedberg, Joseph A. Schumpeter. The Economics and Sociology of Capitalism. Princeton. New Jersey, Princeton University Press. 1991. pp.284-297.

6. 政治的文書

S.351 Politisches Memorandum. Graz, Frühjahr 1916.

S.352 Politisches Memorandum. 1. Dezember 1916.

S.353 Politisches Memorandum. Graz im April 1917. Die politische Lage und die Interessen der Monarchie.

S.354 Politisches Memorandum. Graz, 23. Juni 1917. Die Ursachen des Misserfolges der Regierung und die politische Lage.

S.355 Politisches Memorandum. Graz, Juli/August 1917. Die Aufgabe und die Chancen des österreichischen Cabinetts.

S.356 Politisches Memorandum. Johannisbad (Böhmen), August 1917.

S.357 Politisches Memorandum. Graz, Weihnachten 1917.

S.358 Politisches Memorandum. Frühjahr 1918.

7. 書簡

S.359 Schreiben des Staatssekretärs Schumpeter an Staatskanzler Renner. Herausgegeben von Wolfgang F. Stolper und Christian Seidl, Joseph A. Schumpeter. Aufsätze zur Wirtschaftspolitik. Tübingen, J. C. B. Mohr (Paul Siebeck), 1985. S.336-343.

S.360 Letter to George Garvey. 1 December 1943.

S.361 Letter to Charles A. Gulick. 7 August 1944. Charles A. Gulick, Austria from Habsburg to Hitler. Vol. 1, Berkley and Los Angeles, University of California Press. 1948. p.140.

S.362 Persönliche Briefe Schumpeters. Eduard März, Joseph Alois Schumpeter—— Forscher, Lehrer und Politiker. München, R. Oldenbourg Verlag, 1983. S.169-184.

S.363 Letters by Schumpeter. Richard Swedberg, Joseph. A. Schumpeter. His Life and Work. Polity Press, 1991. pp.209-238(2).Briefe von Joseph A. Schumpeter. Richard Swedberg, Joseph A. Schumpeter. Eine Bibliographie. Aus dem Englischen übersetzt von Johannes G. Pankau. Klett-Cotta, Stuttgart, 1994. S288-329.

S.364 Briefe Schumpeters an Graf Otto Harrach. Herausgegeben von Christian Seidl und Wolfgang F. Stolper, Joseph A. Schumpeter. Politische Reden. Tübingen, J. C. B. Mohr (Paul Siebeck), 1992. S359-375.

S.365 Schumpeter letters〔Bonn, May 28th 1928. Bonn, 7th July 1928. Bonn, Aug. 16th 1928. Bremen, Sept. 9 1930〕.Christian Seidl, Schumpeter Addressing Keynes. *History of Economic Ideas.*IV/1996/3. pp.174-179.

S.366 Joseph Alois Schumpeter. Briefe/Letters. Ausgewählt und herausgegeben von Ulrich Hedtke und Richard Swedberg. Tübingen, J. C. B. Mohr (Paul Siebeck) .2000. S.39-393.

S.367 Ulrich Hedtke, Joseph Alois Schumpeter. Verzeichnis der deutschsprachigen Briefe. Eine Dokumentation zu Joseph A. Schumpeter. Briefe/Letters, ausgewählt und herausgegeben von Ulrich Hedtke und Richard Swedberg, Tübingen 2000. Über arbeitete Fassung, herausgegeben am 25. Juni 2007. www. Schumpeter, info.

8. アフォリズム

S.368 Aphorisms from Schumpeter's Private Diary. Richard Swedberg, Joseph A. Schumpeter. His Life and Work. Polity Press, 1991. pp.199-206(3).Aphorismen aus Schumpeters privatem Tagebuch. Richard Swedberg, Joseph A. Schumpeter. Eine Biographie. Aus dem Englischen übersetzt von Johannes G. Pankau. Klett-Cotta, Stuttgart, 1994. S.267-284.

9. 小 説

S.369 Schumpeter's Novel. *Ships in the Flog* (a Fragment).Richard Swedberg, Joseph A. Schumpeter. His Life and Work. Polity Press, 1991. pp.207-208(4).Schumpeter's Roman. *Schiffe im Nebel* (Ein Fragment).Richard Swedberg, Joseph A. Schumpeter. Eine Bibliographie. Aus dem Englischen übersetzt von Johannes G. Pankau. Klett-Cotta, Stuttgart, 1994. S.285-287.

10. 自筆草稿

S.370 Handwritten manuscript of Joseph A. Schumpeter's Capitalism, Socialism, and Democracy(5).Deciphered and compiled by Shinichi Uraki and Norio Yonekawa.

注

(1) 今まで本著の出版が、1911年か1912年か不明確であった。シュンペーター自身は、論文や書簡で1911年に出版されたと言っている。オックスフォード大学のマーシャル文庫のドイツ語初版本ではフロントページの1911年が、手書きで1912年に訂正して書き直され、その第2ページが1912年となっている。こうしたことから本著初版本は、出版元の図書目録には1912年とあるが、1911年秋に出版されたと見てよいだろう。わが国では1911年版の存在は、未だ確認できない。Markus C. Becker and Thorbjørn Knudsen, Schumpeter 1911, Forsighted Views on Economic Development, *The American Journal of Economics and Sociology*, Vol. 61, No. 2, April 2002, pp.387, 397-399.

(2) 米川紀生「J. A. シュンペーターのアフォリズム・小説・書簡」「法経論叢」第12巻第1号, 1995年1月20日, pp.10-29.

(3) 米川紀生「J. A. シュンペーターのアフォリズム」「法経論叢」第12巻第1号, 1995年1月20日, pp.2-8.

(4) 米川紀生「J. A. シュンペーターの小説―「霧の中の船」（一断片）」「法経論叢」第12巻第1号, 1995年1月20日, pp.8-10.

(5)この文書類(手書き原稿、イエローペーパー等)は全て、米国留学中の古谷弘が、シュンペーターの形見としてエリザベスから受け取り、友子夫人の父ゆずりのトランクに納められ、古谷夫妻とともに熱海丸で太平洋を越えて1954年10月7日頃恩師東畑精一に直接届けられた。古谷夫人は2006年11月5日に50年ぶりにシュンペーター遺品と再会し、シュンペーター・東畑・古谷の麗しくも親しい人間関係に思いを致し、感激を新たにした。同文書は現在、東畑文庫(東畑記念館より三重県立図書館に移管)の隣り奥の桐箱に保管されている。同文庫を訪れ、記念帳にサインの上、地下のシュンペーターのドアを拓くことができる。「シュンペーター幻の草稿」「日本経済新聞」1992年8月11日、p32。2006年11月15日付古谷友子書簡。杉浦祥夫「日本にあるシュンペーターの代表作原稿(東畑精一教授と古谷弘教授)」「級友」168号, 2007年6月10日, pp.48-54.

資料　自筆原稿

Advent?

Capitalism, Socialism, and Democracy

by

Joseph A. Schumpeter

Professor of Economics in Harvard University

Memo.

I suggest that, ~~on the outside of the jacket,~~ the headings of the five Parts should appear on the outside of the jacket, thus:

Part I The Marxian Doctrine
Part II Can Capitalism Survive?
Part III Can Socialism Work?
Part IV Socialism and Democracy
Part V A Historical Sketch of Socialist Parties

59

(1) シュンペーター自筆原稿『資本主義・社会主義・民主主義』ジャケット

（三重県立図書館所蔵）

I

Preface

This volume is the result of an effort to weld into a readable form the bulk of almost forty years' thought, observation and research on the subject of socialism. The problem of democracy forced its way into the place it now occupies in this volume because it proved impossible to state my views on the relation between the socialist order of society and the democratic method of government without a rather extensive analysis of the latter.

My task turned out more difficult than I thought it would be. Part of the heterogeneous material that had to be marshalled, reflected the views and experiences of an individual who at various stages of his life had more opportunity for observation than nonsocialists usually have and who reacted to what he saw in an unconventional manner. I had no wish to obliterate the traces of this: much of what interest this book may command would have gone if I had tried to smooth them away.

New paragraph

Moreover, those that

CO

(1) シュンペーター自筆原稿『資本主義・社会主義・民主主義』序文

（三重県立図書館所蔵）

II

materials also reflected the analytic efforts of an individual who, while always honestly trying to probe below the surface, never made the problems of socialism the principal subject of his professional research for any length of time and therefore has much more to say on some topics than on others. In order to avoid creating the impression that I aimed at writing a well-balanced treatise, I have thought it best to group my stuff around five central themes. Links and bridges between them have been provided of course and something like systematic unity of presentation has, I hope, been achieved. But in essence they are almost—though not independent—self-contained pieces of analysis.

The First Part sums up, in a nontechnical manner, what I have to say—and what, as a matter of fact, I have been teaching for some decades—on the subject of the Marxian Doctrine. To preface a discussion of the main problems of socialism by an exposition of the Gospel would be the natural thing to do for a Marxist. But what has it got to do in the hall of a house built by one who is not a Marxist? It stands there to bear witness to this non-Marxist's belief in the unique importance of that message, an importance that is completely independent of acceptance or rejection. But it makes difficult reading. And no Marxian tools are used in the subsequent work. Though the results of the latter are again and again compared with the tenets of the one great socialist thinker, readers who are not interested in Marxism may start directly with Part II.

61

111

In the Second Part — Can Capitalism Survive? — I have tried to show that a socialist form of society will inevitably emerge from an equally inevitable decomposition of capitalist society. Many readers will wonder why I thought so laborious and complex an analysis necessary in order to establish what is rapidly becoming the general opinion, even among conservatives. The reason is that, while most of us agree as to the result, we do not agree as to the nature of the process that is killing capitalism and as to the precise meaning to be attached to the word "inevitable." Believing that most of the arguments offered — both on Marxian and on more popular lines — are wrong, I felt it my duty to take, and to inflict upon the reader, considerable trouble in order to lead up effectively to my paradoxical conclusion: capitalism is being killed by its achievements.

Having seen, as I think we shall see, that socialism is a practical proposition that may become immediately practical in consequence of the present war, we shall in the Third Part — Can Socialism Work? — survey a large expanse of problems that bear

62

IV.

upon the conditions in which the socialist order may be expected to be an economic success. This Part comes nearest to being a balanced treatment of its various topics including the "transitional" problems. Love and hate have blurred the results of such serious work as has been done on this problem — it is not much — that even mere restatements of widely accepted views seemed justified here and there.

The Fourth Part — Socialism and Democracy — is a contribution to a controversy that has been going on in this country for some time. [illegible] But it should be noticed that only a question of principle is dealt with in that Part. Facts and comments relevant to the subject are scattered all over the book particularly in Parts III and V.

I said that I offer no Marxist. Neither [illegible] a Marxologist [illegible] Marx's major publications

63

V

The Fifth Part is what it purports to be, a sketch. More than in the other Parts I wished to confine myself to what I had to say from personal observation and very fragmentary research. Therefore the material that went into this Part is no doubt woefully incomplete. But what there is of it, is alive.

No part of the contents of this volume has ever appeared in print. An early draft of the argument of Part II has however provided the basis for a lecture delivered at the U.S. Department of Agriculture Graduate School on January 18, 1936, and has been mimeographed by the latter. I wish to thank Mr. A. C. Edwards, chairman of the Arrangements Committee, for the permission to include an extended version in this volume.

Harvard University
March 1942.

Joseph A. Schumpeter

64

VI

Table of Contents.

65

(1) シュンペーター自筆原稿『資本主義・社会主義・民主主義』目次

（三重県立図書館所蔵）

V4

Contents

Page

66

VIII

Page

67

IX

Page

Part IV. Socialism and Democracy 343–460

68

X

Page

Part V. A Historical Sketch of Socialist Parties 461–575

~~[illegible]~~

69

Contents

Page

VI. The Present War and the Future of Socialist Parties 571

70

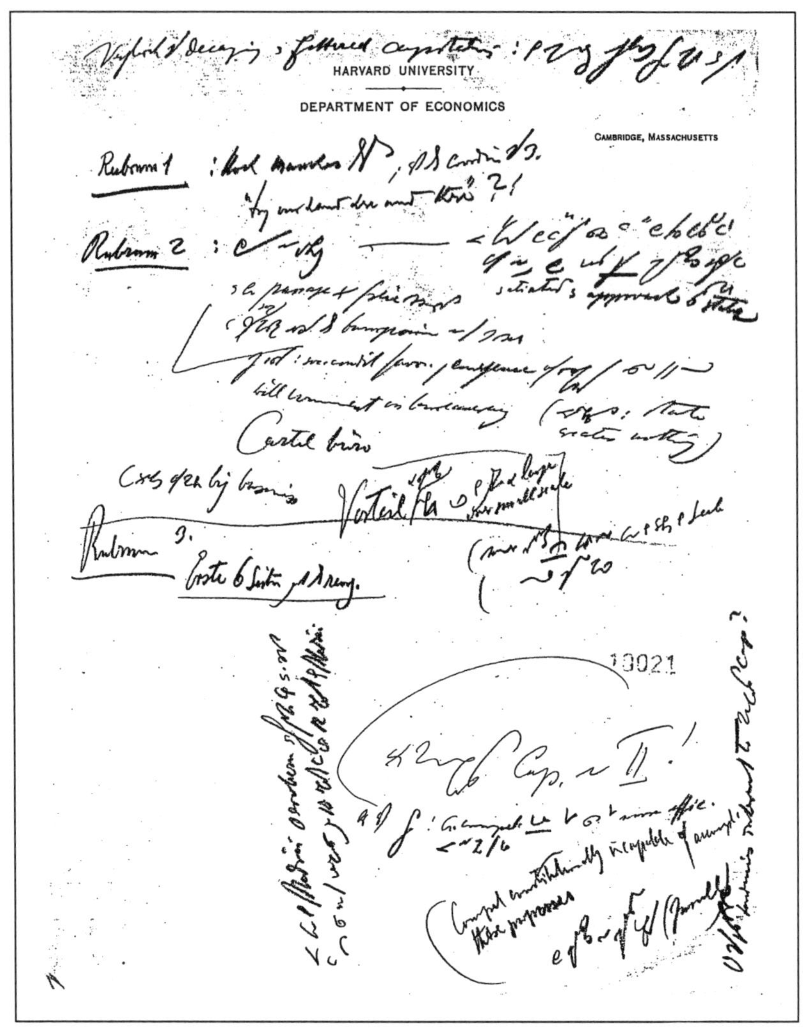
HARVARD UNIVERSITY

DEPARTMENT OF ECONOMICS

CAMBRIDGE, MASSACHUSETTS

10021

(1) シュンペーター自筆原稿『資本主義・社会主義・民主主義』手書き原稿

(三重県立図書館所蔵)

(1) シュンペーター自筆原稿『資本主義・社会主義・民主主義』イエローページ

(三重県立図書館所蔵)

II　参考文献目録

II 参考文献目録

1. 著作の邦訳

1936年

001 シュムペーター, 木村健康, 安井琢磨訳『理論経済学の本質と主要内容』日本評論社, 1936年2月8日第1刷.1937年12月1日再版.1939年3月25日3版.1939年7月15日4版.1940年8月15日5版.1941年9月20日7版.1941年12月30日8版.1942年12月30日第9刷.1943年10月10日第10刷.6+18+12+607p.

002 改訂版 シュムペーター著, 大野忠男, 木村健康, 安井琢磨訳『理論経済学の本質と主要内容』岩波書店〔上・下全2冊, 文庫版〕.(上)1983年12月16日第1刷.1993年3月16日第2刷.499p.(下)1984年2月16日第1刷.1993年3月16日第2刷.510p.

1937年

003 シュムペーター, 中山伊知郎, 東畑精一共訳『経済発展の理論 企業者利潤・資本・信用・利子及び景気の回転に関する一研究 (原著第二版より)』岩波書店, 1937年7月20日第1刷.1938年7月10日第2刷.1939年9月20日第3刷.1940年8月第4刷.1941年8月第5刷.36+6+706+3p.

004 増訂版 岩波書店, 1951年1月15日第1刷.1951年2月25日第2刷.1951年8月5日第3刷.1953年5月第4刷.1955年5月30日第5刷.1956年5月第6刷.36+6+693+19p.

005 改訂版 シュムペーター, 塩野谷祐一, 中山伊知郎, 東畑精一訳『経済発展の理論 企業者利潤・資本・信用・利子および景気の回転に関する一研究(原著第二版より)』岩波書店〔上・下全2冊, 文庫版〕.(上)1977年9月16日第1刷.1977年10月20日第2刷.1979年12月第3刷.1980年12月20日第4刷.1982年2月10日第5刷.1983年6月10日第6刷.1983年12月20日第7刷.1989年9月18日第8刷.1990年5月15日第9刷.1993年2月16日第10刷.1993年12月5日第11刷.362P.(下)1977年11月16日第1刷.1977年12月20日第2刷.1979年8月10日第3刷.1980年12月20日第4刷.1982年3月10日第5刷.1983年12月20日第6刷.1989年9月18日第7刷.1990年5月15日第8刷.1993年2月16日第9刷.275p.

006 机上版 シュムペーター, 塩野谷祐一, 中山伊知郎, 東畑精一訳『経済発展の理論 企業者利潤・資本・信用・利子および景気の回転に関する一研究(原著第二版より)』岩波書店, 1980年9月26日改訳第1刷.546+17P.

1950年

007　シュムペーター, 中山伊知郎, 東畑精一共訳『経済学史—学説竝びに方法の諸段階—』岩波書店, 1950年12月15日第1刷.1951年2月10日第2刷.1951年3月第3刷.1953年9月1日第4刷.1957年2月第7刷.1958年11月30日第8刷.1961年3月20日第9刷.1963年1月20日第10刷.1964年5月10日第11刷.1966年2月20日第12刷.1967年1月30日第13刷.1967年11月30日第14刷.1970年5月20日第15刷.1971年6月30日第16刷.6+3+355+9p.

008　改訂版　シュムペーター, 中山伊知郎, 東畑精一訳『経済学史—学説ならびに方法の諸段階—』岩波書店〔文庫版〕, 1980年9月16日第1刷.1984年4月10日第2刷.1991年12月16日第3刷.1993年3月3日第4刷.386+10p.

1951年

009　シュムペーター, 中山伊知郎, 東畑精一共訳『資本主義・社会主義・民主主義第三版』東洋経済新報社〔上・中・下全3巻〕.

009a　上巻 1951年2月15日第1版.1951年4月20日第2刷.1952年5月15日第3刷.1953年5月25日第4刷.1953年10月20日第5刷, 1955年8月30日第7刷, 3+8+288p.

009b　中巻 1951年12月25日第1刷, 1952年2月10日第2刷, 1953年2月20日第3刷, 5月25日第4刷, 1953年10月20日第5刷, 1955年8月30日第7刷, 4+4p.+pp.289-548.

009c　下巻 1952年12月15日発行, 1953年1月25日第2刷, 10月20日第3刷, 1954年8月30日第4刷, 1955年8月30日第5刷, 1956年9月5日第6刷, 3+4p.+pp.549-778+22+7p.

010　改訂版 シュムペーター, 中山伊知郎, 東畑精一訳『資本主義・社会主義・民主主義 第三版』東洋経済新報社〔上・中・下全3巻〕.

010a　上 1962年4月28日第1刷.1964年3月20日第6刷.1965年1月20日第7刷.1967年7月1日第14刷.1967年7月10日第15刷.1969年6月15日第16刷.1969年11月10日第19刷.1970年7月10日第20刷.1970年12月8日第21刷.1971年5月10日第22刷.1971年10月25日第23刷.1972年7月10日第24刷.1973年3月2日第25刷.1973年11月15日第26刷.1974年8月13日第27刷.1975年7月1日第28刷.1976年5月10日第29刷.1977年8月11日第30刷.1978年7月21日第31刷.1979年7月16日第32刷.1982年8月6日第33刷.1984年4月10日第34刷.1986年8月27日第35刷.1988年7月15日第36刷.1990年7月5日第37刷.1991年9月5日第38刷.1992年11月10日第39刷.48+298p.

010b　中 1962年6月8日第1刷.1964年3月20日第5刷.1965年1月30日第6刷.1965年11月20日第9刷.1969年6月15日第16刷.1970年7月7日第17刷.1971年2月25日第18刷.1971年12月20日 第19刷.1973年2月20日 第20刷.1973年11月27日 第21刷.1974年8月13日 第22刷.1975年12月4日第23刷.1977年12月15日第24刷.1979年7月12日第25刷.1984年4月10日第26刷.1986年7月15日第27刷.1989年8月10日第28刷.1991年2月5日第29刷.1992年11月10日第30刷.12p.+pp.299-568.

010c　下 1962年6月28日第1刷.1964年3月20日第4刷.1965年2月5日第5刷.1966年11月25日第9刷.1969年11月25日第14刷.1970年8月24日第15刷.1971年9月5日第16刷.1972年

7月10日 第17刷.1974年1月10日 第18刷.1974年8月19日 第19刷.1975年12月4日 第20刷.1978年2月15日 第21刷.1979年5月17日 第22刷.1981年9月28日 第23刷.1984年10月25日 第24刷.1989年4月5日 第25刷.1991年2月5日 第26刷.1992年10月5日 第27刷.1993年7月12日 第28刷.7p.+pp.569-807+8p.下巻初版第1刷(1952年12月15日)付録「シュムペーター関係文献目録」(pp.1-22)に替わって, 下巻改訂版第1刷(1962年6月28日)巻末「シュムペーター邦訳著作目録」(pp.7-8).

011 J・A・シュンペーター, 編集部訳「資本主義の存続は必然的に不可能」〔『資本主義・社会主義・民主主義』第二部プロローグ, 第12, 14章を参考〕「季刊現代経済」1(創刊号), 1971年6月8日.pp.234-237.

012 ヨーゼフ・シュンペーター「創造的破壊―資本主義の本質」〔『資本主義・社会主義・民主主義』の抜録〕, 米誌NPQ(New Perspectives Quarterly)編小林勇次/森平慶司訳『勝ち誇る資本主義への警告 資本主義は勝利したか?』JICC出版局, 1991年3月1日第1刷, pp.34-40.

013 J. A. Schumpeter〔J・A・シュムペーター〕, 木村元一訳『租税国家の危機』勁草書房, 1951年5月15日発行, 2+8+1+144p.

014 改訳版 シュムペーター著, 木村元一, 小谷義次訳『租税国家の危機』岩波書店〔文庫版〕, 1983年7月18日第1刷.141p.

1952年

015 シュムペーター, 中山伊知郎・東畑精一監修『十大経済学者　マルクスからケインズまで』日本評論新社, 1952年5月30日第1版第1刷.1952年7月10日第1版第2刷.1966年5月25日第1版第6刷.8+430p.

015a 中山伊知郎, 東畑精一「監修者序文」pp.1-5.

015b エリザベス・ブーディ・シュムペーター, 中山伊知郎訳「シュムペーター夫人による原著序文」pp.1-10.

015c 中山伊知郎・東畑精一訳「マルクス(1818―1883)」pp.11-108.

015d 安井琢磨訳「ワルラス(1834―1910)」pp.109-118.

015e 安井琢磨訳「メンガー(1840―1921)」pp.119-131.

015f 山田雄三訳「マーシァル(1842―1924)」pp.133-156.

015g 古谷弘訳「パレート(1848―1923)」pp.157-202.

015h 東畑精一訳「ボェーム・バヴェルク(1851―1914)」pp.203-263.

015i 都留重人訳「タウシッグ(1859―1940)」pp.265-311.

015j 久武雅夫訳「フィッシャー(1867―1947)」pp.313-334.

015k 高橋長太郎訳「ミッチェル(1874―1948)」pp.335-361.

015l 塩野谷九十九訳「ケインズ(1883―1946)」pp.363-414.

015m 宮田喜代蔵訳「クナップ(1842―1926)」pp.417-420.

015n 永田清訳「ウィーザー(1851―1926)」pp.421-425.

015o 森田優三訳「ボルトキウィッツ(1868―1931)」pp.427-430.

015l1　ヨゼフ・A・シュンペーター「経済学者ケインズ(その二)」, 日本銀行調査局訳『新しい経済学 理論と政策にたいするケインズの影響 I』東洋経済新報社, 1949年10月20日第1版.1949年11月25日第2版.1950年2月10日第3版.1950年5月25日第4版.pp.110-156.

015h1　シュンペーター, 一杉哲也訳「ボェーム＝バウェルク論」, H. W. シュピーゲル編, 伊坂市助, 越村信三郎, 山田長夫, 伊藤豊三郎, 長州一二, 古沢友吉監訳『限界効用学派 ―経済思想発展史IV―』東洋経済新報社, 1954年12月10日発行.pp.191-208.

1955年

016　シュムペーター, 東畑精一訳『経済分析の歴史』岩波書店〔全7巻〕.

016a　1　1955年10月30日第1刷.1959年2月第2刷.1961年9月30日第3刷.1963年9月20日第4刷.1965年9月15日第5刷.1967年6月20日第6刷.1969年3月20日第7刷.1970年10月30日第8刷.1980年9月26日第9刷.1992年9月3日第10刷.38+438p.

016b　2　1956年11月1日第1刷.1959年8月第2刷.1962年10月30日第3刷.1964年8月20日第4刷.1967年2月25日第5刷.1969年3月20日第6刷.1980年9月26日第8刷.1992年9月3日第9刷.10p.+pp.435-794+4p.

016c　3　1957年8月26日第1刷.1961年7月25日第2刷.1963年9月20日第3刷.1966年8月30日第4刷.1968年10月20日第5刷.1971年2月20日第6刷.1980年9月26日第7刷.1992年9月3日第8刷.11p.+pp.795-1206+4p.

016d　4　1958年2月25日第1刷.1962年10月30日第2刷.1964年7月20日第3刷.1967年4月10日第4刷.1969年7月30日第5刷.1971年10月30日第6刷.1980年9月26日第7刷.1992年9月3日第8刷.8p.+pp.1207-1573+4p.

016e　5　1958年11月29日第1刷.1962年11月30日第2刷.1964年12月10日第3刷.1967年7月30日第4刷.1969年9月30日第5刷.1972年7月10日第6刷.1980年9月26日第7刷.1992年9月30日第8刷.12p.+pp.1575-2006+4p.

016f　6　1960年2月20日第1刷.1961年11月10日第2刷.1963年9月20日第3刷.1966年8月30日第4刷.1968年5月20日第5刷.1970年5月20日第6刷.1980年9月26日第7刷.1992年9月3日第8刷.10p.+pp.2007-2391+4p.

016g　7　1962年4月30日第1刷.1963年9月20日第2刷.1966年11月20日第3刷.1968年12月20日第4刷.1971年7月20日第5刷.1980年9月26日第6刷.1992年9月3日第7刷.5p.+pp.2393- 2533＋181p.

016h　編集部訳「経済分析の歴史〔目次〕」「経済研究」第1巻第3号, 1950年7月5日.pp.226-227.

1956年

017　シュンペーター, 都留重人訳『帝国主義と社会階級』岩波書店, 1956年12月20日第1刷.1959年2月第2刷.1961年4月30日第3刷.1963年2月20日第4刷.1964年8月30日第5刷.1966年7月20日第6刷.1967年7月30日第7刷.1968年7月20日第8刷.1969年6月20日第9刷.1971年3月

30日第10刷.1972年1月20日第11刷.1972年12月20日第12刷.1974年3月20日第13刷.1975年1月30日第14刷.1977年7月30日第15刷.1980年9月10日第16刷.1983年4月8日第17刷.1993年9月1日第18刷.6+262+8p.

1958年

018 シュムペーター, 吉田昇三監修, 金融経済研究所訳『景気循環論―資本主義過程の理論的・歴史的・統計的分析―』有斐閣〔全5巻〕

018a I　1958年12月20日初版第1刷.1963年7月30日初版第3刷.1966年2月10日初版第4刷.復刻1985年9月10日第7刷復刻版第1刷.4+1+6+12+6+326+4p.

018b II　1959年10月30日初版第1刷.1965年9月20日初版第2刷.復刻1985年9月10日第4刷復刻版第1刷.4p.+pp.327-670-4p.

018c III　1960年12月5日初版第1刷.1964年5月30日初版第2刷.復刻1985年9月10日第4刷復刻版第1刷.5p.+pp.671-1022+4p.

018d IV　1962年2月25日初版第1刷.1971年7月20日初版第3刷.復刻1985年9月10日第4刷復刻版第1刷.4p.+pp.1023-1354+6p.

018e V　1964年12月1日初版第1刷.1969年12月20日初版第2刷.復刻1985年9月10日第3刷復刻版第1刷.3p.+pp.1355-1653+30p.

018f 内田幸登訳「Joseph A. Schumpeter, Business Cycle, A Theoretical and Statistical Analysis of the Capitalist Process. Chapter III, How the Economic System generates Evolution」, 立命館大学経済学部浜崎ゼミナール『J. A・シュムペーターの経済学について』「学生論集」(昭和32年度), 1958年3月.pp.304-337.

1961年

019 シュムペーター, 三輪悌三訳『貨幣・分配の理論』東洋経済新報社, 1961年9月25日.6+266+2p.

019a 第一部　社会生産物と計算貨幣―今日の貨幣論に対する批判と貢献―〔1917〕.pp.1-120.

019b 第二部　分配理論の基礎原理〔1916〕.pp.121-266.

1972年

020 シュムペーター, 玉野井芳郎監修, 谷嶋喬四郎, 佐瀬昌盛, 中村友太郎, 島岡光一訳『社会科学の過去と未来』ダイヤモンド社, 1972年3月16日初版.13+519p.

020a 玉野井芳郎「はじめに―監修者のことば―」pp.1-8.

020b 玉野井芳郎「シュムペーターの今日的意味」pp.1-48. 1部が「人間シュムペーター」『転換する経済学 科学の総合化を求めて』東京大学出版会, 1975年11月30日初版.pp.9-

65.

020c　谷嶋喬四郎訳「社会科学の過去と未来」〔1915〕pp.149-289.

020d　佐瀬昌盛訳「国民経済の全体像」〔『経済発展の理論』初版(1912年)第7章〕pp.311-405.

020e　中村友太郎・島岡光一訳「歴史と理論—シュモラーと今日の諸問題—」〔1926〕pp.421-503.

020f　佐瀬昌盛作成者「主要著作一覧」pp.510-519.

1973年

021　シュムペーター, 大野忠男訳『資本主義と社会主義』創文社, 1973年5月25日第1刷.1+246p.

021a　「資本主義」〔1946年〕pp.3-40.

021b　「戦後の世界における資本主義」〔1943年〕pp.41-64.

021c　「英国経済学と国家管理経済」〔1949年〕pp.65-95.

021d　「今日における社会主義の可能性」〔1920年〕pp.96-178.

021e　「英国ならびにわが国における社会主義」〔1924年〕pp.179-200.

021f　「共産党宣言の社会学と経済学」〔1949年〕pp.201-237.

021bb　シュンペーター, 大蔵省理財局調査部財政経済実勢研究室訳「戦後世界における資本主義」〔Seymour Harris編 Postwar Economic Problems(1943)所載〕「大蔵省調査部調査月報」第37巻第16号, 1948年11月25日.pp.1-19.

1977年

022　シュムペーター著, 大野忠男訳『今日における社会主義の可能性』創文社, 1977年7月10日改題増補版第1刷.1980年4月20日改題増補第2刷.1+282p.シュムペーター, 大野訳『資本主義と社会主義』創文社, 1973年5月25日第1刷に以下の二論文追加.

022a　「私的企業の将来—現代の社会主義的傾向に直面して—」〔1946年〕pp.238-246.

022b　「社会主義への前進」〔1950年〕pp.247-268.

1980年

023　シュムペーター, 谷嶋喬四郎訳『社会科学の未来像』講談社〔文庫版〕, 1980年5月10日第1刷.227p.シュムペーター, 玉野井芳郎監修『社会科学の過去と未来』ダイヤモンド社, 1972年3月16日初版の谷嶋喬四郎訳の改訳.

1988年

024 シュンペーター「現時と向こう三年間の財政政策の基準線」〔1919年〕, 米川紀生「J. A. Schumpeterの財政政策構想」「法経論叢」第6巻第1号, 1988年10月1日.pp.29-61.

1991年

025 シュムペーター, 金指基編訳『景気循環分析への歴史的接近』八朔社, 1991年4月10日第1刷.1+221p.

025a 「景気循環の理論(1931)」pp.1-21.

025b 「沈滞—過去の経験から学ぶことができるか(1934)」pp.23-41.

025c 「経済変動の分析(1935)」pp.43-70.

025d 「20年代の10年間(1946)」pp.71-90.

025e 「経済成長の理論的諸問題(1947)」pp.91-108.

025f 「まだインフレを止める時間はある(1948)」pp.109-111.

025g 「景気循環分析への歴史的接近(1949)」pp.133-147.

025h 「シュンペーター年譜」(金指基)pp.149-187.

025i 「シュンペーター著作目録」(金指基)pp.189-212.

025ee ジョセフ・A・シュンペーター, 宇佐美和彦訳「経済変動の分析」, G・ハーバラー編, 後藤誉之助訳『景気変動の理論 上』実業之日本社, 1951年3月5日.pp.3-25.

2. 論文・講演

1909年

026 政治科小泉信三「社会価値の概念」「三田学会雑誌」第2巻第4号, 1909年12月1日.pp.88-95.「(本年〔1909年〕2月発行Quarterly Journal of Economics pp.213-232. ヨセフシュムペーター氏の所説三田読書会報告)」(p.88), 福田徳三附言(pp.95-96).

026a 永安幸正訳「〔資料〕J. A. シュムペーター 社会的価値の概念について」「高崎経済大学論集」第14巻第1・2号, 1971年11月10日.pp.294-314.

1931年

027 ボン大学教授 シュンペーター「最近の景気学説」「エコノミスト」第9年第4号, 1931年2月15日.pp.33-36. 付記「本稿は, 1月30日東京帝大における博士の講演主旨である。」.

028　ジェー・エー・シュムペーター「恐慌の理論」「経済往来」第6巻第3号, 1931年3月1日, pp.23-38. 本稿は1931年1月30日東京帝国大学に於ける講演速記.1931年2月3日付シュンペーター自身のサインあり.

029　「シュンペーター博士の講演」「公民講座」第76号, 1931年3月1日, p.136. 1931年1月29日東京〔日本工業の誤り〕倶楽部での講演及び神戸商大講演の第一回「商業政策の現状」.

030　ジョセフ・シュンペーター「世界不況の原因と今後の景気予測」「東京工場懇話会々報」第53号, 1931年2月20日, pp.14 - 19

031　ヨセフ・シュムペーター教授述『世界不況に就て—特に米国の事情を参照したる—』日本経済連盟会, 日本工業倶楽部, 1931年3月, 1+19p.(代謄写).

032　ヨセフ・シュムペーター教授述「世界不況に就て—特に米国の事情を参照したる—」「日本工業倶楽部会報」第16号, 1931年5月25日.pp.20-28. 本稿は, 1931年1月29日日本工業倶楽部での講演速記.

033　ヨゼフ・シュムペーター博士「政治経済生活に於ける貨幣政策」「大阪商工会議所月報」第286号, 1931年3月25日.pp.14-16.

034　ヨセフ・シュンペーター「現下の恐慌理論に就て」「東京工場懇話会々報」第61号, 1931年12月20日.pp.17-21.

1938年

035　ヨゼフ・シュムペーター博士, 伊藤俊夫訳「StaatsreferendarとStaatsassessor」「司法資料」(司法省調査部)第244号, 1938年9月.pp.1-33.

1949年

036　ジョセフ・A・シュムペーター「科学とイデオロギー」「思想」303号, 1949年9月5日.pp.1-16.

037　田村倉一訳「Essays of J. A. Schumpeter, edited by R. V. Clemence. Science and Ideology」, 立命館大学経済学部浜崎ゼミナール『J. A. シュムペーターの経済学について』「学生論集」(昭和32年度)1958年3月.pp.338-358.

1951年

038　ワシリー・レオンティエフ, 山田勇訳「計量経済学 批判者J・A・シュムペーター, W・アレン・ウォリス」.H・S・エリス編, 都留重人訳監修『現代経済学の展望　理論篇II』岩波書店, 1951年12月10日第1刷.pp.211-251.

1966年

039 ジョセフ・A・シュンペーター, 竹内靖雄訳「選択の係数としての価格」.W・A・リーマン, 玉野井芳郎監訳『比較経済体制論(上)』日本評論社, 1966年3月25日第1版第1刷.pp.179-185.

040 J. A. シュンペーター, 金原実翻訳「経済理論と企業者史」「金融経済」第100号, 1966年10月25日.pp.215-233.

1983年

041 ジョウゼフ・A・シュンペーター, 杉山忠平訳「経済学の「危機」—50年前の……」, 編集発行人・大石進『別冊経済セミナー　シュンペーター再発見 生誕100年記念』日本評論社, 1983年7月30日.pp.17-26.

1990年

042 J. A. Schumpeter, 米川紀生訳「政治経済学の最近の発展」〔1931年〕「J. A・Schumpeter『資本主義・社会主義・民主主義』の準備的考察」「法経論叢」第8巻第1号, 1990年12月20日.pp.11-34.

1991年

043 J. A. Schumpeter, 米川紀生訳「社会諸科学における合理性の意義」〔1940年〕「J. A. Schumpeterから見た「社会諸科学における合理性の意義」」「法経論叢」第8巻第2号, 1991年3月20日.pp.2-29.

3. 関連著書・論文・書評・回想

1913年

044 〔森林太郎〕「むく鳥通信—無名氏—」「昴」第5年第1号, 大正2年1月1日発行.p.112. 木下杢太郎, 小島政二郎, 斎藤茂吉, 佐藤春夫, 平野萬里, 森於菟編輯『鷗外全集著作篇』第17巻, 岩波書店, 昭和11年12月25日発行.p.913. 木下杢太郎, 小島政二郎, 斎藤茂吉, 佐藤春夫, 平野萬利, 森於菟, 佐藤佐太郎, 澤柳大五郎編輯『鷗外全集』第27巻, 岩波書店, 昭和49年1月22日発行.p.750. 森鷗外は,「Gratz大学で理財学教授Schumpeterが苛酷なので学生が反抗した」と報じる。

1923年

045　土方成美『財政学の基礎概念　経済社会と財政現象』岩波書店, 1923年12月23日発行.1924年11月25日改訂.1926年5月25日改訂第3刷.6+4+3+612p.

1924年

046　土方博士述『財政学 大正一三年度東大講義』(非売品)編集兼発行者石田正七, 文信社, 1924年2月13日.2+2+6+193p.

047　土方成美講述『財政学』(非売品)国文社出版部, 山田余所治編集兼発行者, 1928年10月1日.2+160p.

048　高田保馬『経済学研究』岩波書店, 1924年9月15日第1刷.2+2+822p.

1925年

049　福田徳三『経済学全集第一集　経済学講義』同文館, 1925年3月12日発行.1925年3月15日再版.1925年3月18日3版.3月25日4版.15+33+30+1424+29p.

049a　福田徳三『経済学全集第一集　経済学講義 第一分冊』同文館, 1927年1月25日発行.33+14+432p.廉刷版.

049b　福田徳三『経済学全集第一集　経済学講義 第一分冊』同文館, 1927年3月10日発行.pp.433-928. 廉刷版.

050　高田保馬「経済静態に就て」「経済研究」第2巻第2号, 1925年4月15日.pp.1-33.

051　徳重伍介「Joseph Schumpeterの「貨幣理論基本方程式」に就て」「国民経済雑誌」第39巻第4号, 1925年10月1日.pp.35-54.

1926年

052　土方成美『経済生活の理論　上巻』岩波書店, 1926年4月25日第1刷.6+3+429+9p.

053　菊田太郎「シュームペーターのシュモッラー観」「経済論叢」第23巻第5号, 1926年11月1日.pp.156-161.

054　高島善哉「シュムペーターの経済静学」「ヘルメス」第6号, 1926年12月12日.pp.46-79.

1927年

055　ハンス・ホネッガー原著.安部浩, 谷口武彦共訳『最近の経済思潮』中外文化協会, 1927年2月20日.14+9+311p.

056　荒木光太郎「ウヰーン学界の人々」「経済往来」第2巻第5号, 1927年5月1日.pp.150-157.『現代貨幣問題』改造社, 1935年4月20日発行.pp.540-551.

057　高島佐一郎『動態経済の研究』同文館, 1927年7月1日発行.1927年7月25日再版.15+11+539p.

058　今井久次郎「価格論に於ける静態と動態」「ヘルメス」第9号, 1927年12月25日.pp.39-55.

1928年

059　高橋次郎「シュムペーターとオッペンハイマーの静態論」「商学討究」第3巻上冊, 1928年6月30日.pp.123-160.

060　土方成美『経済学総論』日本評論社, 1928年9月25日発行.6+9+547p.

061　高田保馬『景気変動論』日本評論社, 1928年11月15日発行.4+4+485p.

062　高島善哉「静観的経済学止揚の方法」1928年11月18日（1929年2月加筆）, 未公刊〔助手論文〕, 山田秀雄編『高島善哉 市民社会論の構想』新評論, 1991年12月25日初版第1刷.1992年2月29日初版第2刷.pp.129-171.

1929年

063　高田保馬『価格と独占』千倉書房, 1929年3月25日.2+1+384p.

064　岸本誠二郎「シュンペーター」「新興科学の旗のもとに」第2巻第5号, 1929年5月1日.pp.65-85,「新興科学の旗のもとに」復刻版, 1982年11月20日全15冊揃, 岩波ブックセンター株式会社信山社.

065　高田保馬「労銀の理論（二）」「経済論叢」第29巻第1号, 1929年7月1日.pp.20-44.

066　米田庄太郎「経済静学と経済動学(一)」「経済論叢」第29巻第3号, 1929年9月1日.pp.51-80.

067　米田庄太郎「経済静学と経済動学(二)」「経済論叢」第29巻第4号, 1929年10月1日.pp.45-57.

068　米田庄太郎「経済静学と経済動学(三)」「経済論叢」第29巻第5号, 1929年11月1日.pp.56-69.

069　高田保馬『経済学新講 第一巻（総説生産の理論）』岩波書店, 1929年11月10日第1刷.1932年5月25日第3刷.1937年11月5日第7刷.2+3+255p.

1930年

070　大北文次郎「ハーンの銀行信用理論」「商学論集」第1巻, 1930年3月.pp.203-321.

071　高田保馬『経済学新講 第二巻（価格の理論）』岩波書店, 1930年6月25日第1刷.1932年5月10日第2刷.1937年2月5日第6刷.9+5+370p.

072　柴田敬「帰属理論の一考察（一）」「経済論叢」第31巻第4号, 1930年10月1日.pp.69-95.

073　高田保馬『経済学新講 第三巻（貨幣の理論）』岩波書店, 1930年10月5日第1刷.1937年9月1日第4刷.2+4+426p.

074　高田保馬「勢力と経済—勢力説に対する批判—」「経済論叢」第31巻第5号, 1930年11月1日.pp.32-50.

075　柴田敬「帰属理論の一考察(二)」「経済論叢」第31巻第5号, 1930年11月1日.pp.107-127.

1931年

076　「シュムペーター博士の片影(1)」「エコノミスト」第9年第4号, 1931年2月15日.p.31.

077　「シュムペーター博士の片影(2)」「エコノミスト」第9年第4号, 1931年2月15日.p.32.

078　「シュムペーター博士の片影(3)」「エコノミスト」第9年第4号, 1931年2月15日.p.33.

079　「シュムペーター博士の片影(4)」「エコノミスト」第9年第4号, 1931年2月15日.p.34.

080　「シュムペーター博士の片影(5)」「エコノミスト」第9年第4号, 1931年2月15日.P. 35

081　「シュムペーター博士の片影(6)」「エコノミスト」第9年第4号, 1931年2月15日.p.36.

082　中山伊知郎「シュムペーター教授を語る」「経済往来」第6巻第3号, 1931年3月1日.pp.39-47. 続いて「シュムペーター著作目録」pp.47-49.

083　五十嵐直三「シュムペーター博士を見る」「経済往来」第6巻第3号, 1931年3月1日.pp.89-90.

084　岸本誠二郎「静態動態論経済学研究への序説」「法政大学論集」第5巻第2号, 1931年6月13日.pp.131-183.

085　高田保馬『経済学新講 第四巻(分配理論)』岩波書店, 1931年6月15日第1刷.1937年7月15日第3刷.8+4+556p.

086　木村元一「財政社会学の発展」「一橋論叢」第8巻第4号, 1931年10月15日.pp.63-83. J. A. シュムペーター, 木村元一訳『租税国家の危機』勁草書房, 1951年5月15日発行の「解説」pp.1-32.

1932年

087　中山伊知郎「数理経済学方法論」高田保馬・高垣寅次郎・中山伊知郎『経済学全集第5巻経済学の基礎理論』改造社, 1932年3月22日発行.pp.3-254. 『中山伊知郎全集 第二集数理経済学説研究I』講談社, 1973年1月20日第1刷.pp.3-97, 196-281, 359-376.

088　岸本誠二郎「静態動態論の純粋理論的根拠」「経済志林」第6巻第1号, 1932年3月31日.pp.1-37.

089　岡橋保「シュムペーターの貨幣本質観と貨幣数量説」「内外研究」第5巻第2号, 1932年5月25日.pp.13-42.

090　高田保馬『経済学新講 第五巻(変動の理論)』岩波書店, 1932年6月10日第1刷.1939年3月1日第4刷.2+4+4+514+2p.

091　岡橋保「シュムペーターの貨幣本質観と貨幣数量説(二・完)」「内外研究」第5巻第3号, 1932年9月30日.pp.1-40.

1933年

092 岸本誠二郎「分配論の二途」「経済志林」第7巻第1号, 1933年2月5日.pp.1-79. 岸本誠二郎『分配の理論』森山書店, 1993年12月19日発行のpp.3-44. 59-71, 73-89, 91-93, 99-120.

093 木村健康「シュンペーターの貨幣理論」「経済学論集」第3巻第3・4号合冊, 1933年4月15日.pp.310-326.

094 大畑文七「租税国家の概念（一）」「内外研究」第6巻第1号, 1933年4月25日.pp.1-44.

095 大畑文七「租税国家の概念（二・完）」「内外研究」第6巻第2号, 1933年7月5日.pp.1-46.

096 木村健康「二つの分配理論―「勢力と経済法則」について」「経済学論集」第3巻第8号, 1933年8月15日.pp.40-81.

097 杉本栄一「静態的経済学の破綻」「中央公論」第48年第10号, 1933年10月1日.pp.19-33.『理論経済学の基本問題―経済発展の過程と弾力性概念―』日本評論社, 1939年6月3日第1版第1刷, 1939年6月10日再版, 1940年12月20日第4版, 1948年7月5日第7版第9刷.pp3-44.

098 中山伊知郎『純粋経済学』岩波書店, 1933年12月10日第1刷.1934年12月10日第4刷.1940年12月20日第12刷.1941年9月10日第13刷.1942年9月20日第15刷.1948年6月30日第19刷.7+255p.増補版1954年6月10日第20刷『中山伊知郎全集 第一集純粋経済学の拡充』講談社, 1972年4月24日第1刷.pp.1-165.

099 岸本誠二郎『分配の理論』森山書店, 1933年12月19日発行.4+1+8+387+11p.

1934年

100 木村健康「労銀における社会的なるもの―「勢力と経済法則」について―」「経済学論集」第4巻第1号, 1934年1月15日.pp.93-146.

101 中山伊知郎「経済動態論の構造」「経済学論集」第4巻第2号, 1934年2月15日.pp.1-28.『中山伊知郎全集 第一集』講談社, 1972年4月24日第1刷.pp.438-464.

102 塩野谷九十九「シュンペーターに於ける経済循環の構造」「横浜市立横浜商業専門学校研究論集」第7輯, 1934年2月28日.pp.1-26.

103 安井琢磨「帰属理論と限界生産力説―帰属理論と限界生産力説―純粋経済学の二問題―」「経済学論集」第4巻第4号, 1934年4月15日.pp.28-89.

104 シュランニー・ウンゲル「シュンペーターの静態論及び動態論」, シュランニー・ウンゲル著, 堀経夫, 三谷友吉共訳『現代経済学概観』日本評論社, 1934年4月19日.pp.92-95.

105 安井琢磨「中山教授の経済学体系―「純粋経済学」に就て」「経済学論集」第4巻第5号, 1934年5月15日.pp.134-140.

106 田中精一「均衡理論に於ける動態論―「純粋経済学」に於ける中山伊知郎氏―」「経済集志」第7巻第3号, 1934年5月30日.pp.9-35.

107 山下覚太郎「「財政社会学」の意義および方法（その一）」「国民経済雑誌」第56巻第6号, 1934年6月1日.pp.88-106.

108 山下覚太郎「「財政社会学」の意義および方法（その二）」「国民経済雑誌」第57巻第1号, 1934年7月1日.pp.91-110.

109　木村健康「雑録 岸本誠二郎「分配の理論」「経済学論集」第4巻第7号, 1934年7月15日.pp.85-99.

110　波多野鼎「信用と景気変動の問題—シュムペーター及びハーンの理論の吟味—」「経済学研究」第4巻第3号, 1934年9月.pp.43-82.

111　波多野鼎『景気論』千倉書房, 1934年10月30日.227p.

112　塩野谷九十九「シュンペーターに於ける経済発展理論の基本構造」「横浜市立横浜商業専門学校研究論集」第8輯, 1934年12月15日.pp.1-31.

1935年

113　東畑精一「シュムペーターの統制経済批判」, 東京日日新聞社経済部編『新説を探る』日本評論社, 1935年6月20日発行.pp.128-136.

114　柴田敬『理論経済学 上』弘文堂書房, 1935年8月1日発行.10月10日再版, 3+16+560p.

115　豊崎稔『景気論序説』高陽書院, 1935年9月10日.6+2+162+15p.

116　井口政一「均衡理論を中心とせる経済学体系の吟味—主としてシュンペーターに就いて—」「ヘルメス」第22号, 1935年9月15日.pp.1-57.

117　豊崎稔『景気論』改造社, 1935年12月16日.5+286p.

118　波多野鼎「シュムペーター—経済静学と経済動学—」『現代経済学論』改造社, 1935年12月18日発行.pp.217-273. 『現代の経済学』日本評論社, 1940年11月17日発行.1942年1月25日16版.pp.260-326. 春秋社, 1948年2月15日第1刷.1948年11月25日重版.pp.213-267.

1936年

119　高田保馬「費用としての勢力」「経済論叢」第42巻第1号, 1936年1月1日.pp.39-52.

120　東畑精一『日本農業の展開過程』東洋出版社, 1936年1月16日発行.4+4+385p.

121　東畑精一『増訂日本農業の展開過程』岩波書店, 1936年6月25日第1刷.1940年6月30日第5刷.1947年8月15日第8刷.3+11+436p.近藤康男編『昭和前期農政経済名著集第3巻東畑精一日本農業の展開過程』農山漁村文化協会, 1978年12月10日第1刷.pp.33-354.

122　土方成美『経済学』日本評論社, 1936年2月18日発行.1936年4月20日再版, 1936年4月30日2版, 1936年9月20日3版, 1936年10月2日4版, 1937年3月26日5版, 1937年12月10日6版, 2+8+732p.

123　高田保馬「労銀理論の破綻」「経済論叢」第42巻第3号, 1936年3月1日.pp.18-36.

124　柴田敬『理論経済学 下』弘文堂書房, 1936年3月25日発行.2+12p.+pp.561-1039+16p.

125　高田保馬『経済と勢力』日本評論社, 1936年11月20日発行.3+5+260p.

1937年

126 波多野鼎『景気学説批判』日本評論社, 1937年3月30日発行.1939年3月3日再版, 1940年9月1日3版, 1942年6月25日第5版, 2+6+464p.

127 波多野鼎「シュムペーターの景気学説」『景気学説批判』岩崎書店, 1948年3月10日発行.pp.85-119.

128 波多野鼎「景気上昇の理論」「経済学研究」第7巻第1号, 1937年5月15日.pp.1-48.

129 高田保馬「貨幣本質に関する若干の問題」「経済論叢」第45巻第4号, 1937年10月1日.pp.46-60.

130 宮川実「シュムペーターの『経済循環』について」「内外研究」第10巻第3-6合併号, 1937年10月21日.pp.453-463.

131 大熊信行『経済本質論 配分と均衡』同文館, 1937年10月25日.1938年8月10日第2版, 1939年8月1日第2版第2刷.12+18+4+340p.

132 中山伊知郎『数理経済学研究』日本評論社, 1937年11月25日発行.1939年9月10日再版, 1941年8月20日3版, 2+5+579+4p.

1938年

133 難波田春夫『国家と経済 第一巻序説』日本評論社, 1938年2月25日第1刷.1941年9月20日7版, 1942年5月5日第8刷.1943年6月20日第10刷.1943年6月25日第11刷.2+3+1+407p.『難波田春夫著作集6』早稲田大学出版部, 1982年12月25日発行.7+357+13p.

134 中山伊知郎「貨幣の本質とその価値(上)—高田博士に答ふ—」「経済論叢」第46巻第4号, 1938年4月1日.pp.13-30. 『中山伊知郎全集第五集 発展過程の均衡分析』講談社, 1972年10月26日第1刷.pp.247-280. 中山伊知郎「貨幣の本質とその価値(下)—高田博士に答ふ—」「経済論叢」第46巻第5号, 1938年5月1日.pp.45-59. 『中山伊知郎全集 第九集経済の安定と進歩』講談社, 1972年8月24日第1刷.pp.193-203.

135 中山伊知郎『均衡理論と資本理論』岩波書店, 1938年9月30日第1刷.1942年12月20日第5刷.1948年1月10日第6刷.12月30日第7刷.7+4+403p.

136 『中山伊知郎全集 第一集』pp.389-464. 『中山伊知郎全集 第四集資本の理論』講談社, 1973年3月20日第1刷.pp.235-283, 387-402. 『中山伊知郎全集 第五集発展過程の均衡分析』講談社, 1972年10月20日第1刷.pp.323-383. 『中山伊知郎全集 第六集近代経済学の展開』講談社, 1972年7月24日第1刷.pp.149-189. 『中山伊知郎全集 第九集経済の安定と進歩』講談社, 1972年8月24日第1刷.pp.193-203.

137 中谷実『新金融理論—預金通貨と中立貨幣—』有斐閣, 1938年10月25日.408+5+2p.

138 岸本誠二郎「変動に於ける価格の考案」「経済志林」第12巻第3号, 1938年12月15日.pp.1-68.

1939年

139 武村忠雄「純粋経済学体系(静態経済学体系)—シュンペーター」—『独逸経済学(三)』慶應義塾大学講座経済学第15回配本慶應出版社1939年1月25日.pp.123-137.

140 エミール・レーデラー著, 田中精一訳『景気変動と恐慌』有斐閣, 1939年9月15日発行.3+3+61+1+135p.

141 高田保馬「シュムペエタア教授の印象」『貧者必勝』千倉書房, 1939年2月18日発行.1940年3月20日再版, 4月10日5版, 5月20日10版, 1941年9月15日11版.pp.44-52.

142 中山伊知郎『発展過程の均衡分析 発展を含む経済均衡の性質に関する一研究』岩波書店, 1939年4月20日第1刷.1941年9月20日第3刷.1942年9月20日第4刷.1949年7月25日第6刷.3+4+345p.『中山伊知郎全集 第五集』pp.1-243

143 武村忠雄「純粋景気理論の方法論的構造」「三田学会雑誌」第33巻第7号, 1939年7月1日.pp.31-65.

144 安井琢磨「中山伊知郎著「発展過程の均衡分析」〔書評〕」「経済学論集」第9巻第7号, 1939年8月1日.pp.124-131.

145 辻六兵衛「シュンペーター貨幣理論の一研究—貨幣理論と価格との綜合に関する一の試み—」「ヘルメス」第25号, 1939年8月10日.pp.37-82.

146 武村忠雄『景気変動論』中山伊知郎, 東畑精一編輯『新経済学全集 第三巻 経済学特殊理論〔下〕』日本評論社, 1939年12月1日発行.141+2p.

147 中山伊知郎「前書」中山伊知郎編『ケインズ一般理論解説』日本評論社, 1939年12月21日発行.1941年9月15日5版.pp.1-16『中山伊知郎全集 第一集 純粋経済学の拡充』講談社, 1972年4月24日第1刷.pp.465-470.

1940年

148 岸本誠二郎『価格の理論』日本評論社, 1940年4月25日第1刷.1941年9月1日3版, 1942年7月25日第4刷.10+12+532p.

149 高田保馬「貨幣本質に関する若干の問題」,「利子動態説について—二の批評に答ふ—」『新利子論研究』岩波書店, 1940年7月2日第1刷.1943年10月1日第3刷.pp.272-290, 328-346.

150 大熊信行『政治経済学の問題—生活原理と経済原理—』日本評論社, 1940年10月5日発行.26+4+12+602p., 1940年11月10日再版, 1941年11月30日7版, 26+4+12+604p.

151 豊崎稔『現代景気変動論』三笠書房, 1940年11月28日.263p.

1941年

152 勝田貞次『経済機構の歴史的転換』東洋経済新報社, 1941年2月20日発行.7+7+330p.

153 宮田喜代蔵『貨幣の生活理論—貨幣経済の本質に関する生活経済学的研究—』日本評論社, 1941年2月20日第1刷.1943年1月25日第4刷.5+10+708+10p.

154 波多野鼎『景気変動論』日本評論社, 1941年4月28日第1刷.1942年7月10日第3刷.3+1+256p.

155 一谷藤一郎「シュムペーター景気理論に於ける貯蓄と投資」「経済論叢」第53巻第2号, 1941年8月1日.pp.64-79.

156 東畑精一「資本主義の運命」「中央公論」第56年第1号第641号, 1941年6月1日.pp.4-20.

157 大熊信行『経済本質論 配分原理第一巻』日本評論社, 1941年9月1日.1941年11月20日再版, 1942年3月15日第3版, 17+6+558p.

158 高田保馬『勢力説論集』日本評論社, 1941年12月5日発行.1942年9月25日第4刷.5+4+272p. 惇信堂, 1947年10月20日改版再刊, 6+6+272p.

159 武村忠雄「純粋経済学体系(静態経済学体系)―シュンペーター」『経済学体系論全』慶應出版社, 1941年12月15日.pp.102-116.

1942年

160 カール・フェール著, 日下藤吾訳『経済循環の貨幣的構造』大鵬社, 1942年10月1日発行.8+5+1+587+13p.

1943年

161 柏祐賢『経済科学の構造』弘文堂書房, 1943年1月15日初版, 6+2+435p.『柏祐賢著作集 第一巻経済科学の一構造』京都産業大学出版会, 1985年7月30日第1刷.pp.1-300.

162 アルバート・ハーン著, 大北文次郎訳『銀行信用の国民経済的理論』実業之日本社, 1943年8月20日発行1946年10月30日再版, 1+22+290p.

1944年

163 栗村雄吉「静態経済学」, 神戸商大新聞部編『経済及経済学の再出発』日本評論社, 1944年1月20日第1刷.pp.171-188.

164 中山伊知郎『経済学一般理論』日本評論社, 1944年9月20日第1版第1刷.2+6+417p.1945年2月15日第2版第1刷.384p.1948年1月20日第3版第1刷.4月1日第3版第2刷.8月20日第3版第4刷.12月20日第3版第5刷.1949年11月10日第4版第1刷.1951年10月25日第4版第6刷.1+6+384p.『中山伊知郎全集 第七集経済学一般理論』講談社, 1972年2月24日第1刷.pp.1-417.

1945年

165　柏祐賢「経済の現実理論―シュピートホフの現実理論を中心として―」「理想」第19年第2冊第160号, 1945年4月5日.pp.19-34『柏祐賢著作集 第一巻』京都産業大学出版会, 1985年7月30日第1刷.pp.306-326.

1946年

166　沖中恒幸「シュムペーター（Josef Schumpeter, 1883―）」『経済学説史』廣文社, 1946年5月20日印刷.1946年6月10日3版.pp.246-252.

167　飯田藤次「紹介 シュムペーター『資本主義, 社会主義および民主主義』J. Schumpeter: “Capitalism, Socialism and Democracy”1942」「経済評論」第1巻第7号, 1946年10月1日.pp.32-40.

168　高田保馬「経済学研究回顧（続）」「経済評論」第1巻第8号, 1946年11月1日、pp.37-41.

1947年

169　都留重人「アメリカ経済学界の近状」「世界週報」第28巻第1号, 1947年1月1日.pp.12-15.『アメリカ経済学の旅』理想社, 1949年2月20日初版.pp.2-20.

170　都留重人「その後のシュンペーター」「世界」第17号, 1947年5月1日.pp.19-28. 『アメリカ経済の旅』思想社，1949年2月20日初版pp.21-43.

171　中山伊知郎『現代の経済学』実業之日本社, 1947年5月15日第1刷.1948年2月1日第2刷.2+145p.『中山伊知郎全集 第八集初等経済学講義』講談社, 1972年6月24日第1刷.pp.207-268.

172　東畑精一『一農政学徒の記録』酣燈社, 1947年5月20日発行.1947年10月10日再版, 1947年.2+3+312p.

173　土方成美『経済原論』厳松堂, 1947年5月20日.1+2+265p.

174　飯田藤次「紹介 シュムペーター「ジョン・メイナード・ケインズ」」「経済評論」第2巻第7号, 1947年7月1日.pp.41-47.

175　中山伊知郎「シュムペーター・オン・マルクス」「法律新報」第737号, 1947年8月1日.pp.34-36.

176　土方成美『資本主義と社会主義』廣文社, 1947年9月20日.1948年6月30日発行.307p.

177　高田保馬「研究の回顧」『洛北雑記 第一集』大丸印刷株式会社, 1947年11月15日発行.pp.110-133.

178　中山伊知郎「マルクスとシュムペーター」「社会」第2巻第12号, 1947年12月1日.pp.8-14.『近代経済学の展開―完全雇傭の理論―』有斐閣, 1950年11月20日初版, 12月20日再版.pp.285-300. 『中山伊知郎全集 第一集』講談社, 1972年4月14日第1刷.pp.372-382.

179　柏祐賢『経済秩序個性論―中国経済の研究― 第一分回』人文書林, 1947年12月10日発行.6+5+306p.『柏祐賢著作集 第三巻経済秩序個性論（I）―中国経済の研究』京都産業大学出版会, 1985年11月30日第1刷.379p.

180 柏祐賢『企業者―資本主義経済の構造と発展―』弘文堂書房, 1947年12月20日初版, 155p. 『柏祐賢著作集 第六巻企業者/資本主義のメカニズム』京都産業大学出版会, 1986年5月31日第1刷.pp.3-120.

181 高橋泰蔵「経済発展の理論(5)完」, 東京経済学研究所編『経済学講座第5巻』東京経済学研究所出版部, 1947年12月25日発行.pp.249-319.

1948年

182 友岡久雄「ジョセフ・シュムペーター著『資本主義・社会主義及び民主主義』について」「ブック・レヴキウ」第4巻, 1948年2月10日.pp.123-186.

183 高橋泰蔵『経済発展の理論―構想的試論―』青也書店, 1948年5月10日初版, 3+6+205p.

184 高橋泰蔵『経済発展と雇用問題―スミス―マルサス―ケインズ―』富士出版株式会社, 1948年6月1日.224p.

185 友岡久雄「シュンペーター著「資本主義・社会主義及び民主主義」」, 理論社編集部編『近代理論経済学とマルクス主義経済学―現代経済学と価値論―』理論社, 1948年6月10日.pp.336-340.

186 都留重人「世界の学界 ハーヴァード大学 リッタウアー行政学院」「思想」第289号, 1948年7月20日.pp.56-64. 「リッタウアー・センターのことども―ハーヴァード大学リッタウアー行政学院―」『アメリカ経済学の旅』pp.211-229, 「リッタウアー・センターのことども」『アメリカ遊学記』岩波書店, 1950年9月5日第1刷.1950年11月15日第2刷.pp.71-91. 『都留重人著作集 第12巻随想と思い出』講談社, 1976年5月12日第1刷.pp.60-74.

187 青山秀夫『近代国民経済の構造』白日書院, 1948年10月20日第1刷.18+5+282p.

188 田村実「経済学に於ける実体概念と関係概念―マルクスとシュムペーター」「神戸商科大学研究と資料」第23・4号, 開学記念論文集(第1輯), 1948年11月3日.pp.25-46.

1949年

189 中山伊知郎「説苑 経済展望一九四九年 シュムペーター教授「資本主義・社会主義・民主主義」に依據して」「週刊東洋経済新報」2354号1949年1月8日 pp.25-29.

190 「「世界の社会科学」シュンペーターにおける社会主義」「世界の社会科学」2, 1949年1月10日.pp.64-68.

191 豊崎稔『経済変動論』創元社, 1949年1月25日.251p.

192 三谷友吉「動態の問題 シュムペーターの経済発展の理論」『近代経済学史』創元社, 1949年1月30日.pp.109-139.

193 吉田昇三「数理経済学の方法論的基礎」「松山経専論集」7号, 1949年2月1日.pp.23-41.

194 都留重人「シュンペーターとマルクス―景気循環と資本主義―」『アメリカ経済学の旅』pp.126-156. 「景気循環と資本主義―シュンペーター対マルクス―」『都留重人著作集第2巻国民所得と再生産』講談社, 1975年7月20日第1刷.pp.441-466. 学位論文の一部で

1941年に英文で執筆。原文は『都留重人著作集 第13巻(Towards a new political economy)』講談社, 1976年6月12日第1刷.pp.117-137.

195 中山伊知郎「アメリカ経済学の動向」「思索」第20号, 1949年3月1日.pp.2-7.

196 竹中久七「ヴァルガとシュンペーター」「経営評論」第4巻第3号, 1949年3月1日.pp.26-29.

197 東畑精一氏述 J. シュペイター, 1949年6月18日.於工業クラブ, 137p.

198 杉本栄一「近代経済学とマルクス経済学」『近代経済学の基本的性格—近代性の探究—』日本評論社, 1949年6月20日.pp.16212.

199 青山秀夫「「科学とイデオロギー」を読んで 社会科学的認識の客観性とその実質的条件」「思想」303号, 1949年9月5日.pp.17-27.

200 川崎己三郎「「科学とイデオロギー」を読んで 科学の階級性と真理性」「思想」303号, 1949年9月5日.pp.32-36.

201 近藤洋逸「「科学とイデオロギー」を読んで 理論と実践との連関」「思想」303号, 1949年9月5日.pp.28-31.

202 阿部源一「計画経済下の自由」「青山経済論集」第1巻第1号, 1949年11月16日.pp.29-52.

203 中山伊知郎「ヨーゼフ・シュムペーター」「季刊理論経済学」第1巻第1号, 1949年12月5日.pp.1-12. 「シュムペーターの純粋性」『近代経済学の展開—完全雇傭の理論—』有斐閣, 1950年11月20日初版, 1950年12月20日再版.pp.257-285. 「理論の純粋性」『中山伊知郎全集第一集』講談社, 1972年4月24日第1刷.pp.257-285.

204 石田興平「信用と資本蓄積—信用理論の基本的視角について—」「彦根論叢」開学記念創刊号, 1949年12月15日.pp.54-68.

205 吉田昇三「近代経済学とイデオロギーの問題」「内外研究」第19巻第1・2合併号, 1949年12月15日.pp.27-40.

1950年

206 岩崎秀二「シュムペーター動態利子論」「東北学院論集」第2号, 1950年1月1日.pp.131-153.

207 杉本栄一『近代経済学の解明 その系譜と現代的評価』理論社, 1950年1月10日発行.1953年1月15日発行296p.1965年5月第29刷.1968年4月第38刷.246+4p.『近代経済学の解明(上)第1巻』岩波書店〔文庫版〕, 1981年9月16日第1刷.pp.330+4p.

208 杉本栄一『近代経済学の解明 現代的主潮流と新展開』理論社, 1950年10月10日第1刷.478p.1952年3月1日発行.1962年11月5日発行.397+5p.1968年4月第36刷.『近代経済学の解明(下)第2巻』岩波書店〔文庫版〕, 1981年10月16日第1刷.473+5p.

209 荻山健吉「景気の波及理論」「商経法論叢」復刊第1号, 1950年1月20日.pp.1-17.

210 中山伊知郎「追想 シュムペーター先生」「週刊東洋経済新報」第2406号, 1950年1月21日.pp.59-60. 「シュムペーター教授への追憶」『近代経済学の展開』pp.300-304, 『中山伊知郎全集 第一集』pp.383-385.

211 都留重人「シュンペーターを悼む」「世界週報」第31巻第4号, 1950年1月25日.p.7.

212 東畑精一, 中山伊知郎, 都留重人「シュンペーター教授の「思い出」を語る」「経済評論」第5巻第2号, 1950年2月1日.pp.50-59.

213 生田豊朗「シュムペーターの「共産党宣言」論」「国民経済」第5巻第2号, 1950年2月5日.pp.50-5
214 中山伊知郎「学界餘滴 ボンのことども」「一橋論叢」第23巻第3号, 1950年3月1日.pp.90-93.
215 豊川卓三「紹介 J・Aシュムペーター「社会学および経済学における『共産党宣言』」」「金融経済」第3号, 1950年3月10日.pp.78-82.
216 酒井正三郎「経済の発展と企業者の変質」「商業経済論叢」第24巻第2号, 1950年3月15日.pp.1-42.
217 麻田四郎「シュムペーターの資本主義観―資本主義・社会主義及び民主主義第二編の紹介―」「小樽商科大学開学記念論文集第二分冊」1950年3月25日.pp.205-238.
218 巽博一「学界消息 シュムペーター教授の生涯と業績」「政治経済論叢」第1巻第2号, 1950年3月25日.pp.107-113.
219 伊達邦春「シュムペーター二元論の特有性について―シュムペーターのcircular flowとフリッシュ=サミュエルソン流のstationary state―」「早稲田政治経済学雑誌」第103号, 1950年4月3日.pp.73-96. 若干の修正・改筆『シュンペーターの経済学』創文社, 1991年10月30日第1刷.pp.3-22.
220 東畑精一「シュムペーター教授逝く」「季刊理論経済学」第1巻第2号, 1950年4月10日.pp.137-139, 「シュムペーターの死」『書物と人物』新評論社, 1954年8月30日.pp.37-42.
221 阿部源一「シュムペーターの民主主義」『経済学史概論』千倉書房, 1950年5月10日.pp.244-247.
222 飯田藤次「シュムペーターの「共産党宣言」批判」「理想」第205号, 1950年6月1日.pp.75-77.
223 緑川敬「純粋科学としての景気循環論―シュムペーターの学問的生涯―」「経済学」第2号, 1950年6月15日.pp.174-179.
224 福岡正夫「ヨーゼフ・A・シュンペーター―革新の経済学―」「三田学会雑誌」第43巻第1号, 1950年7月1日.pp.3-23.
225 編集部訳「シュンペーター教授の一生―ハーヴァード大学教授会記録―」「経済研究」第1巻第3号, 1950年7月5日.pp.224-226.
226 古谷弘「動向 現代イギリス経済とシュンペーター」「経済学論集」第19巻第10・11号, 1950年8月1日.pp.67-79.
227 都留重人『アメリカ遊学記』岩波書店, 1950年9月5日第1刷.1950年11月15日第2刷.3+2+166p.
228 エドウァード・ハイマン著, 喜多村浩訳『経済学説史』中央公論社, 1950年9月25日初版.1951年12月10日4版.1969年6月30日13版.5+400+10p.
229 沓水勇「ヴィクセル図式について―シュンペーター「景気論」におけるヴィクセル批判の研究―」「経済志林」第18巻第4号, 1950年10月20日.pp.29-80.
230 荻山健吉「景気理論の方法論とハイエク」「商経法論叢」第1巻第2号, 1950年10月30日.pp.54-76.
231 中山伊知郎『近代経済学の展開―完全雇傭の理論―』有斐閣, 1950年11月20日初版.1950年12月20日再版.4+5+304p.『中山伊知郎全集 第一巻』講談社, 1972年4月24日第1刷
232 吉田昇三「シュムペーター体系の二元論について」「経済理論」第1号, 1950年11月20日.pp.25-42. 加筆「シュムペーター体系の二元的構造の発展」『シュムペーターの経

済学』法律文化社, 1956年11月5日発行.1964年6月10日改訂第1刷.1967年9月1日改訂第2刷.pp.33-72.

233 古谷弘「シュンペーター」, 弘文堂編集部編『社会科学講座 第II巻 社会科学の諸系譜』弘文堂, 1950年11月25日初版.1953年4月10日4版.pp.214-221.

234 伊達邦春「景気循環の一構想としての新機構理論について—衝撃現象の一つの典型としてのInnovation—」「早稲田政治経済学雑誌」第107号, 1950年12月3日.pp.85-108.

235 泉三義『レーデラー「景気変動・技術的進歩と失業」』春秋社, 1950年12月15日学生版第1刷.2+4+288+23p.

236 坂本二郎「紹介 シュムペーター社会学及経済学に於ける『共産党宣言』」「ヘルメス」第2集, 1950年12月20日.pp.28-34.

237 岩崎秀二「シュムペーターの経済理論(その一)—シュムペーターの著作(続き)—」「新潟大学法経学会誌」第11号, 1950年12月25日.pp.3-4.

238 石田興平「貨幣的均衡と資本蓄積」「彦根論叢」第3号, 1950年12月30日.pp.1-26.

1951年

239 P. M. スウィージー, 野々村一雄訳「社会主義は労働と能率に刺激を與之得るか」『社会主義』岩波書店, 1951年1月25日第1刷.1951年5月25日第4刷.1961年2月15日第15刷.1969年4月30日第21刷.1970年10月30日第22刷.pp.242-271.

240 平実「資料 シュムペーターの均衡賃銀」「経済学雑誌」第24巻第1·2号, 1951年2月1日.pp.37-62.

241 坂本二郎「The Schumpeteriam System, by Richard V. Clemence and Francis S.Doody (Addison-Wiseley Press, Inc. 1950)〔書評〕」「季刊理論経済学」第2巻第1号, 1951年2月5日.pp.56-59.

242 近澤敏里「シュムペーター経済学史—学説並びに方法の諸段階—中山伊知郎 東畑精一 訳」「富士論集」第7号, 1951年2月.pp.147-148.

243 都留重人「書評 東畑精一, 中山伊知郎訳『シュムペーター経済学史』」「図書」第18号, 1951年3月5日.pp.18-19.

244 岩崎秀二「シュムペーターの経済理論(その二)—シュムペーターの著作(続き)」「新潟大学法経学会誌」第13号, 1951年3月10日.pp.3-4.

245 中山伊知郎「経済学とヴィジョン」「季刊理論経済学」第2巻第2号, 1951年4月5日.pp.65-72.「経済学とビジョン」『中山伊知郎全集 第一集』講談社, 1972年4月24日第1刷.pp.535-550.

246 東畑精一「シュムペーター夫人を訪ふ」「季刊理論経済学」第2巻第2号, 1951年4月5日.pp.101-108.『書物と人物』pp.101-108.

247 宇野弘蔵「シュンペーターとスヰージー」「読書人」第1号, 1951年4月5日.pp.17-18.「シュンペーターとスウィージー」『宇野弘蔵著作集 別巻学問と人と本 随想・書評・未定稿他』岩波書店, 1974年8月16日発行.pp.16-19.

248 吉田昇三『近代経済理論』法律文化社, 1951年4月5日1版.1952年4月5日2版.2+5+218p.

249 安井琢磨「資本主義は生き延び得るか シュムペーター著「資本主義・社会主義・民主主義」(上)を読んで」「週刊東洋経済」第2466号, 1951年4月21日.pp.31-32.

250 板垣與一『世界政治経済論』新紀元社, 1951年5月5日初版.1953年5月10日再版.4+6+371p.

251 土方成美『経済講話』東洋経済新報社, 1951年5月18日第1刷.1951年6月20日第2刷.3+8+351p.

252 三輪悌三「シュムペーター経済学の二元性—とくに信用創造論との関連において—」「経済評論」第6巻第6号, 1951年6月1日.pp.47-55.

253 坂本二郎「ヨーゼフ・シュムペーター」「経済評論」第6巻第6号, 1951年6月1日.pp.56-69.

254 高田保馬「経済の変動—其二・経済の前進」『小経済学 経済学入門篇二冊原理篇』有斐閣, 1951年6月1日初版.1951年9月20日再版.1956年6月20日8版.pp.100-109.

255 岩崎秀二「シュムペーターの経済静態論—批判への道—」「新潟大学社会科学研究」第1集, 1951年6月25日.pp.79-98.

256 佐藤豊三郎「シュムペーター理論—静学と動学—」, 監修『理論経済学I』評論社, 1951年6月30日初版.1952年12月10日3版.1956年2月29日改訂第1刷.1958年改訂第2刷.pp.86-97.

257 都留重人「シュンペーターとスウィージー」『官僚と大学教授』勁草書房, 1951年8月1日発行.pp.151-155.

258 高田保馬『経済学説の展開 経済学入門第一冊学説篇』有斐閣, 1951年8月25日第1刷.1951年9月1日再版.6+3+157p.

259 吉田昇三「シュムペーター体系と零利子率」「経済理論」第4号, 1951年8月31日.pp.1-18.『シュムペーターの経済学』pp.72-104.

260 中山伊知郎「シュムペーターの発展理論」『現代の経済学』勁草書房, 1951年9月1日第1刷.pp.59-78.

261 山田雄三『経済学はいかに進歩したか—経済学史要—』春秋社, 1951年9月20日第1刷.1952年11月10日第2刷.2+4+168+3p.

262 生川栄治「近代における利潤理論の変質過程—企業形態発展との関連—」「経済学雑誌」第25巻第4号, 1951年10月1日.pp.44-88.

263 伊達邦春「シュンペーター利子論への若干の反省—ロビンズ, サミュエルソン, ハーバラーの見解の吟味を通じて—」「早稲田政治経済学雑誌」第112号, 1951年10月3日.pp.89-110.

264 塩野谷九十九『経済発展と資本蓄積』東洋経済新報社, 1951年10月5日発行.3+386+11p.

265 土方成美「アメリカ資本主義は何處へ行く—シュンペーター, 社会主義への行進」『資本主義の変貌とその将来—並びに各国計画経済の動向—』廣文社, 1951年10月10日発行.pp.178-192.

266 沓水勇「金融市場の理論(一)—シュムペーター『景気論』の研究—」「経済志林」第19巻第3・4合併号, 1951年10月30日.pp.84-113.

267 佐藤豊三郎「シュムペーターの貨幣資本」, 監修『理論経済学II—資本の理論—』評論社, 1951年11月10日初版.1952年11月20日再版.pp.49-55.

268 喜多村浩「書評 J. A. シュムペーター著中山伊知郎, 東畑精一訳『経済学史 学説並びに方法の諸段階』岩波書店, 昭和25年12月」「季刊理論経済学」第2巻第4号, 1951年11月13日.pp.236-240, 248.

269 武藤光朗「経済の計画化と自由の問題—ウェーバー・シュムペーターにおける問題の所在—」「経商論纂」第41号, 1951年12月1日.pp.32-51.

1952年

270 東畑精一「序文の運命」「総研月報」第34号, 1952年1月.pp.24-30, 「序文」「図書」第34号, 1952年7月5日.pp.2-4, 「序文の話」『書物と人物』pp.3-9. 「シュムペーター先生の序文」『わが師わが友わが人間』柏書房, 1984年8月25日.pp.13-19.

271 「書評 シュムペーター著資本主義・社会主義・民主主義(中巻)」「北海道労働経済」第3巻第1号, 1952年1月.pp.20-21.

272 坂本二郎「書評 ハリマ編「社会科学者シュムペーター」」「経済評論」第1巻第2号〔復刊第2号〕, 1952年2月1日.pp.63-72.

273 福岡正夫「シュムペーターとケインズ」「季刊理論経済学」第3巻第1号, 1952年3月8日.pp.38-45.

274 中山伊知郎「対決の焦点—特集に寄す—」「季刊理論経済学」第3巻第1号, 1952年3月8日.pp.1-4.

275 坂本二郎「社会主義必然論におけるスウィージー・ドッブ・シュムペーター」「季刊理論経済学」第3巻第1号, 1952年3月8日.pp.54-62.

276 高田保馬「資本主義の変質」「季刊理論経済学」第3巻第1号, 1952年3月8日.pp.5-11.

277 内田忠壽「イギリス社会主義の理論的基準」「季刊理論経済学」第3巻第1号, 1952年3月8日.pp.63-69.

278 三輪悌三「信用創造論の二形態—シュムペーター「経済発展の理論」とケインズ「雇傭, 利子及び貨幣の一般理論」とその関連において—」「金融経済」第12号, 1952年3月10日.pp.16-37.

279 坂本二郎「マルクスとシュムペーター シュムペーターの国家企業主義論」「理論経済学研究I」第1号, 1952年4月11日.pp.27-38.

280 坂本二郎「蓄積—マルクスとシュムペーターの資本理論」, 中山伊知郎編『資本経済学新体系第一巻』河出書房, 1952年5月15日第1刷.普及版.特製版.pp.135-173.

281 新井嘉之作「O. H. テイラー シュンペーターとマルクス O. H. Taylor, Schumpeter and Marx:Imperialism and Social Classes in the Schumpeteriam System〔The Quarterly Journal of Economics, 1951, vol. LXV, No. 4〕」「史学雑誌」第61編第6号, 1952年6月20日.pp.83-88.

282 吉田義三「シュムペーターの動学的独占理論」, 豊崎稔編『独占 経済学新大系第三巻』河出書房, 1952年6月23日第1刷.普及版.特製版.pp.202-209.

283 阿部源一「「社会化」概念の歴史的発展」「青山経済論集」第4巻第1号, 1952年6月30日.pp.45-74.

284 武藤光朗「マックス・ウェーバーとシュムペーター」『社会主義的自由への道—実存哲学的研究—』創元社, 1952年6月30日初版.pp.95-116.

285 戸田武雄「シュムペーター「十大経済学者」について—マルクスからケインズまで—」「金融経済」第15号, 1952年8月15日.pp.40-49.

286 吉田昇三「シュムペーター体系と『成長』の経済学」「経済理論」第9号, 1952年9月1日.pp.1-23. 加筆「ケインズとシュムペーター」『シュムペーターの経済学』pp.152-208.

287　阿部源一「社会化と「成熟」問題—シュムペーターの成熟論を基軸として—」「青山経済論集」第4巻第2号, 1952年9月10日.pp.157-190.

288　伊藤善市「サール・フェールの公共投資論〔1〕—貨幣造出と経済循環—」「山形大学紀要（人文科学）」第2巻第2号, 1952年10月10日.pp.201-223.

289　泉三義『日本産業構造論—産業構造の変動理論—』中央経済社 1952年10月15日発行.353+228+8p.

290　石田興平『再生産と貨幣経済』有斐閣, 1952年11月1日発行.7+6+300p.1956年4月10日増訂3版.1+3+7+6+325p.

291　小泉信三「ケインズとシュムペエタア（上）」「新文明」第2巻第11号, 1952年11月1日.pp.42-48. 『大学と私』岩波書店, 1953年6月30日第1刷.1953年10月15日第2刷.pp.204-213.『私の敬愛する人びと』角川書店, 1968年11月20日初版.1968年12月20日再版.pp.220-229.

292　戸田武雄「シュムペーター」『近代経済学批判』青木書店, 1952年11月1日.1954年4月30日再版.pp.95-110.

293　上月保「シュムペーター経済学に関する一考察」「理論経済学研究」第2号, 1952年11月10日.pp.11-20.

294　小泉信三「ケインズとシュムペエタア（中）」「新文明」第2巻第12号, 1952年12月1日.pp.30-34. 『大学と私』pp.214-220. 『私の敬愛する人びと』pp.229-235.

1953年

295　小泉信三「ケインズとシュムペエタア（下）」「新文明」第3巻第1号, 1953年1月1日.pp.56-61. 『大学と私』pp.220-228. 『私の敬愛する人びと』pp.235-242. 224と225とともに『小泉信三全集 第十一巻』文芸春秋, 1967年12月10日発行.pp.429-448.

296　山部徳雄「独占と競争 シュムペーターについて」「三田学会雑誌」第46巻第1号, 1953年1月1日.pp.39-52.

297　酒井正三郎『経済體制と人間類型』岩波書店, 1953年2月10日第1刷.1954年8月30日第2刷.8+329+12p.

298　浜崎正規「〈研究ノート〉Overton H. Taylorのシュムペーター学説における「帝国主義論」「社会階級論」の位置づけについて」「立命館経済学」第2巻第1号, 1953年2月25日.pp.113-138. 『シュムペーター経済学の基本問題』雄渾社, 1955年4月1日発行.pp.155-189.

299　西村允克「シュムペーターの利子論」「学術論叢」第3号, 1953年3月10日.pp.79-87.

300　杉本栄一『近代経済学史』岩波書店, 1953年3月14日第1刷.1953年4月15日第2刷.17+326+10p.

301　難波田春夫『国家と経済 経済学の基礎』講談社, 1953年3月20日発行.1+3+215+16p.

302　塩野谷九十九「ジョセフ・シュンペーター—人と思想—」「出版ニュース」第232号, 1953年4月上旬号.p.7.

303　上月保「シュムペーターの貨幣観」「理論経済学研究」第3号, 1953年4月15日.pp.42-48.

304　坂本二郎「『十大経済学者』を通じて見たるシュムペーター像」「理論経済学研究」第3号, 1953年4月15日.pp.49-62.

305 鎌倉昇「シュンペーターの資本主義論」「経済論叢」第71巻第5号, 1953年5月1日.pp.23-43.

306 向坂逸郎「シュムペーターとマルクス」「経済学研究」第18巻第4号, 1953年5月1日.pp.1-18.

307 浜崎正規「(紹介)C. S.ソロー著「資本主義過程における革新」—シュムペーター理論の批判—(Carolin S.Solo:Innovation in the Capitalist Process:A Critique of the Schumpeteriam System(Quarterly Journal of Economics, vol. LXV. 1951. No. 3)」「立命館経済学」第2巻第3号, 1953年6月25日.pp.116-123.

308 高田保馬「紙上講座㉖ 今日の経済学新しい歩みと方向 経済学の回顧と展望 高田保馬氏に聴く=第二回=」「週刊エコノミスト」第31年第31号, 1953年8月1日.pp.48-50.

309 高田保馬「紙上講座㉘ 今日の経済学 新しい歩みと方向 経済学の回顧と展望 高田保馬氏に聴く=第四回=」「週刊エコノミスト」第31年第33号, 1953年8月15日.pp.48-51.

310 浜崎正規「「企業者」と資本主義過程の「革新」について—シュムペーター学説の主要問題—」「立命館経済学」第2巻第4号, 1953年8月25日.pp.93-122. 『シュムペーター経済学の基本問題』pp.75-114.

311 波多野鼎『景気変動論』ダイヤモンド社, 1953年10月15日初版.1955年8月15日再版.2+3+228p.

312 B. S.ケアステッド著, 酒井正三郎訳『経済変動の理論』東洋経済新報社, 1953年11月20日発行.12+322p.

313 吉田昇三「オーストリア学派経済学の基本的性格とシュムペーター体系」「経済理論」第15~18合併号, 1953年12月1日.pp.11-25. 書改め「シュムペーター小伝」『シュムペーターの経済学』pp.3-32.

314 小宮隆太郎「資本主義・社会主義・民主主義—シュムペーターの理論—」, 木村健康編『社会主義 経済学新大系第10巻』河出書房, 1953年12月25日第1刷.普及版.特製版.pp.175-209.

1954年

315 杉本金馬「二つのソ連観 シユムペーターとラスキ」「ソ連研究」第3巻第3号(通巻23号), 1954年3月11日.pp.17-21.

316 浜崎正規「シュムペーター経済学の方法論的一考察」「立命館経済学」第3巻第2号, 1954年4月25日.pp.42-71. 『シュムペーター経済学の基本問題』pp.31-72.

317 山部徳雄「シュムペーター体系に於ける貨幣と経済変動」「バンキング」第74号, 1954年5月1日.pp.42-50.

318 坂本二郎「シュムペーター」「理想」第253号, 1954年6月1日.pp.38-41.

319 土方成美『ケインズ以前とケインズ以後』学芸書房, 1954年5月10日発行.2+3+242p.

320 吉村一雄「シュムペーターのスコラ経済学観」「ソフィア」第3巻第2号, 1954年6月30日.pp.80-87.

321 浜崎正規「C・ワーバートン『シュムペーター学説における貨幣および景気変動』Clark Warburton. "Money and Business Fluctuations in the Schumpeterian System", The Journal of Political Economy, LXI, December, 1953」「立命館経済学」第3巻第4号, 1954年8月25日.pp.102-118.

322 東畑精一『書物と人物』新評論社, 1954年8月30日発行.2+4+305p.

323　岸本誠二郎編「シュムペーターJoseph Alois Schumpeter (1883-1950)」『経済学演習講座経済学史』青林書院, 1954年9月25日第1版.『新経済学演習講座 経済学史』青林書院新社, 1962年1月20日第1版.pp.532-537.

324　塩野谷九十九「理論経済学の方法と課題」「経済評論」第3巻第10号, 1954年10月1日.pp.49-57.

325　東畑精一「シュムペーター「経済分析の歴史」」「経済研究」第5巻第4号, 1954年10月20日.pp.324-330.

326　P. M. スウィージー, 都留重人監訳「シュンペーターの新機軸理論」『歴史としての現代—資本主義・社会主義に関する論改—』岩波書店, 1954年11月1日第1刷.1955年3月5日第4刷.1965年7月20日第13刷.pp.318-328.

327　寺川末治郎「シュンペーターの「本質」に対するヴイザーの「本質」」「奈良学芸大学紀要」第4巻第1号, 1954年11月25日.pp.1-9.

328　吉田昇三「資本主義・経済発展の論理—マルクスとシュムペーター—」「経済理論」第22号, 1954年12月1日.pp.13-32. 『シュムペーターの経済学』pp.105-151.

329　山本正「ヨゼフ・シュンペーターの時系列解析批判をめぐって—景気変動研究に於ける統計的方法の地位—」「山梨大学学芸学部研究報告」第5号, 1954年12月20日.pp.91-98.

330　浜崎正規「景気変動理論についての一試論—シュムペーターをめぐって—」「立命館経済学」第3巻第6号, 1954年12月25日.pp.124-149. 『シュムペーター経済学の基本問題』pp.117-151.

1955年

331　吉田昇三「書評 シュムペーター著『経済分析の歴史』について」「理論経済学研究」第6号, 1955年1月25日.pp.29-33.

332　吉田昇三「社会思想家評伝 シュムペーター」「社会理想研究」第7巻第2号, 1955年2月15日.pp.17-21, 33.

333　東畑精一「一巻の人, 一書の徒—ある日の日誌—」「図書」第65号, 1955年2月5日.pp.2-7.

334　伊達邦春「衝撃の問題と適応機構の問題—シュムペーター景気循環理論を中心にして—」「季刊理論経済学」第5巻第3・4号, 1955年3月25日.pp.119-126. 『シュンペーター・企業行動・経済変動』早稲田大学出版部, 1992年3月10日初版第1刷.pp.107-121.

335　浜崎正規「ヴィジョンと経済法則との関連—理論経済学における方法論上の一問題—」「立命館大学人文科学研究所紀要」第3号, 1955年3月31日.pp.142-154. 『シュムペーター経済学の基本問題』pp.1-29.

336　浜崎正規『シュムペーター経済学の基本問題』雄渾社, 1955年4月1日発行.2+193p.

337　高田保馬『ケインズ論難—勢力説の立場から—』有斐閣, 1955年5月5日発行.2+3+4+210p.

338　セイモア・E・ハリス編, 中山伊知郎, 東畑精一監訳, 坂本二郎訳『社会科学者シュムペーター』東洋経済新報社, 1955年5月10日発行.20+417p.

338a　中山伊知郎「序文」pp.5-7.

338b　セイモア・E・ハリス「はしがき」p.9. G・ハーバラー, S・E・ハリス, W・W・レオンティエフ, E・S・メーソン(委員長)「ヨーゼフ・アロイス・シュムペーター教授」〔覚書 1950年2月7日ハーヴァード大学連合教授の公式記録〕pp.15-20. 161と同内容.

338c　セイモア・E・ハリス「緒論」pp.3-24.

338d　ラグナー・フリッシュ「一人の偉大な人物についてのある利的回想」pp.27-34.

338e　アーサー・スミッシーズ「追憶―ヨーゼフ・アロイス・シュムペーター, 一八八三――九五〇年」pp.35-71.

338f　アーサー・スミッシーズ「シュムペーターとケインズ」pp.381-399.

338g　ゴットフリート・ハーバラー「ヨーゼフ・アロイス・シュムペーター, 一八八三――九五〇年」pp.72-137. 同論文はハーバラー, 一杉哲也訳「シュンペーター論」, H・W・スピーゲル編, 伊坂市助, 越村信三郎, 山田長夫, 佐藤豊三郎, 長州一二, 古沢友吉監訳『近代経済学―経済思想発展史V―』東洋経済新聞新報社, 1955年2月20日発行.pp.189-235.

338h　ゴットフリート・ハーバラー「シュムペーターの利子論」pp.204-222.

338i　ポール・A・サミュエルソン「教師および経済理論家としてのシュムペーター」pp.138-154. 同論文は、ポエル・A・サミュエルソン〔編集部訳〕「教師, 経済理論家としてのシュンペーター〔経済学者のプロフィール―II〕」「季刊現代経済」第9号, 1973年6月22日.pp.214-222及びサミュエルソン, 坂本二郎訳「教師および経済理論家としてのシュムペーター」, 篠原三代平, 佐藤隆三編集『サミュエルソン経済学体系9 リカード, マルクス, ケインズ …… 』勁草書房, 1979年10月25日第1刷.pp.234-247.

338j　エーリッヒ・シュナイダー「シュムペーターの初期のドイツ語の労作, 一九〇六――九一七年」pp.157-169.

338k　J・ティンバーゲン「シュムペーターと経済学における計量的研究」pp.170-177.

338l　アーサー・W・マーゲット「シュムペーター体系の貨幣的側面」pp.178-203.

338m　アルヴィン・H・ハンセン「景気循環理論に対するシュムペーターの貢献」pp.223-231.

338n　エドワード・H・チェンバリン「最近の独占理論がシュムペーター体系に与える影響」pp.232-245.

338o　エドワード・S・メーソン「シュムペーターの独占理論および大規模企業論」pp.246-260.

338p　フリッツ・マハループ「シュムペーターの経済学方法論」pp.261-280.

338q　ウォルフガング・F・ストルパー「シュムペーターの諸労作についての省察」pp.281-303.

338r　ヘルバート・フォン・ベッケラート「社会学者としてのヨーゼフ・A・シュムペーター」pp.307-331.

338s　ポール・M・スウィージー「シュムペーターの『帝国主義および社会階級』」pp.332-349.

338t　A・P・アッシャー「経済発展の理論の歴史的意味内容」pp.350-361.

338u　デヴィド・マッコート・ライト「シュムペーターの政治哲学」pp.362-378.

338v　坂本二郎「解説―シュムペーター入門として読まれる方のために―」pp.401-413.

338w　坂本二郎「あとがき」pp.415-407.

339　大内兵衛「シュンペーターと東畑精一君―『経済分析の歴史』について―」「図書」第74号, 1955年11月5日.pp.2-3, 『我・人・本』岩波書店, 1958年12月1日第1刷.pp.327-332.

1956年

340 吉田昇三「ケインズとシュムペーター「経済理論」」第29・30合併号, 1956年3月1日.pp.1-26. 加筆『シュムペーターの経済学』pp.152-207.

341 岩崎秀二「シュンペーター理論の科学的性格」「法経論集(新潟大学)」第5巻第3号, 1956年3月30日.pp.23-46.

342 山田雄三「理論経済学―シュムペーター著『経済分析の歴史』の紹介を通じて―」「一橋論叢」第35巻第4号.1956年4月10日.pp.16-34.

343 緑川敬『景気変動の研究方法―経済変動の一般理論へ―』日新出版, 1956年5月20日.2+10+300p.

344 石田興平「貨幣理論におけるシュムペーターとケインズ」「バンキング」第101号, 1956年8月1日.pp.12-25.

345 山部徳雄「シュムペーター著東畑精一訳『経済分析の歴史I』」「三田学会雑誌」第49巻第8号, 1956年8月1日.pp.47-51.

346 R・V・クレメンス, F・S・ドーディ著, 伊達春監訳『シュムペーター経済学入門』ダイヤモンド社, 1956年9月15日初版.238p.

347 伊達邦春「シュムペーター型モデルとケインズ型モデル―循環分析と成長分析との統合という視点にたって―」「早稲田政治経済学雑誌」第141号, 1956年10月1日.pp.47-68.『シュンペーター・企業行動・経済変動』pp.150-167.

348 高橋泰蔵「技術の進歩と経済理論」「エコノミスト別冊 技術革新と明日の生活」1956年10月15日.pp.21-24.

349 都留重人「シュンペーター」, 岸本誠二郎, 都留重人監修『講座近代経済学批判 第一巻』東洋経済新報社, 1956年10月30日発行.pp.293-306「シュンペーター論」『都留重人著作集第2巻』pp.556-579.

350 吉田昇三『シュムペーターの経済学』法律文化社, 1956年11月5日発行.5+3+207p.1964年6月10日改訂第1刷.1967年改訂第2刷.9+3+230p.

351 武藤光朗「経済的進化の非人格化と自由化―シュムペーターの理論的パースペクティヴ―」『経済倫理―経済学と世界観―』春秋社, 1956年11月20日第1刷.pp.66-76.

352 熊谷尚夫『近代経済学』日本評論社, 1956年12月25日第1版第1刷.1966年3月31日第1版第20刷.1970年2月20日第1版第28刷.10+275+12p.

1957年

353 安井琢磨「経済学史の人々 J・A・シュムペーター」「法学セミナー」〔学生版法律時報〕No. 10, 1957年1月1日.pp.58-62. 日本評論新社編集局編『経済学史上の十二人』日本評論新社, 1957年8月20日第1版第1刷.pp.161-176.「J・A・シュムペーター」『経済学とその周辺』木鐸社, 1979年9月25日第1版第1刷.p.189-201.

354 向井利昌「カーリン「シュンペーターにおける構成型としての企業」」「国民経済雑誌」第95巻第1号, 1957年1月10日.pp.71-75.

355　高田保馬『学問遍路』東洋経済新報社, 1957年2月5日発行.7+184p.

356　吉田昇三「シュムペーターの独占論について」「経済理論」第35・36号, 1957年3月1日.pp.1-26. 修正補筆「シュムペーターの動態的競争・独占理論の再検討」『競争・独占と経済発展』春秋社, 1959年11月15日第1刷.pp.97-122.

357　T. W. ハチスン, 長守善, 山田雄三, 武藤光朗共訳『近代経済学説史 上巻』東洋経済新報社, 1957年3月30日発行.20+315p.

358　T. W. ハチスン, 長守善, 山田雄三, 武藤光朗共訳『近代経済学説史 下巻』東洋経済新報社, 1957年5月10日発行.10+237p.

359　L. ロビンズ, 中山伊知郎監修, 辻六兵衛訳『経済学の本質と意義』東洋経済新報社, 1957年4月20日第1刷.1959年3月20日第2刷.964年10月25日第10刷.28+238+9p.

360　岡崎陽一「独占と経済発展―シュンペーターの動学的独占論の吟味―」, 明治学院大学経済学部編『近代社会の諸問題―経済発展と社会関係―』有信堂, 1957年5月1日.pp.183-206.

361　大熊信行「マルクス経済学と近代経済学の交流点」『経済本質=計画経済学の基礎』東洋経済新報社, 1957年5月20日第1刷.1958年5月1日第4刷.pp.255-283.

362　正井敬次「貨幣資本における利子発生の根拠―マルクス, シュムペーター, ケインズの立場を繞って―」「関西大学経済論集」第7巻第3号, 1957年6月1日.pp.1-24.

363　柴山幸治「独占と経済発展―シュムペーター理論の批判を手がかりとして―」「季刊理論経済学」第8巻第1, 2号, 1957年7月15日.pp.24-32, 8.

364　吉田昇三「シュムペーター体系と独占」「季刊理論経済学」第8巻第1, 2号, 1957年7月15日.pp.9-15加筆して『シュムペーターの経済学』法律文化社, 1956年11月5日発行のpp.208-230.

365　伊達邦春「シュムペーターにおける均衡の近傍の概念について―特にシュムペーターの統計的手法との関連において―」, 久保田明光先生還暦記念会編『久保田明光教授還暦記念論文集』創元社, 1957年9月8日発行.pp.307-324.

366　静田均「シュンペーター帝国主義論序説」「経済論叢」第80巻第4号, 1957年10月1日.pp.174-189.

367　山田雄三『近代経済学史要 経済学はいかに進歩したか』春秋社, 1957年11月5日第1刷.6+4+181+4p.

368　柏祐賢『資本主義のメカニズム』関書院, 1957年11月15日初版.4+3+326p.『柏祐賢著作集第6巻』pp.121-370.

369　大野忠男, 熊谷尚夫「シュンペーター体系と社会主義の問題」「大阪大学経済学」第7巻第3号, 1957年11月25日.pp.146-182. 付記「実質的にはこれは主として大野の労作」.大野忠男「シュムペーター体系序説」『シュムペーター体系研究―資本主義の発展と崩壊―』創文社, 1971年1月30日第1刷.1972年4月15日第2刷.1979年11月30日第4刷.pp3-37.

370　山部徳雄「ハリス編『社会科学者シュムペーター』」「三田学会雑誌」第48巻第11号, 1957年12月1日.pp.64-68.

1958年

371　ダヴィッド・マッコード・ライト, 田口芳弘訳『資本主義』みすず書房, 1958年1月15日第1刷.325+10p.

372　岡村久雄「社会遺制説—シュムペーター」『戦争・民族・階級—国際緊張の社会学(上)—』関書院, 1958年2月1日.pp.96-142.

373　立命館大学経済学部浜崎ゼミナール『「学生論集」(昭和32年度)J. A. シュムペーターの経済学について』1958年3月.4+8+2+358+4p.

374　中山伊知郎「与件と日本経済の分析」「経済評論」第7巻第5号, 1958年5月1日.pp.2-10.『中山伊知郎全集 第九集 経済の安定と進歩』講談社, 1972年8月24日第1刷.pp.339-352.

375　清水嘉治「帝国主義の型について—ウインズロー教授の見解を中心として—」「一橋論叢」第40巻第1号, 1958年7月1日.pp.82-88. 越村信三郎編『最近の独占研究』東洋経済新報社, 1959年6月10日.pp.278-291.

376　村田稔「シュムペーターの資本主義没落論の一検討」「フェビアン研究」9巻7号, 1958年7月15日.pp.19-32.

377　村田稔「シュムペーターの資本主義没落論の一検討(二)」「フェビアン研究」9巻8号, 1958年8月15日.pp.21-32.

378　早川泰三『経済変動理論—拡張と崩壊の経済理論—』東洋経済新報社, 1958年9月15日発行.6+226p.

379　青山秀夫「資本と景気循環」, 編集委員代表篠原三代平『中山伊知郎博士還暦記念論文集 経済の安定と進歩』東洋経済新報社, 1958年9月25日発行.pp.665-681.

380　馬場啓之助「経済発展の思想と理論」『中山伊知郎博士還暦記念論文集』pp.79-94.

381　高橋泰蔵「経済発展と金融機構—シュムペーター『経済発展の理論』を中心として—」『中山伊知郎博士還暦記念論文集』pp.339-352.

382　静田均「シュンペーターの帝国主義論」「経済論叢」第82巻第4号, 1958年10月1日.pp.24-38.

383　河野善隆「シュムペーターの革新概念の変化」「研究紀要(長崎県立短期大学佐世保商英部)」第6集, 1958年11月1日.pp.9-20.

384　近代経済学研究会編「シュムペーターの経済学」『マルクスとケインズ世界十五大経済学』柏林書房, 1958年11月25日初版.pp.140-158. 富士書店, 1969年4月20日改訂16版.1979年10月20日改訂42版.pp.143-161.

385　T. パーソンズ, N. J. スメルサー, 富永健一訳『経済と社会I　経済学理論と社会学理論の統合についての研究』岩波書店, 1958年11月29日第1版.1977年3月20日第14刷.1992年10月30日第16刷.24+293p.

1959年

386　大野忠男「シュムペーターと資本主義の変貌」「季刊理論経済学」第9巻第1, 2号, 1959年1月25日.pp.36-43. 「資本主義の変貌」『シュムペーター体系研究』pp.251-268.

387　静田均「シュンペーター帝国主義論への補説」「経済論叢」第83巻第2号, 1959年2月1日.pp.1-20.

388　中山伊知郎「「景気循環論」邦訳を手にして(有斐閣刊,「景気循環論」序文より)」「書斎の窓」(有斐閣)第65号, 1959年3月1日.pp.15-16.「始めにも述べたように」を除いて吉田昇三監修, 金融経済研究所訳『景気循環論I』の序文pp.1-4.

389　白杉庄一郎「シュムペーターの独占理論—最近における独占肯定の諸理論その1—」「彦根論叢」第53号, 1959年3月5日.pp.1-20,『独占理論の研究』ミネルヴァ書房, 1961年4月15日第1刷.1968年9月5日第3刷.pp.236-266.

390　力石定一「複合循環のモデルと経済予測—シュンペーターの景気循環論によせて—」「国民経済」通巻第37号, 1959年3月30日.pp.2-28.

391　高橋泰蔵「ヨーゼフ・アロイス・シュムペーター—理論と歴史との接点—」「一橋論叢」第41巻第4号, 1959年4月1日.pp.106-120.『経済学巡礼記』東洋経済新報社, 1977年3月10日発行.pp.119-139.

392　緑川敬『技術革新と景気変動　初等経済学講義』日新出版, 1959年5月10日初版.1+9+252+20p.

393　長州一二「独占評価の諸類型」, 越村信三郎編『最近の独占研究』pp.84-121.

394　小西唯雄「—研究—シュムペーターの独占企業論」「経済学論究」第13巻第2号, 1959年6月25日.pp.97-116.『反独占政策と有効需要』有斐閣, 1967年11月30日初版第1刷.1968年4月5日初版第2刷.pp.12-32. 増補版1975年9月30日.pp.9-32.

395　河野善隆「経済成長と技術的革新をめぐる問題—シュムペーターの経済学について—」「研究紀要(長崎県立短期大学佐世保商英部)」第7集, 1959年9月30日.pp.58-74.

396　吉田昇三『競争・独占と経済発展』春秋社, 1959年11月15日第1刷.5+226+6p.

397　高島善哉「理論におけるヴィジョンとイデオロギー」「一橋論叢」第42巻第6号, 1959年12月1日.pp.52-70. 山田秀雄編『高島善哉 市民社会論の構想』pp.378-399.

1960年

398　吉田昇三「独占理論の新視点について」「経済評論」第9巻第3号, 1960年2月1日.pp.45-53.

399　東畑精一『一巻の人』私家本, 1960年3月25日発行.2+4+286p.

400　中山伊知郎「経済学の広場」「経済セミナー」42号, 1960年4月1日.pp.1-4.

401　吉田昇三「シュムペーター「経済発展の理論」」「経済セミナー」43号別冊経済学必修書解明, 1960年5月1日.pp.73-88.

402　横尾邦夫「租税国家論についての一考察」「経済論叢」第86巻第1号, 1960年7月1日.pp.36-46.

403　伊達邦春「シュンペーター・モデルにおける循環と趨勢」「季刊理論経済学」第11巻第1, 2号, 1960年7月15日.pp.35-42.

404　伊達邦春「図式化された経済発展の諸理論—B・ヒギンス教授の所説の吟味を道じて—」「早稲田政治経済学雑誌」第164号, 1960年8月1日.pp.71-88.

405　永友育雄「シュンペーターの景気変動理論」「経済論叢」第86巻第4号, 1960年10月1日.pp.43-57.

406　阿部源一「シュムペーターの社会主義論の二元性―価値判断論争の―問題―」, 井藤半弥博士退官記念事業会記念論文集編集委員会編『井藤半弥博士退官記念論文集　社会政策の基本問題』千倉書房, 1960年11月20日発行.pp.343-362.

407　加藤芳太郎「財政社会学ということ」『井藤半弥博士退官記念論文集』pp.129-144.

408　山下覚太郎「「財政社会学」の意義および方法」『井藤半弥博士退官記念論文集』pp.109-128.

1961年

409　緑川敬「シュムペーター経済学の再評価―現代成長経済学の視点から―」「経済往来」第13巻第1号, 1961年1月1日.pp.71-79.

410　伊達邦春「書評 シュムペーター『景気循環』吉田昇三監修, 金融経済研究所訳(全五巻), 現在三巻まで発刊, 有斐閣」「早稲田政治経済学雑誌」第167号, 1961年2月1日.pp.71-74.

411　坂本市郎「〈研究ノート〉 シュムペーター体系における企業者と革新に関する一考察―マックス・ウェーバーのカリスマ的支配者との比較をめぐって―」「経済経営論集」第21号, 1961年2月5日.pp.53-62.

412　三島康雄『経営史学の展開』ミネルヴァ書房, 1961年6月25日第1刷.12+220+8p.増補版1970年4月1日.12+231+9p.

413　白杉庄一郎『独占理論の研究』ミネルヴァ書房, 1961年4月15日第1刷.1968年9月5日第3刷.4+2+390+2p.

414　吉田昇三「書評『シュムペーター体系研究』大野忠男著, 独創的な「大きなシュムペーター体系」」「週刊東洋経済」等3608号, 1961年7月19日.pp.112-113.

415　中川敬一郎「経済発展と企業者活動(上)―企業者史研究の立場から―」「思想」446号, 1961年8月5日.pp.49-55.

416　中川敬一郎「経済発展と企業者活動(下)―企業者史研究の立場から―」「思想」447号, 1961年9月5日.pp.105-116.「経済発展と企業者活動(上)」とともに『比較経営史序説　比較経営史研究1』東京大学出版会, 1981年3月20日初版.1993年6月25日8刷.pp.15-48.

417　岩野茂道「シュムペーター景気循環論の一考察」「経済論究」第10号, 1961年10月20日.pp.1-18.

418　高津英雄「シュムペーターにおける二つの利子理論」「法経論集」第9巻第1号, 1961年11月20日.pp.1-24.

1962年

419　永友育雄「シュンペーターの投資理論」「経済論叢」第89巻第2号, 1962年2月1日.pp.37-50.

420　森田優三「序文」『The CATALOGUE of Prof. Schumpeter Library　The Hitotsubashi Library　Tokyo 1962』一橋大学, 1962年3月1日.p.3.

421　東畑精一「由来記」『The CATALOGUE of Prof. Schumpeter Library　The Hitotsubashi Library　Tokyo 1962』pp.7-12.「シュムペーター文庫の由来記」『農書に歴史あり』家の光協会, 1973年2月3日第1版.1973年4月20日第2版.pp.241-251.

422　高津英雄「シュムペーターにおける二つの利子理論(二)」「法経論集」第9巻第2号, 1962年3月20日.pp.1-31.

423　東畑精一「翻訳苦楽談―『経済分析の歴史』を訳了して―」「図書」152号, 1962年4月1日.pp.2-6. 『農書に歴史あり』pp.252-263.

424　吉田昇三「シュムペーター」, 堀経夫編『原典経済学史 下巻』創元社, 1962年5月5日.pp.68-74.

425　馬場啓之助「経済発展と企業者」「季刊理論経済学」第12巻第3号, 1962年6月30日.pp.60-63.

426　末永隆甫「シュムペーターの帝国主義論」, 赤松要・堀江薫・名和統一・大来佐武郎監修『講座国際経済　第5巻帝国主義と後進国開発』有斐閣, 1962年6月30日初版第1刷.1972年4月10日初版第6刷.pp.101-103.

427　中山伊知郎「経済十話」, 著者代表湯川秀樹『十人十話』毎日新聞社, 1962年8月10日発行.pp.63-83. 『中山伊知郎全集　第十六集 日本経済への発言』講談社, 1973年2月20日第1刷.pp.1-28.

428　カール・ヤスパース, 小倉志祥記「マックス・ウェーバーの政治的思考」「実存主義」第26号, 1962年10月6日.pp.2-11.

429　高津英雄「価値打歩の二面性―シュムペーターにおける二つの利子理論(三)―」「法経論集」第10巻第2号, 1962年12月1日.pp.1-21.

1963年

430　岩野茂道「シュムペーター信用理論に関する覚書」「経済学研究」第28巻第6号, 1963年2月25日.pp.21-49.

431　清水嘉治「非マルクス主義帝国主義論の検討」, 井汲卓一, 今井則義, 宇高基輔, 江口朴郎, 吉村正晴編『現代帝国主義講座　第V巻 現代帝国主義の経済法則』日本評論新社, 1963年3月30日第1版第1刷.pp.255-302. 『帝国主義論研究序説』有斐閣, 1965年11月30日.pp.229-262.

432　永友育雄「シュンペーターの資本理論」「経済論叢」第91巻第6号, 1963年6月1日.pp.65-83.

433　岩野茂道「国際金融機構についての一考察―金ブレーキ論批判―」「経済学研究」第29巻第2号, 1963年6月25日.pp.75-91.

434　坂垣與一「帝国主義の社会学―シュンペーターの帝国主義論」『国際関係論の基本問題』新紀元社, 1963年7月15日.1976年12月5日第2刷.pp.151-157, 『国際関係論の基本問題I』アジア書房出版部, 1982年4月5日, 初版第1刷.pp.151-157.

435　坂本二郎「革新の社会経済学者シュンペーター」, 大河内一男編『経済学を築いた人々　ペティーからシュンペーターまで』青林書院新社, 1963年11月30日第1刷.1964年2月20日第2刷.1965年9月20日第4刷.pp.335-362. 『増補 経済学を築いた人々』1966年9月30日増補第1刷.1968年4月15日増補第3刷.1969年10月15日増補第6刷.pp.391-418.

1964年

436 吉田昇三「経済学者の横顔(その一)—ベームとシュムペーター」「理論経済学研究」復刊1, 1964年1月28日.pp.3-10.

437 東畑精一『日本資本主義の形成者—さまざまの経済主体—』岩波書店, 1964年2月20日第1刷.1964年3月5日第2刷.1967年4月20日第5刷.1970年12月10日第9刷.3+190p.

438 米川伸一「経営史学の生誕と展開(一)—第二次大戦以前における「経営史」Business Historyの発達を廻って—」「商学研究」8, 1964年3月31日.pp.177-278.

439 R・ダーレンドルフ著, 富永健一訳『産業社会における階級闘争』ダイヤモンド社, 1964年6月30日初版.1974年4月10日6版.27+454+34p.

440 都留重人『近代経済学の群像　人とその学説』日本経済新聞社, 1964年9月10日発行.1977年6月20日20版1刷.1981年4月30日20版4刷.1983年8月20日20版5刷.245p.,『都留重人著作集　第11巻人と旅と本』講談社, 1976年4月12日第1刷.pp.1-160. 末尾の「エピローグ—ハーヴァード黄金時代」は割愛.『近代経済学の群像　人とその学説』社会思想社, 1993年12月30日初版第1刷.254p.

441 馬場啓之助「シュムペーターの理論」, 木村健康監修『現代経済理論のエッセンス　ケインズ以後の18大理論』ぺりかん社, 1964年9月15日第1刷.1965年4月10日第2刷.1966年4月30日第3刷.1968年3月1日第4刷.1969年4月10日増補第1刷.pp.33-47.

442 吉田昇三「ヴェーバーとシュムペーター」「経済理論」第82号, 1964年11月1日.pp.1-21.「はじめに」,「人間型の比較」,「「倫理」の企業者と『発展』の企業者」『ウェーバーとシュムペーター—歴史家の眼・理論家の眼』筑摩書房, 1974年10月30日初版第1刷.pp.3-12, 13-23, 105-120.

1965年

443 高橋泰蔵「技術革新と経済と金融」「金融経済」第90号, 1965年2月25日.pp.1-12.

444 速水保「シュムペーターとケインズの利潤概念の比較」「一橋論叢」第53巻第3号, 1965年3月1日.pp.75-81.

445 酒井正三郎「シュムペーター『経済発展の理論』」「オイコノミカ」第1巻1・2合併号, 1965年3月31日.pp.13-22.

446 米川伸一「経営史学の生誕と展開(二)——九四〇年代の学界状況を廻って—」「商学研究」9, 1965年3月31日.pp.27-129.

447 中山伊知郎「シュムペーター『理論経済学の本質』」, 朝日新聞東京本社学芸部編『一冊の本2』雪華社, 1965年4月1日.1968年9月20日3版.pp.78-80,『一冊の本(全)』雪華社, 1976年11月25日新装発行.pp.165-167.『中山伊知郎全集　第十七集エッセイ集』講談社, 1973年4月20日第1刷.pp.202-203.

448 中山伊知郎「経済学者のことば　衰退に導く成功シュンペーター」「エコノミスト」第43巻第24号増刊号, 1965年5月31日.p.117.

449　速水保「シュムペーターとケインズの利子概念の比較」「一橋論叢」第53巻第6号, 1965年6月1日.pp.89-96.

450　渡辺文夫「シュンペーターの「企業者史」について」, 渡辺信一教授退官記念論文集刊行会編『経済発展の論理 渡辺信一教授記念論文集』東洋経済新報社, 1965年6月10日発行.pp.249-266.

451　高橋泰蔵「企業者機能についての一解釈」「ビジネス レビュー」13巻1号, 1965年6月25日.pp.1-9.

452　伊東光晴「シュンペーター」, 内田義彦, 小林昇, 宮崎義一, 宮崎犀一編『経済学史講座第3巻　経済学の展開』有斐閣, 1965年6月30日初版第1刷.1967年3月30日初版第2刷.1970年9月10日初版第4刷.pp.199-224.

453　宮崎義一「近代経済学における現代資本主義観」, 内田義彦他編『経済学史講座3』pp.277-323.

454　T・B・ボットモア著, 綿貫譲治訳『エリートと社会』岩波書店, 1965年7月30日第1刷.1978年8月30日第11刷.3+188+15p.

455　岸本誠二郎「人と学説　シュンペーター」「経済往来」17巻10号, 1965年10月1日.pp.75-84.

456　広江真助「J. A. Schumpeterと利子理論」「神戸外大論叢」第16巻第4号, 1965年10月15日.pp.19-36.

457　小野進「シュンペーターの景気循環論—その批判的考察—」「立命館経済学」第14巻第4号, 1965年10月20日.pp.2-129.

458　川田俊昭「シュムペーターの動学—その方法論的註解—」「経営と経済」第45巻第2・3号, 1965年10月25日.pp.57-94.

459　エミール・ジャム, 久保田明光, 山川義雄訳『経済思想史 上』岩波書店, 1965年10月25日第1刷.1978年4月20日第9刷.22+388p.

460　エミール・ジャム, 久保田明光, 山川義雄訳『経済思想史 下』岩波書店, 1967年1月10日第1刷.6p.+pp.389-631+18p.

461　A・H・コール著, 中川敬一郎訳『経営と社会—企業者史学序説—』ダイヤモンド社, 1965年11月27日初版.1971年3月25日5版.19+257+21p.

1966年

462　森本三男「企業者機能と経営者」, 古川栄一博士還暦記念論文集編集委員会編『現代経営学と財務管理』同文館, 1966年2月4日発行.pp.117-129.

463　藻利重隆「経営者の革新的職能—シュンペーターの所論を中心として—」, 古川栄一博士還暦記念論文集編集委員会編『現代経営学と財務管理』pp.87-116.

464　F. レックスハウゼン著, 鈴木辰治訳『経営者と経済発展』未来社, 1966年2月28日第1刷.234p.

465　青山秀夫・吉田昇三「シュムペーター『経済分析の歴史』の輪郭と問題点—邦訳の完成にちなんで—」「季刊理論経済学」第16巻第2号, 1966年3月30日.pp.48-60.

466　小野進「シュンペーターの景気循環論批判」「経済」第23号, 1966年4月1日.pp.163-170.

467　中山伊知郎「私の古典③　シュムペーター「経済発展の理論」」「エコノミスト」第44巻第15号(通巻1593号), 1966年4月19日.pp.74-77.『中山伊知郎全集　第十七集』pp.204-210.

468　中山伊知郎「対話……現代日本経済論1　日本の工業化と伝統社会　中山伊知郎　きき手 小泉明, 宮崎義一」「週刊東洋経済」第3284号, 1966年5月21日.pp.26-36. 小泉明, 宮崎義一編『日本経済を見る眼』東洋経済新報社, 1967年9月20日発行のpp.5-26. 坂本二郎「私の見た中山博士―人とその学説」「週刊東洋経済」第3284号, 1966年5月21日.pp.36-41. 小泉明, 宮崎義一編『日本経済を見る眼』の「相反するものを統一する才能―中山博士―」pp.27-38.

469　清水嘉治「非マルクス主義帝国主義論の原型―とくにホブソンとシュムペーターの所説を中心として―」「経済系」第69集, 1966年6月3日.pp.1-16.

470　酒井正三郎「シュムペーター『経済発展理論』と企業者概念」『経営学方法論〔第二版〕』森山書店, 1966年6月15日初版.1971年7月27日第2版.pp.233-253.

471　井上忠勝「個別企業史はいかに研究すべきか」「経営史学」第1巻第1号, 1966年6月20日.pp.96-104.

472　桂芳男「経営主体の諸概念」「経営史学」第1巻第1号, 1966年6月20日.pp.71-89.

473　高田保馬「仁智勇の人」「三田評論」第652号, 1966年8月1日.pp.49-51.『小泉信三全集2』月報18, 文芸春秋, 1968年9月.pp.1-2.

474　高橋泰蔵「「利潤」概念におけるケインズとシュムペーター」「国民経済雑誌」第114巻第3号, 1966年9月10日.pp.1-14.

475　大原静夫「シュンペーターの貨幣論―信用創造論を中心として―」「山陽女子短期大学研究紀要」第1号, 1966年9月30日.pp.63-71.

476　高橋泰蔵「技術の進歩と経済理論」「エコノミスト」別冊「技術革新と明日の生活」1966年10月15日.pp.21-24.

477　高橋泰蔵「経済における「変化」と「企業者」」「金融経済」第100号, 1966年10月25日.pp.205-213.

478　有沢広己, 中山伊知郎, 東畑精一, 安井琢磨「戦前戦後の経済学　創刊二〇年によせて」「経済評論」第15巻第14号, 1966年12月1日.pp.26-41.

479　東畑精一「対話……現代日本経済論⑥ 経済の進歩とそのにない手　東畑精一氏 きき手小泉明, 宮崎義一」「週刊東洋経済」第3318号, 1966年12月3日.pp.42-50. 小泉明, 宮崎義一編『日本経済を見る眼』東洋経済新報社, 1967年9月20日発行のpp.203-222.

480　馬場啓之助「東畑精一先生」「週刊東洋経済」第3318号, 1966年12月3日.pp.51-54. 小泉明, 宮崎義一編『日本経済を見る眼』東洋経済新報社, 1967年9月20日発行の「ゆたかな直観力―東畑精一先生―」pp.223-230.

1967年

481　大野忠男「シュンペーター」, 小林昇, 杉原四郎編『経済学史』有斐閣, 1967年2月15日初版第1刷.1972年7月20日第9刷.pp.219-239.『新版経済学史』有斐閣, 1986年8月15日初版第1刷.pp.209-227.「シュムペーターの経済学」『シュムペーター体系研究』pp.38-58.

482　今井賢一「企業行動と革新」, 石原善太郎, 宮川公男, 今井賢一『経営革新』講談社, 1967年2月20日第1刷.pp.55-72.

483　小泉明, 宮崎義一「対話……現代日本経済論⑨ 日本経済を見る眼」「週刊東洋経済」第3332号, 1967年3月18日.pp.40-48. 小泉明, 宮崎義一編『日本経済を見る眼』東洋経済新報社, 1967年9月20日発行の「日本経済を見る眼の構造」pp.301-318.

484　高田保馬「経済学と私」「経済セミナー」通巻第132号, 1967年4月1日.pp.2-6.

485　伊達邦春「シュンペーター『経済発展の理論』―現代経済学古典案内―」「経済セミナー」通巻第134号別冊付録, 1967年6月1日.pp.105-126.

486　永友育雄『景気変動の経済理論』有斐閣, 1967年6月30日初版第1刷.3+3+238p.

487　大熊信行『資源配分の理論』東洋経済新報社, 1967年7月25日第1刷.1973年5月15日第5刷.21+396+14p.

488　小泉明, 宮崎義一編『日本経済を見る眼』東洋経済新報社, 1967年9月20日発行.9+318p.

489　羽鳥忠「Schumpeterの企業者」, 編集責任者蓁目英三『手塚寿郎先生の追憶』「緑丘」編集部, 1967年10月13日.pp.194-197.

490　土方成美「経済学における独創 J. SchumpeterとPaul Leroy―Beaulieu」「独協大学経済学研究」第2号, 1967年10月20日.pp.106-111.

491　小野進「帝国主義論―シュンペーターとレーニン―」「立命館経済学」第16巻第304号, 1967年10月20日.pp.122-134.

492　宮崎義一「長期停滞論と独占観」『近代経済学の史的展開―「ケインズ革命」以後の現代資本主義像―』有斐閣, 1967年10月30日初版第1刷.1970年3月10日初版第4刷.pp.215-266.

493　ウインチエンツオ・ヴィテッロ, 中村文夫訳「資本主義的発展の理論　シュンペーターの分析とマルクスの分析との類似と差異」『近代経済思想入門』合同出版, 1967年11月5日第1刷.pp.55-77.

494　小谷義次「シュムペーターの帝国主義論について―ブルジョア帝国主義論批判―」「経済」第44号, 1967年12月1日.pp.254-263.

1968年

495　渡辺徳二「―表紙写真解説―J. A. シュンペーター著『資本主義, 社会主義, 民主主義』「労働資料(日本労働協会労働図書館)」No32, 1968年1月1日.表紙裏面.

496　伊東光晴「シュンペーターの小説」「図書」第222号, 1968年2月1日.pp.38-41.

497　長州一二「創造的破壊, 『資本主義・社会主義・民主主義』」『現代資本主義の名著』日本経済新聞社, 1968年6月26日初版.1973年5月10日6版.pp.13-30.

498　浜崎正規「シュムペーター・モデルの再検討(上)―開発理論形成のための適応論争をめぐって―」「立命館経済学」第17巻第3・4号, 1968年10月20日.pp.153-214.

499　吉原英樹「経営史学と革新の行動科学的理論」「経営史学」第3巻第3号, 1968年12月20日.pp.56-82.

1969年

500 馬場啓之助『社会科学としての経済学—新版経済学方法論—普及版』春秋社, 1969年4月15日第1刷.5+268p.

501 川田俊昭「学説並びに方法—J・A・シュムペーター」「経営と経済」第49巻第1号, 1969年4月30日.pp.77-132.

502 安部一成「寡占と技術革新」, 馬場正雄, 新野幸次郎編『寡占の経済学』日本経済新聞社, 1969年6月20日.pp.123-158.

503 高田保馬「高田保馬先生の巻」, 京都大学経済学部『創立五十年記念　思い出草』京都大学経済学部, 1969年7月10日発行.pp.1-50.

504 吉田昇三「シュムペーター体系と組織上の革新」「経済理論」第111号, 1969年9月1日.pp.1-32.

505 大谷龍造『景気変動の理論』東洋経済新報社, 1969年9月25日.7+264p.

506 山下博「シュムペーター」, 山口勇蔵編『経済学史入門』有斐閣, 1969年10月20日初版第1刷.1980年12月20日初版第18刷.pp.194-202.

507 吉田昇三「ウェーバー体系とシュムペーター体系」「経済理論」第112号, 1969年11月1日.pp.1-29. 「補論」『ウェーバーとシュムペーター』pp.206-241.

1970年

508 丸山恵也「シュンペーターの「企業者」論」「経済経営論集」第55号, 1970年2月20日.pp.21-54.

509 大野忠男「シュムペーターと経済社会学の根本問題(I)」「岡山大学経済学会雑誌」第1巻第2号, 1970年2月28日.pp.1-23.

510 吉田昇三「ウェーバーの『カリスマ的指導者』とシュムペーターの『企業者』」「経済理論」第114号, 1970年3月1日.pp.1-41. 「「カリスマ的指導者」とシュムペーターの「企業者」」『ウェーバーとシュムペーター』pp.121-171.

511 岡田純一「シュムペーター経済学についての一試論」「上智経済論集」第16巻第3号, 1970年3月15日.pp.12-27.

512 大野忠男「シュムペーターと経済社会学の根本問題(II)」「岡山大学経済学会雑誌」第1巻第3・4号, 1970年3月31日.pp.34-62. 「シュムペーターと経済社会学の根本問題(I)」とともに「経済社会学の根本問題」『シュムペーター体系研究』pp.59-111.

513 中山伊知郎「近代経済学について」「季刊理論経済学」第21巻第1号, 1970年4月4日.pp.1-10. 「中山伊知郎全集 第六集近代経済学の展開」講談社, 1772年7月24日第1刷.pp.293-311.

514 高田保馬「近代経済学とはどういう学問か」「経済セミナー」通巻第172号, 1970年5月1日.pp.1-18.

515 十川広国「経営理念論からみた経営者の職能と役割—シュムペーターの「企業者論」の吟味を中心として—」「三田商学研究」第13巻第2号, 1970年6月30日.pp.199-219.

516　中山伊知郎「〈連載〉現代史を創る人びと⑮ 中山伊知郎〔第一回〕純粋経済学の誕生　聞き手.中村隆英, 伊藤隆」「エコノミスト」1970年8月4日.pp.76-83. , 中村隆英/伊藤隆/原朗編『現代史を創る人びと(1)中山伊知郎』毎日新聞社, 1971年4月10日.pp.173-224.

517　大野忠男「資本主義発展と社会構造の変化について(1)—シュムペーターの資本主義崩壊論—」「岡山大学経済学会雑誌」第2巻第2号, 1970年8月10日.pp.1-30.

518　米倉一良「シュムペーターの「企業者」の心理学的分析」「経済理論」第117号, 1970年9月1日.pp.141-159.

519　吉田昇三「『方法論争』とウェーバー, シュムペーターの方法論的考察」「経済理論」第117号, 1970年9月1日.pp.1-31. , 「「方法論争」と両者の方法論的考察」『ウェーバーとシュムペーター』pp.24-61.

520　岩崎秀二「シュムペーターの利子理論」「千葉敬愛経済大学研究論集」第3号, 1970年9月15日.pp.39-58.

521　岡田純一『経済思想史』東洋経済新報社, 1970年10月12日第1刷.1975年3月20日第5刷.1993年2月15日第19刷.7+308p.

522　大野忠男「シュムペーターとマルクス—経済発展の論理について—」「大阪大学経済学」第20巻第1号, 1970年10月17日.pp.12-42. 「シュムペーターとマルクス—資本主義発展の論理について—」『シュムペーター体系研究』pp.112-162.

523　岩崎秀二「シュムペーターの景気理論研究序説」「現代科学論叢」第4集, 1970年12月21日.pp.1-9.

1971年

524　吉田昇三「ウェーバーとシュムペーターとの方法論的考察の比較」「経済理論」第119号, 1971年1月1日, pp.1-34. 「方法論的考察の比較」『ウェーバーとシュムペーター』pp.62-104.

525　大野忠男『シュムペーター体系研究—資本主義の発展と崩壊—』創文社, 1971年1月30日第1刷, 1972年4月15日第2刷, 1979年11月30日第4刷, 8+4+445+6p.

526　金指基「シュムペーターの経済思想的展開—方法論的研究の視角から—」「商学集志」第40巻第4号, 1971年2月10日, pp.57-75.

527　大野忠男「資本主義発展と社会構造の変化について(2)—シュムペーターの資本主義崩壊論—」「岡山大学経済学会雑誌」第2巻第4号, 1971年3月24日, pp.63-86. 435とともに加筆して『シュムペーター体系研究』pp.163-242.

528　大野忠男「シュムペーターとウェーバーの会見の記」「創文」95号, 1971年4月1日, pp.9-14.

529　橋本昭一「新刊紹介 エリッヒ シュナイダー著『ヨセフA. シュンペーター, 一人の偉大な社会経済学者の生涯と著作』」「関西大学経済論集」第21巻第2号, 1971年6月20日, pp.117-122.

530　吉田昇三「書評『シュムペーター体系研究』大野忠男著, 独創的な「大きなシュムペーター体系」論」「週刊東洋経済」第3608号, 1971年7月17日, pp.112-113.

531　川田俊昭「シュムペーターとケインズ—彼等における動学の条件—」「経営と経済」第51巻第2号, 1971年7月31日, pp.193-228.

532 ライオネル・ロビンズ著井手口一夫, 伊東正則監訳『経済発展の学説』東洋経済新報社, 1971年9月27日発行, 10+223p.

533 川田俊昭「シュムペーターとマルクス—彼等における進化主義について—(その一)」「経営と経済」第51巻第3号, 1971年10月31日, pp.161-190.

534 金指基「シュムペーター経済学の源泉—ボェームとワルラスの関係を中心に—」「商学集志」第41巻第2号, 1971年11月25日, pp.81-94.

535 I. アデルマン, 山岡喜久男訳「シュムペーター」, 『経済発展の諸理論』同文館出版株式会社, 1971年11月30日初版発行, 1975年3月20日3版発行, pp.116-135.

536 藻利重隆「企業者職能と資本主義体制—シュムペーター学説の検討—」「会計」第100巻第7号, 1971年12月1日, pp.1-19.

537 トム・ケンプ, 時永淑訳『帝国主義論史』法政大学出版局, 1971年12月25日初版第1刷, 1972年12月25日第2刷, 9+355+19p.

538 伊達邦春「書評 大野忠男『シュムペーター体系』シュムペーター体系の巨峰に挑む」「季刊現代経済」第3号, 1971年12月10日, pp.196-200.

1972年

539 藻利重隆「企業者職能と資本主義体制(二・完)—シュムペーターの所論を中心として」「会計」第101巻第1号, 1972年1月1日, pp.103-114.

540 M. S.カーン著, 金指基記『シュムペーターの資本主義発展論』現代書館, 1972年1月13日第1版, 1974年6月20日第2刷, 1977年8月15日第5刷, 7+179p.

541 河野善隆「シュムペーター理論の現代的意義」「長崎県立 国際経済大学論集」第5巻第3号, 1972年1月15日, pp.55-76.

542 板垣與一「シュムペーター教授と」『中山伊知郎全集 第七集』月報第1号, 1972年2月24日, p.1. 「中山先生の軌跡1 シュムペーター教授と」『中山伊知郎全集 別巻』講談社, 1973年8月30日第1刷, p.29. 「シュムペーター教授—偉大な教育者魂」『続アジアとの対話』論創社, 1988年4月15日, pp.54-55.

543 東畑精一, 山田雄三, 安井琢磨, 中山伊知郎, 板垣與一, 巽博一, 倉林義正, 藤井隆(司会)「座談会 近代経済学の展開 その一 中山教授の出発点」『中山伊知郎全集 第七集』月報第1号, 1972年2月24日pp.4-8. 『中山伊知郎全集』講談社, pp.24-30.

544 東畑精一, 山田雄三, 安井琢磨, 中山伊知郎, 板垣與一, 巽博一, 倉林義正, 藤井隆(司会)「座談会 近代経済学の展開 その二 『純粋経済学』「前後の経済学会」」『中山伊知郎全集 第十三集 経営者労働者の新時代』月報第2号, 1972年3月24日, pp.3-8. 『中山伊知郎全集 別巻』pp.31-37.

545 川田俊昭「シュムペーターとマルクス—彼等における進化主義について—(その二)」「経営と経済」第51巻第4号.1972年3月31日, pp.123-156.

546 松坂矢三郎「シュムペーターの経済発展理論」『成長・循環・開発の基本問題』千倉書房, 1972年3月31日発行.非売品.pp.15-21.

547 東條隆進「産業社会の理論と政策—ケインズとシュムペーターの根底にあるもの—」「下関商経論集」第15巻第2・3合併号, 1972年3月31日.pp.127-160.

548　玉野井芳郎「経済学総点検の時代―シュムペーターの問題意識をめぐって―」「経済セミナー」通巻第200号, 1972年4月1日.pp.2-9. 「シュムペーター体系とドイツ歴史学派」『転換する経済学』pp.67-83.

549　中山伊知郎「シュムペーターの経済学」, 「シュムペーター(小伝)」『中山伊知郎全集　第一集』pp.305-387, 311-312.

550　東畑精一, 山田雄三, 安井琢磨, 中山伊知郎, 板垣與一, 巽博一, 倉林義正, 藤井隆(司会)「座談会　近代経済学の展開と背景その三　中山教授におけるシュムペーターとケインズ」『中山伊知郎全集　第一集』月報第3号, 1972年4月24日, pp.3-8.

551　『中山伊知郎全集　別巻』講談社, 1973年8月30日第1刷, pp.37-43.

552　東畑精一, 山田雄三, 安井琢磨, 中山伊知郎, 板垣與一, 巽博一, 倉林義正, 藤井隆(司会)「座談会　近代経済学の展開と背景 その四　中山経済学体系とこれからの経済学」『中山伊知郎全集　第十五集』月報第4号, 1972年5月24日.pp.3-8. 『中山伊知郎全集　第七集』pp.44-50.

553　中山伊知郎『中山伊知郎全集　第十五集 近代化と工業化の民主主義』講談社, 1972年5月24日第1刷.11+10+516+2p.

554　大野忠男「経済学の軌道修正を求める.シュムペーター, 玉野井芳郎監訳『社会科学の過去と未来』」「エコノミスト」50巻第25号(通巻1926号), 1972年6月13日.pp.95-96.

555　大野忠男「シュムペーターと経済政策の問題」「大阪大学経済学」第22巻第1号, 1972年8月30日.pp.1-20.

556　吉田昇三「woher—wohin問題とウェーバー, シュムペーター」「経済理論」第127—131合併号, 1972年11月1日.pp.1-27. 「資本主義の運命—woher—wohin問題」『ウェーバーとシュムペーター』pp.172-206.

557　中山伊知郎『中山伊知郎全集　第十四集労使関係の基盤』講談社, 1972年12月20日第1刷.11+6+375+15p.

1973年

558　安井琢磨「私と近代経済学　ある学究のあゆみ3　きき手早坂忠」「経済セミナー」通巻第211号, 1973年1月1日, pp.44-60. , 安井琢磨編『近代経済学と私.—安井琢磨対談集—』木鐸社, 1980年6月30日第1版第1刷.pp.39-71.

559　金指基「シュムペーターの経済発展論と信用創造論」「商学集志」第42巻第3号, 1973年1月10日.pp.27-40.

560　p.シロス=ラビーニ, 尾上久雄訳「マルクスとシュムペーターにおける経済発展の問題」『経済発展—理論と現実—』平凡社, 1973年1月25日初版第1刷.pp.22-86.

561　安井琢磨「私と近代経済学　ある学究のあゆみ4　きき手早坂忠」「経済セミナー」通巻第212号, 1973年2月1日.pp.50-65, 安井琢磨編『近代経済学と私』pp.71-99.

562　東畑精一『農書に歴史あり』家の光協会, 1973年2月3日第1版.1973年4月20日第2版, 268p.

563　米川伸一『経営史学—生誕・現状・展望—』東洋経済新報社, 1973年3月15日発行.8+222p.

564　公文俊平「時代を超越する冷徹な視点シュムペーター著大野忠男訳『資本主義と社会主義』創文社(読書)」「エコノミスト」第51巻第31号通巻1987号, 1973年7月31日.pp.92-93.

565　大野忠男「現代の経済像—人と学説第8回シュムペーター—経済学の伝統と資本主義経済理論の発展—」「経済セミナー」通巻第223号, 1973年11月1日.pp.92-101.

566　金指基「シュムペーターの経済発展論と企業者」「商学集志」第43巻第3号, 1973年11月25日.pp.23-48.

567　大野忠男「シュムペーター『資本主義・社会主義・民主主義』」, 玉野井芳郎, 松浦保編『経済学の名著12選』学陽書房, 1973年12月15日初版.pp.215-236.

1974年

568　大野忠男「シュムペーターと近代経済学」「大阪大学経済学」第23巻2・3合併号, 1974年3月4日.pp.17-29.

569　伊達邦春「わたしの経済学遍歴—シュンペーター・イコール安井先生とともに歩んだ二十八年—」「東洋経済 書窓」第16号, 1974年4月1日.pp.2-7.

570　都留重人「連載・社会科学五〇年の証言 ㉞ 聞き手伊東光晴, 都留重人第三回 黄金時代のハーバード」「エコノミスト」第52巻第14号, 通巻2024号, 1974年4月2日.pp.80-85.

571　都留重人「連載・社会科学五〇年の証言 ㉟ 聞き手伊東光晴, 都留重人第四回 30年代のアメリカ」「エコノミスト」第52巻第15号通巻2025号, 1974年4月9日.pp.86-92.

572　伊達邦春「シュムペーターと資本主義」, 福岡正夫編『経済学の潮流』日本評論社, 1974年6月30日第1版第1刷.pp.127-162.

573　金指基「シュムペーターの景気循環モデル」「商学集志」第44巻第1号, 1974年6月30日.pp.35-50.

574　亀畑義彦「在庫循環の理論について—シュムペーターの理論を考察するための序説—」「北海道教育大学紀要第1部B 社会科学編」第25巻第1号, 1974年8月25日.pp.24-36.

575　宮沢健一「発展と独占の経済学」, 中山伊知郎, 荒憲治郎, 宮沢健一『原典による経済学の歩み　原典による学術史』講談社, 1974年10月20日第1刷.pp.521-552.

576　吉田昇三『ウェーバーとシュムペーター 歴史家の眼・理論家の眼』筑摩書房, 1974年10月30日初版第1刷.9+241p.

1975年

577　亀畑義彦「ケインズ体系とシュムペーター体系との融合のための序説I(シュムペーターの理論について)」「北海道教育大学紀要第1部B社会科学編」第25巻第2号, 1975年2月25日, pp.1-13.

578　松浦保「日本経済学史上における中山経済学」「季刊理論経済学」第26巻第1号, 1975年4月25日.pp.14-28.

579　都留重人「師友雁信録1ジョセフ・シュンペーター」「『都留重人著作集　第1巻経済学を学ぶ人のために』講談社(第1回配本)月報」第1号, 1975年6月12日.pp.10-16. 『師友雁信録』講談社, 1976年10月10日第1刷.pp.9-19. 『都留重人交友抄』講談社, 1976年6月29日.非売品.pp.10-16.

580 楊天溢「シュムペーターとウェーバーの「企業者」について(上)」「日本経済短期大学紀要」第7号, 1975年6月30日.pp.1-21.

581 亀畑義彦「シュムペーターとポスト.ケインジアンの理論との比較検討について」「北海道教育大学紀要第1部B社会科学編」第26巻第1号, 1975年9月20日.pp.35-42.

582 北條勇作「シュムペーターの景気循環分析」「青山社会科学紀要」第4巻第1号, 1975年9月30日.pp.85-102.

583 井上和雄「シュムペーターの経済学方法論—とくに方法と現実について—」「神戸商船大学紀要第一類文科論集」第24号, 1975年10月1日.pp.1-36.

584 大野忠男「シュムペーター体系の現代的意義」「経済セミナー」通巻250号, 1975年11月1日.pp.11-17.

585 楊天溢「シュムペーターとウェーバーの「企業者」について(中)」「日本経済短期大学紀要」第8号, 1975年12月30日.pp.1-22.

1976年

586a 金指基「《資料》シュムペーター著作目録」「商学集志」第45巻第3号, 1976年1月30日.pp.83-100.

586b 金指基「《資料》シュムペーター著作目録第2版 1983 」「商学集志」第53巻第1, 2号, 1983年11月30日.pp.75-95.

586c 金指基「《資料》シュムペーター著作目録第3版 」「商学集志」第57巻第1号, 1987年8月25日.pp.61-84.

586d 金指基「《資料》シュムペーター著作目録 第4版, 1991 」「商学集志」第61巻第2号, 1991年9月25日.pp.59-95.

587 亀畑義彦「過剰投資理論の検討について」「北海道教育大学紀要第1部B社会科学編」第26巻第2号, 1976年2月25日.pp.1-11.

588 白石孝『経済革新と競争の世界—経済発展と対外投資—』秀潤社, 1976年4月15日第1刷.239p.

589 東畑精一, 木村健康, 安井琢磨「座談会 東京大学経済学部における近代経済学の発展」東京大学経済学部編『東京大学経済学部の五十年史』東京大学出版会, 1976年4月20日初版.PP.575-608.

590 井上和雄「シュムペーター—資本主義衰退の理論—」, 野尻武敏編『現代の経済体制思想』新評論, 1976年4月25日初版第1刷.1982年3月15日初版第7刷.pp.169-190.

591 西川潤「支配の理論」『経済発展の理論』1976年4月30日第1版第1刷.1978年6月10日第25第1刷.pp.210-232.

592 大野忠男「J・シュンペーター—経済学の伝統と資本主義経済理論の発展」, 新野幸次郎編『セミナー経済学教室　現代の経済学　理論と思想通巻第12号』日本評論社, 1976年4月30日.pp.19-26.

593 亀畑義彦「シュムペーター体系とポスト・ケインジアン体系—総合のための序説—」泉文堂, 1976年6月30日第1刷.3+4+211p.

594 北條勇作「革新における企業者行動と信用創造の役割に関する一考察—シュムペーターの経済発展の理論を中心として」「青山社会科学紀要」第5巻第1号, 1976年9月30日.pp.1-24.

595 斎藤謹造「資本主義社会の未来」, 熊谷尚夫編『経済思想と現代世界』日本経済新聞社, 1976年10月25日.pp.23-47.

596 柴田敬「連載 経済学と歩いて五〇年(3)ハーバードの人びと」「週刊エコノミスト」第54巻第47号通巻2167号, 1976年10月26日.pp.48-53,『経済の法則を求めて—近代経済学の群像—』日本経済評論社, 1978年4月20日第1刷.1978年6月10日第2刷.pp.39-57. 1983年7月30日新装版第1刷.pp.39-57. 1987年12月1日増補第1刷.

1977年

597 大野忠男「続 現代の経済学/No. 2 J. A. シュンペーター その業績と今日的意義」「商業教育資料」第21巻2号, 1977年2月1日.pp.8-11.

598 大野忠男「シュンペーターの経済学体系」, 杉原四郎・鶴田満彦・菱山泉・松浦保編『限界革命の経済思想　経済思想史(3)』有斐閣, 1977年4月30日初版第1刷.pp.41-56.

599 金指基「現代資本主義と長期波動—体制論的視点から—」「商学集志」第46巻第2・3号, 1977年3月15日.pp.33-45.

600 堀江正男「ヴェブレン, ケインズ, シュムペーターにおける資本主義観の研究1」「秋田大学教育学部研究紀要, 人文科学・社会科学」第27集, 1977年3月28日.pp.63-74.

601 中井春雄(談)「〔インタビュー シュムペーター経済学の教訓〕強く正しく愛される経営者に」「週刊東洋経済」第4010号, 1977年6月11日, pp.46-47.

602 中山伊知郎(談)「〔インタビュー　シュムペーター経済学の教訓〕資本主義の発展を内側から解剖」「週刊東洋経済」第4010号, 1977年6月11日.pp.46-47.

603 対談坂本二郎vs. 神崎倫一「特集・復権するシュムペーター　日本の企業者精神は80年代によみがえる!」「週刊東洋経済」第4010号, 1977年6月11日.pp.48-53.

604 週刊東洋経済「復権する“企業者精神の提唱者”シュムペーター」「週刊東洋経済」第4010号, 1977年6月11日.pp.44-45.

605 浜崎正規「資本主義の運命—「くずれ落ちる城壁」—」『現代と社会思想—修羅の妄執—』玄文社, 1977年6月17日初版.1978年6月1日2版.pp.165-195.

606 ホスト 加藤秀俊, 小松左京, ゲスト 東畑精一「連載座談会　碩学に聞く 農業と農学の間」「本」第2巻第7号, 1977年7月1日.pp.18-26.「人を養い国を養う」「本」第2巻第8号, 1977年8月1日.pp.26-35.

607 東畑精一—農業と農学と農政と, 加藤秀俊+小松左京『学問の世界 碩学に聞く 下』講談社, 1978年7月20日1刷発行.pp.67-88-110.

608 井上和雄「経済理論のもつ経済社会像—シュムペーターの場合—」「神戸商船大学紀要 第一類文科論集」第26号, 1977年7月30日.pp.79-105.

609 金指基「《研究ノート》現代資本主義に関するノート(その1)—シュムペーターにおける資本主義の衰退と体制移行の問題—」「商学集志」第47巻第1号, 1977年7月30日.pp.39-55.

610 楊天溢「シュムペーターとウェーバーの「企業者」について(下)」「日本経済短期大学紀要」第11号, 1977年9月1日.pp.1-32.

611　辻原悟「企業者史学とJ・A・シュムペーター――系譜の一検討―(1)」「商学討究」第28巻第2号.1977年10月31日, pp.53-67.

612　中村静治「技術革新―転倒したマルクス」『技術論入門』有斐閣, 1977年11月25日.pp.209-212.

1978年

613　O. H. テイラー他著, 金指基編訳『シュムペーター経済学の体系』学文社, 1978年1月20日第1版.4+224p.

613a　W. レオンチェフ「ヨーゼフA. シュムペーター(1883―1950)」pp.2-12.

613b　R. C. マクレアー「『理論経済学の本質と主要内容』と『経済発展の理論』」pp.13-23.

613c　S.クズネッツ「『景気循環論』pp.24-45.

613d　C. H. ハーディー「『資本主義, 社会主義, 民主主義』」pp.46-64.

613e　L. ロビンズ「『経済分析の歴史』」pp.65-97.

613f　O. H. テイラー「シュムペーターとマルクス」pp.100-145.

613g　R. マクドナルド「シュムペーターとウェーバー」pp.146-180.

613h　F. G. ベニオン「シュンベーターとケインズ」pp.181-198.

613i　A. C. タイマンズ「タルドとシュムペーター」pp.199-215.

614　辻原悟「企業者史学とJ・A・シュムペーター――系譜の一検討―(2の完)」「商学討究」第28巻第4号, 1978年2月28日.pp.37-52.

615　池本正純「シュムペーターの企業者像」「専修経営研究年報」1977年No.　2, 1978年3月1日.pp.133-146.

616　吉田昇三「スミスとシュムペーター」「大阪経大論集」第121・122号, 1978年3月13日.pp.47-64.

617　ロバート・ハイルブロナー著, 宮川公男訳『企業文明の没落』日本経済新聞社, 1978年3月20日.165p.

618　斎藤高志「近代経済理論研究」「専修経営研究年報」1977年No.　2, 1978年3月31日.pp.131-132.

619　辻村江太郎「シュムペーターを読む」「経済セミナー」通巻279号, 1978年4月1日.pp.2-8.『経済学名著の読み方』日本評論社, 1979年4月20日第版第1刷.pp.164-179.

620　池本正純・樋口進・前田英昭・皆川正・美濃口武雄・山田太門「シュムペーター『資本主義・社会主義・民主主義』―もうひとつの資本主義没落論―」『経済学の古典(下)近代経済学』有斐閣, 1978年4月30日初版第1刷.pp.160-176.

621　辻村江太郎「シュムペーターを読む(下)」「経済セミナー」通巻280号, 1978年5月1日.pp.31-37.『経済学名著の読み方』pp.179-194.

622　金指基「シュムペーター体系における純粋性」「商学集志」第48巻第1号, 1978年6月30日.pp.37-48.

623　北野熊喜男「シュムペーターの経済社会学」, 経済社会学会編『経済社会学思想の史的展開　経済社会学年報・II』新評論, 1978年11月20日初版第1刷.pp.21-23.

624　吉田昇三「シュムペーターにおける経済学と社会学」, 経済社会学会編『経済社会学思想の史的展開 経済社会学年報・II』新評論, 1978年11月20日初版第1刷.pp.141-159.

625　玉野井芳郎「J・A・シュムペーター」, 水田洋, 玉野井芳郎編『経済思想史読本』東洋経済新報社, 1978年11月30日第1刷.1988年3月10日第8刷.pp.257-276.

626　中山伊知郎「ボン時代の東畑君」『昭和前期農政経済名著集第3巻東畑精一「日本農業の展開過程」』農山漁村文化協会, 1978年12月1日第1刷.「月報」1978年12月.pp.1-3.

1979年

627　美濃口武雄「シュンペーターと歴史分析の必要性」『経済学史 近代経済学の生成と発展』有斐閣, 1979年1月15日初版第1刷.pp.347-352.

628　大河内暁男『経営構想力』東京大学出版会, 1979年1月20日初版.1980年3月30日2刷.1993年10月5日3刷.8+237+16p.

629　白石四郎「ケインズとシュムペーター」「政経論叢」第47巻第4号, 1979年1月30日.pp.1-25.

630　中山伊知郎『わが道経済学』講談社, 1979年4月10日第1刷.162p.

631　伊達邦春『シュンペーター』日本経済新聞社, 1979年4月24日1版1刷.198p.

632　金指基『J・A・シュムペーターの経済学』新評論, 1979年5月10日初版第1刷.276p.

633　中山伊知郎, 早坂忠「連載⑦〈対談〉わが国ケインズ経済学事始　シュムペーター経済学からケインズ経済学へ―私の学問遍歴」「週刊東洋経済」臨時増刊第4157号, 1979年7月13日.pp.148-161, 早坂忠編『ケインズとの出遭い　ケインズ経済学導入史』日本経済評論社, 1993年10月25日第1刷.pp.207-238.

634　安井琢磨『経済学とその周辺』木鐸社, 1979年9月25日第1版第1刷.5+274p.

635　サミュエルソン, 堀出一郎訳「ジョセフ・シュムペーター」, 篠原三代平, 佐藤隆三編集『サミュエルソン経済学体系9　リカード, ケインズ, シュムペーター……』勁草書房, 1979年10月25日第1刷.pp.340-343.

636　サミュエルソン「思い出を語る」, 篠原三代平, 佐藤隆三編集『サミュエルソン経済学体系9』pp.361-364.

637　佐藤良一「技術革新と市場構造―J・A・Schumpeterの見解と実証分析について―」「富大経済論集」第25巻第2号, 1979年11月1日.pp.53-62.

638　金指基「方法論争と社会科学の発展―G. シュモラーとJ. シュムペーター」「商学集志」第49巻第2号, 1979年12月10日.pp.13-27.

639　玉井龍象「思想と潮流」金指基「J・A・シュムペーターの経済学」「朝日ジャーナル」vol. 21 No. 49, 1979年12月14日.pp.65-67.

640　井上和雄「シュムペーターにおける経済と社会―社会科学の綜合化への一試論―」, 向井利昌, 百々和編発行人代表者『経済と社会の基礎分析 北野熊喜男博士古稀記念論文集』古稀記念論文集刊行会（神戸大学経済学部内）, 1979年12月25日.pp.136-148.

1980年

641　伊藤美樹子「戦後日本経済の景気循環―シュムペーター『景気循環論』による考察―」「経済と社会」(東京女子大学社会学会紀要)」第8号, 1980年2月15日.pp.63-73.

642　高橋公夫「企業者機能と官僚制化に関する一考察―シュムペーターの企業者機能陳腐化論をめぐって―」「青山社会科学紀要」第8巻第2号, 1980年2月28日.pp.35-52.

643　大野忠男「金指基著「J・A・シュムペーターの経済学」」「世界経済評論」24巻2号, 1980年3月1日.pp.86-88.

644　堀江正男「ヴェブレン, ケインズ, シュムペーターにおける資本主義観の研究2」「秋田大学教育学部研究紀要 人文科学・社会科学」第30集, 1980年3月15日.pp.83-95.

645　金指基「シュムペーターと経済社会学―『景気循環論』における理論と歴史について―」「商学集志」第49巻第4号, 1980年3月15日.pp.31-44.

646　瀬岡誠『企業者史学序説』実教出版, 1980年6月30日第1刷.1985年4月20日第4刷.1987年11月11日第5刷.2+3+268+4p.

647　保坂直達「シュムペーターの経済発展論」, 田中敏弘, 山下博編『テキストブック近代経済学史』有斐閣, 1980年4月30日初版第1刷.1986年11月30日初版第6刷.pp.156-167.

648　伊達邦春「ワルラスとシュムペーター」「経済セミナー」通巻304号, 1980年5月1日.pp.50-56. 『シュンペーター・企業行動・経済変動』pp.168-179.

649　吉田昇三『歴史の流れのなかの経済学』法律文化社, 1980年6月10日.2+2+238p.

650　金指基「社会科学とりわけ経済学の発展について―シュムペーターの所説を中心として―」「商学集志」第50巻第1号, 1980年6月30日.pp.51-65.

651　伊達邦春・玉井龍象・池本正純『シュンペーター経済発展の理論』有斐閣, 1980年7月30日初版第1刷.212+5p.

652　岡田裕之「経済進歩の二形態―利潤率低下傾向の批判的吟味―(上)」「経営志林」第17巻第2号, 1980年7月30日.pp.1-17.

653　東畑精一, 安井琢磨「《対談》シュムペーターを語る」「図書」第373号, 1980年9月1日.pp.2-19.

654　アンソニー・ダウンズ著, 吉田精司監訳『民主主義の経済理論』成文堂, 1980年9月20日初版第1刷.1+2+9+330p.

655　芦田亘「新自由主義的な国家破産理論の源流―シュムペーターの財政危機論の現代的な再評価―」「財政学研究」第4号, 1980年10月18日.pp.7-14.

656　岡田裕之「経済進歩の二形態―利潤率低下傾向の批判的吟味―(中)」「経営志林」第17巻第3号.1980年10月30日, pp.1-14.

657　黒川博「《研究ノート》シュムペーターの「企業者」概念について(1)―「企業者機能の無用化を中心に―」」「青森短期大学研究紀要」第3巻第1号, 1980年10月31日.pp.57-71.

658　金指基「シュムペーターと独占の問題」「商学集志」第50巻第2号, 1980年11月28日.pp.33-47.

1981年

659　岡田裕之「経済進歩の二形態―利潤率低下傾向の批判的吟味―(下)」「経営志林」第17巻第4号, 1981年1月25日.pp.17-37.

660　高田保馬博士追想録刊行会編『高田保馬博士の生涯と学説』創文社, 1981年1月25日第1刷.2+6+538p.

661　高橋公夫「ドラッカーの革新論―現代産業社会の世界観」「青山社会科学紀要」第9巻第2号, 1981年2月25日.pp.1-16.

662　楠井敏朗「資本主義の発展と「企業者」の役割―J・A・シュムペーター「景気循環論」を中心とした一考察」「横浜経営研究」第1巻第3号, 1981年3月1日.pp.159-176.

663　池本正純「市場と企業者機能―シュムペーターとカーズナーの比較を中心に―」「専修経営研究年報」1980年No. 5, 1981年3月31日.pp.3-18.

664　河内寛次「福田=中山=シュムペーター」, 中山知子編集『一路八十年 中山伊知郎先生追想記念文集』中央公論事業出版, 非売本, 1981年4月9日発行.pp.67-68.

665　金指基「シュムペーター仮説をめぐって」「商学集志」第51巻第2号, 1981年9月30日.pp.29-42.

666　相葉洋一「技術進歩と景気循環―シュムペーター・タイプのモデル―」「六甲台論集」第28巻第3号, 1981年10月20日.pp.1-14. 『貨幣と景気循環』相葉洋一君遺稿集編集刊行実行委員会, 1991年2月16日.pp.11-29.

667　小澤光利「A・シュピートホフの経済変動論―批判的再検討―」『恐慌論史序説』梓出版社, 1981年11月10日第1刷.pp.177-324.

668　岩井克人「シュムペーター経済動学―革新と模倣の動態的モデル」「季刊現代経済」第46号, 1981年12月7日.pp.28-42.

1982年

669　吉田昇三「経済学的分析と社会学的分析との統合としてのマーシャル体系とシュムペーター体系との比較」「商経論叢」第28巻第3号, 1982年3月20日.pp.1-33.

670　岩井克人「シュムペーター経済動学(2), 技術進歩・企業成長・「経済淘汰」」「季刊現代経済」第47号, 1982年4月16日.pp.162-175.

671　相葉洋一「J・A・シュムペーター『経済発展の理論』〔文献解題〕」「経済」第217号, 1982年5月1日.pp.235-237. 『貨幣と景気循環』pp.217-222.

672　山口正之「技術革新と社会革命―シュムペーターの現代的意味―」「経済」第217号, 1982年5月1日.pp.180-194.

673　今井賢一「企業活動と市場―企業者機能との関係において―」, 米川伸一, 平田光弘編『企業活動の理論と歴史』千倉書房, 1982年5月25日.pp.121-141.

674　難波田春夫『経済学革新の道 難波田春夫著作集4』早稲田大学出版部, 1982年5月25日発行.5+282p.

675　フィリス・ディーン著, 奥野正寛訳『経済思想の発展』岩波書店, 1982年5月28日第1刷.4+375+16p.

676　岩井克人「シュムペーター経済動学(3), 産業の長期的構造と動学的有効需要原理」「季刊現代経済」第48号, 1982年6月18日.pp.120-131.

1983年

677　林田睦次『経済変動理論の構造—経済変動の近代理論と現代理論の理論構造に関する—研究—』多賀出版, 1983年1月20日.18+655p.

678　永友育雄「シュンペーターの精髄を生かして, シュンペーターとは異なった仕方で, 経済発展の問題に接近する」「甲南経済学論集」第23巻第3号, 1983年1月25日.pp.35-62.

679　金指基「シュムペーター体系と帝国主義の問題」「商学集志」第52巻第3号, 1983年1月30日.pp.23-46.

680　金指基「人物列伝　シュムペーター—決して幸福とはいえない天才的経済学者の生涯—」「砧通信」12, 1983年.pp.17-21.

681　岩井克人「シュムペーター—遅れてきたマルクス」「経済セミナー」通巻337号, 1983年2月1日.pp.29-36. 「遅れてきたマルクス」『ヴェニスの商人の資本論』筑摩書房, 1985年1月10日初版第1刷.1985年2月15日初版第3刷.1985年5月15日初版第6刷.pp.79-99. 筑摩文庫, 1991年6月26日第1刷.1992年7月20日第2刷.pp.89-110.

682　吉尾博和「シュムペーターにおけるSystemとOrder—体制移行の観点から—」「亜細亜大学大学院経済学研究論集」第7号, 1983年2月15日.pp.33-50.

683　吉田浩「シュムペーターとウェーバー—両者における革新理論の比較・対象を中心として—」「文化紀要」第17号, 1983年2月18日.pp.55-79.

684　若杉隆平「シュムペーターと現代技術革新」「経済セミナー」通巻338号, 1983年3月1日.pp.58-66.

685　大野忠男「シュムペーターと資本主義の将来」「追手門経済論集」第17巻第2・3号, 1983年3月10日.pp.17-34.

686　林田睦次「J. M. ケインズおよびJ. A. シュンペーターとその経済学体系」「徳山大学総合経済研究所紀要」No. 5. 1983年3月15日.pp.25-47.

687　金指基「景気循環論におけるミッチェルとシュムペーター」「日本大学経済学部経済科学研究所紀要」第7号, 1983年3月20日.pp.151-164.

688　小池基之, 竹内靖雄, 早坂忠, 福岡正夫, 丸山徹(司会)「マルクス, ケインズ, シュンペーター—資本主義の将来(座談会)」「三田評論」第835号, 1983年4月1日.pp.4-21.

689　都留重人「現代と経済学の対話　語る人—都留重人 新しいパラダイムの創造を」「エコノミスト」第61巻第14号通巻2508号, 1983年4月5日, pp.112-122. エコノミスト編集部編『現代と経済学の対話(1)新しい経済システムを求めて』毎日新聞社, 1984年6月25日発行.pp.7-31.

690　篠原三代平「経済学の三巨星—下　J. A. シュムペーター　シュムペーターと現代世界いまに生きる壮大なビジョン」「エコノミスト」第61巻第16号通巻2510号, 1983年4月19日.pp.54-62. , 「シュムペーターと現代世界」『世界経済の長期ダイナミクス　長波動と大国の興亡』TBSブリタニカ, 1991年5月27日初版.pp.129-148. 『ヒューマノミクス序説　経済学と現代世界』筑摩書房, 1984年4月30日初版第1刷.pp.59-77.

691 碓井彊「シュムペーターの人と業績」「エコノミスト」第61巻第16号通巻2510号, 1983年4月19日.pp.63-64.

692 都留重人「体制変革の政治経済学」新評論, 1983年4月25日初版第1刷.1983年11月10日初版第4刷.195p.

693 杉山忠平「シュムペーター, ケインズそして日本　示唆に富むそのかかわり合い」「エコノミスト」第61巻第17号通巻2511号, 1983年4月26日.pp.50-56.

694 杉原四郎「「新結合」と「洞察」―シュムペーター生誕100年に寄せて」「バンガード」4(5), 1983年5月1日p.1. 『読書颯々』未来社1987年9月10日第1刷発行.pp.111-113.

695 鶴田満彦「資本主義の運命―マルクス・ケインズ・シュンペーターをめぐって―」「経済」第229号, 1983年5月1日.pp.10-21.

696 水田洋「写真でみるシュンペーターの時代」「経済セミナー」通巻341号, 1983年6月1日.pp.49-61.

697 R. L. ハイルブローナー, 松原隆一郎訳「資本主義から社会主義への前進?―シュンペーターは正しかったか」「季刊現代経済」第54号, 1983年7月1日.pp.55-64.

698 関恒義「マルクス没後百年間の経済学―ケインズとシュンペーター生誕百年に関連させて―」「季刊 科学と思想」第49号, 1983年7月1日.pp.22-34.

699 林田睦次『ケインズ体系とシュンペーター体系』多賀出版, 1983年7月15日.4+4+302p.

700 ピーター・F・ドラッカー, 石川博友訳「いまシュンペーターかケインズか」「週刊ダイヤモンド」第71巻29号, 1983年7月23日.pp.29-34. , P. F. ドラッカー, 上田惇生, 佐々木実智男訳「時代の予言者―シュムペーターとケインズ」『マネジメント・フロンティア』ダイヤモンド社, 1986年10月30日初版.1986年12月17日4版.pp.125-139.

701 編集発行人大石進『別冊経済セミナー シュンペーター再発見　生誕100年記念』日本評論社, 1983年7月30日.192p.

701a 都留重人, 伊東光晴, 金指基(司会)「座談会 人間シュンペーター」pp.2-16. S35.

701b 杉山忠平「新資料の考証と解説」pp.27-30.

701c1 伊達邦春「エッセイ シュンペーターと最初の夫人」p.31.

701c2 伊達邦春「エッセイ シュンペーターとトーマス・マン」p.131.

701c3 伊達邦春「シュンペーターとケインズ・ケインジアン―両体系の総合は可能か―」pp.172-177. 「シュンペーターとケインジアンモデル」『シュンペーター・企業行動・経済変動』pp.180-191.

701d 柴田敬「シュンペーター先生の教え」pp.32-33.

701e 大野忠男「シュンペーターの経済学体系と方法」pp.34-43.

701f1 吉田昇三「シュンペーター体系と歴史的分析」pp.44-51.

701f2 吉田昇三「ウェーバーとシュンペーター―ドイツ歴史学派とオーストリア学派を越えて―」pp.156-160.

701g 谷嶋喬四郎「シュンペーターの社会科学論」pp.52-59.

701h 馬場啓之助「追悼　東畑精一先生のシュンペーター」pp.60-61.

701i 熊谷尚夫「資本主義のビジョン考」pp.62-67.

701j 塩野谷祐一「資本主義文明の衰退と社会主義」pp.68-75.

701k　竹内靖雄「民主主義の条件」pp.76-82.

701l　伊木誠「革新(イノベーション)と長期循環論の復権」pp.83-88.

701m　中村達也「大企業体制と市場の評価―シュンペーターとガルブレイス―」pp.89-94.

701n1　金指基「共生の中の社会階級」pp.95-100.

701n2　金指基「シュンペーター年譜」pp.190-192.

701n3　金指基編「シュンペーター参考文献解説」pp.178-179.

701n4　金指基「シュンペーター著作目録・主要著書解説」pp.180-189.

701o　小野善康「革新(イノベーション)は経済厚生をもたらすか」pp.101-106.

701p　曽根泰教「現代政治におけるリーダーシップ」pp.107-112.

701q　川勝平太「シュンペーターの経済史的読み方」pp.113-118.

701r　佐伯啓思「シュンペーターの現代的読み方」pp.119-125.

701s　佐和隆光「経済学の科学性と数量性」pp.126-130.

701t　斎藤謹造「マルクスとシュンペーター――資本主義社会をどうとらえるか―」pp.132-137.

701u　木村憲二「ワルラスとシュンペーター――新古典派の預言者と経済学最後の巨人―」pp.138-142.

701v　荒憲治郎「ボェームーバヴェルクとシュンペーター――利子論をめぐる静態と動態―」pp.143-148.

701w　池本正純「マーシャルとシュンペーター――経済発展をめぐる二つの企業者像―」pp.149-155.

701x　田中敏弘「ミッチェルとシュンペーター――一般均衡理論の受容と否認―」pp.161-166.

701y　八木紀一郎「ヒルファーディングとシュンペーター――中欧最良の世代の分岐と交錯―」pp.167-171.

702　アーノルド・ヒアチェ編, 西部邁, 松原隆一郎, 八木甫訳『シュムペーターのヴィジョン 『資本主義・社会主義・民主主義』の現代的評価』HBJ出版局(旧ホルトサウンダース/CBS出版), 1983年8月10日第1刷.347p.

702a　A・ヒアチェ「序文」pp.1-4.

702b　ジェル・ジルストラ「序論」pp.9-14.

702c　ポール・A・サミュエルソン「シュムペーターの資本主義, 社会主義および民主主義」pp.15-51.

702d　トム・ボットモア「資本主義衰退の社会学的考察」pp.53-85.

702e　ウィリアム・フェルナー「社会主義への前進か―資本主義の戦後の発展段階」pp.87-120.

702f　ゴットフリート・ハーバラー「『資本主義・社会主義・民主主義』の四〇年」pp.121-162.

702g　R・L・ハイルブローナー「シュムペーターは正しかったか」pp.163-181.

702h　ヘンドリック・ウィルム・ランバース「シュムペーターとヴィジョン」pp.183-221.

702i　アーサー・スミシーズ「シュムペーターの予言」pp.223-254.

702j　ピーター・ワイルス「ソ連学的考察」pp.255-289.

702k　ハーバート・K・ザッセンハウス「資本主義・社会主義・民主主義―「ヴィジョン」と「理論」」pp.291-342.

702l　八木記「訳者あとがき」pp.343-345.

703　熊谷尚夫「マルクス, シュムペーター, ケインズ―資本主義の運命をめぐって」「関西大学通信」第131号, 1983年10月15日.p.8.

704 北條勇作『シュムペーター経済学の研究』多賀出版, 1983年10月25日初版第1刷.1991年4月10日初版第4刷.6+233p.

705 福岡正夫, 早坂忠, 根岸隆『ケインズと現代』税務経理協会, 1983年11月1日初版第1刷.1988年4月1日初版第2刷.1989年初版第3刷.6+359+13p.

706 み「シュムペーターを9倍おもしろく」「経済セミナー」通巻346号, 1983年11月1日.p.87.

707 大野忠男「最近におけるシュムペーター研究の動向〔学会展望〕」「経済学史学会年報」第21号, 1983年11月12日.pp.11-17.

708 A「ルポ 理論・計量経済学会1983年度大会 マルクス・ケインズ・シュンペーターの経済学と現状」「経済セミナー」通巻347号, 1983年12月1日.pp.70-71.

709 早坂忠「シュンペーターと経済学史」「経済セミナー」通巻347号, 1983年12月1日.pp.81-87.

710 小谷義次「シュムペーターにおける資本主義の運命」「経済」第236号, 1983年12月1日.pp.204-218.

711 橋本昭一「シュムペーターとケインズ」「〔関大〕経済学会報」4, 1983年12月15日.pp.1-16.

1984年

712 森本矗「シュムペーターと企業者史」『企業者史』晃洋書房, 1984年1月20日初版第1刷.pp.88-166.

713 福岡正夫「ヨーゼフ・アロイス・シュンペーター―生誕100年―」「三田学会雑誌」第76巻第6号, 1984年2月1日.pp.1-31.

714 嚢谷千凰彦「分析と実践の峻別―シュンペーターの一断面―」「三田学会雑誌」第76巻第6号, 1984年2月1日.pp.62-85.

715 塩野谷祐一「シュンペーターにおける科学とイデオロギー」「三田学会雑誌」第76巻第6号, 1984年2月1日.32-61.

716 住友銀行調査部内国調査班「新年日本経済の展望―新シュンペーター時代の経済回復―」, 住友銀行調査部第一部・第二部「経済月報」第343号, 1984年2月1日.pp.1-14.

717 吉尾博和「シュムペーターにおける体制移行に関する一考察―SystemとOrderの観点から―」「亜細亜大学大学院経済学研究論集」第8号, 1984年2月15日.pp.19-50.

718 永友育雄「グッドウィンの動学について―グッドウィンとシュンペーター」「甲南経済学論集」第24巻第3号, 1984年2月20日.pp.1-29.

719 小谷義次「シュムペーター経済学の理論的性格―資本主義の運命にかんする所説を中心に―」「大阪経済法科大学経済研究所 研究年報」第3号, 1984年3月15日.pp.27-38.

720 金指基「〈資料〉シュンペーター年譜」「商学集志」第53巻第3·4号, 1984年3月24日.pp.73-87.

721 池本正純『企業者とはなにか 経済学における企業者像』有斐閣, 1984年3月25日初版第1刷.16+268p.

722 塩野谷祐一「シュンペーターの問題と方法―方法序説―」「一橋大学研究年報 経済学研究」25, 1984年3月30日.pp.61-108.

723 青木泰樹「シュムペーターと方法論―序説―」「経済学研究年報」23, 1984年3月.pp.207-218.

724 古賀勝次郎「シュンペーターとハイエク―社会主義をめぐって―」, 堀江忠男編『価値転換期の政治経済学』新評論, 1984年3月31日.pp.42-57. 修正加筆「世界経済」第39巻第12号,

1984年12月1日.pp.11-24. 『ハイエク経済学の周辺』行人社, 1986年6月25日.pp.29-54.

725　嚢谷千凰彦「シュンペーターと計量経済学(1)」「三田学会雑誌」第77巻第1号, 1984年4月1日.pp.18-40.

726　篠原三代平「ヒューマノミクス序説—人間の学としての経済学—」『ヒューマノミクス序説 経済学と現代世界』pp.3-36, 『日本経済研究 篠原三代平著作集IV現代経済学の展開と課題』筑摩書房, 1987年6月30日初版第1刷.pp.367-391.

727　佐貫利雄「ハイエク的局面からシュンペーター的局面へ」「日本経済研究センター会報」463号, 1984年5月1日.pp.9-17.

728　東畑精一「私の履歴書」, 日本経済新聞社編『私の履歴書 文化人20』日本経済新聞社, 1984年7月2日1版1刷.pp.179-265.

729　ロバート・F・ヘバート, アルバート・N・リンク著, 池本正純, 宮本光晴訳『企業者論の系譜 18世紀から現代まで』ホルト・サウンダース・ジャパン, 1984年7月10日第1刷.9+199+14p.

730　経商資料室〔関西大〕「マルクス没後100年, ケインズ, シュムペーター生誕100年 記念行事・出版物(国内)目録」「関西大学経済論集」第34巻第3号, 1984年7月25日.pp.115-165.

731　曽根泰教「J・A・シュムペーターと現代民主主義—古典的民主主義批判と「いまひとつの民主主義理論」の提唱—」, 白鳥令, 曽根泰教編『現代世界の民主主義理論』新評論, 1984年7月30日初版第1刷.pp.9-33.

732　P・A・サミュエルソン「経済学百年①」, 佐藤隆三編解説『サミュエルソン 日本の針路を考える 経済と経済学の明日2』勁草書房, 1984年8月20日第1刷.pp.211-222.

733　東畑精一『わが師わが友わが学問』柏書房, 1984年8月25日第1刷.4+236p.

734　池本正純「構造変化が求める商人的企業者像 シュムペーター的企業者論を超えて……」「エコノミスト」第62巻第38号通巻2585号, 1984年9月18日.pp.50-56.

735　八木紀一郎「シュンペーターにおける「資本主義過程」の探究」「経済論叢」第134巻第3・4号, 1984年10月1日.pp.31-49. 『オーストリア経済思想史研究—中欧(ハプスブルク)帝国と経済学者』名古屋大学出版会, 1988年4月15日初版第1刷.pp.145-162.

736　永友育雄「シュンペーターの精髄を生かす経済発展論のために」「甲南経済学論集」第25巻第2号, 1984年10月25日.pp.77-102.

737　経商資料室〔関西大〕「マルクス没後100年, ケインズ, シュムペーター生誕100年記念行事・出版物(国内)目録—3—」「関西大学経済論集」第34巻第5号, 1984年11月25日.シュンペーター関係は, pp.189-190, 207-214, 220-222.

738　水田洋「たそがれのウィーン ヨーゼフ・アロイス・シュンペーター」『十大の経済学者』日本評論社, 1984年11月25日第1版第1刷.pp.185-208.

739　青沼吉松「経営者革命と体制問題—シュムペーターとマルクス, ケインズの所説に関連して—」, 経済社会学会編『資本主義の運命 経済社会学会年報・VI』時潮社, 1984年11月30日初版第1刷.pp.27-54.

740　大野忠男「シュンペーターの未来学について」, 経済社会学会編『資本主義の運命』pp.55-75.

741　東條隆進「ケインズ・シュンペーターそして未来—二〇世紀の歴史的定位—」, 経済社会学会編『資本主義の運命』pp.1-25.

742　金指基「経済発展と社会階級—シュンペーターの社会進化に関する歴史解釈の方法—」「商学集志」第54巻第1・2・3号合併号, 1984年12月1日.pp.89-105.

1985年

743　ナガイ・ケイ「サミュエルソンとシュムペーター」『お手上げのサミュエルソン』富士書房, 1985年1月25日初版.1989年10月20日2版.pp.151-157.

744　吉尾博和「〔研究ノート〕シュムペーター「体制転形」論の再考察」「亜細亜大学大学院経済学研究論集」第9号, 1985年2月15日.pp.73-88.

745　堀江正男「ヴェブレン, ケインズおよびシュムペーターにおける資本主義観の研究3」「秋田大学教育学部研究紀要 人文科学・社会科学」第35集, 1985年2月28日.pp.103-114.

746　金指基「シュンペーターの社会科学に関する基本的見解について」「日本大学経済学部経済科学研究所紀要」第9号, 1985年3月20日.pp.23-37.

747　青木昌彦, 伊丹敬之『企業の経済学』岩波書店, 1985年3月28日第1刷.6+259p.

748　青木泰樹「シュムペーター利子論の再検討」「経済学研究年報」24, 1985年3月.pp.144-158.

749　三上隆三「つれづれ・けいざいがく 伝説の種まく人:シュムペーター」「経済セミナー」通巻363号, 1985年4月1日.pp.80-83. 『経済の博物誌』日本評論社, 1987年9月20日第1版第1刷.pp.1-16.

750　金指基「景気循環におけるミッチェルとシュムペーター」, 佐々木晃編『ヴェブレンとミッチェル』ミネルヴァ書房, 1985年4月15日.pp.178-205.

751　永友育雄「発展の波と単なる波―シュンペーター型発展論のために―」「甲南経済学論集」第26巻第1号, 1985年7月25日.pp.63-85.

752　カーズナー, 田島義博監訳, 江田三喜男, 小林逸太, 佐々木実雄, 野口智雄共訳『競争と企業者精神―ベンチャーの経済理論―』千倉書房, 1985年7月25日発行.2+2+2+3+245p.

753　マーク・ブラウグ, 馬渡尚憲解題・チェック, 佐々木憲介訳「マルクス, シュンペーターの企業者像―経済学における「企業者精神」」「経済評論」第34巻第9号, 1985年9月1日.pp.8-20.

754　巽博一「ケインズとシュムペーター」「成蹊大経済学部論集」第16集第1号, 1985年10月30日.pp.31-37.

755　岩井克人「ケインズ, シュムペーター, 現代資本主義」, 日本経済新聞社編『現代経済学ガイド 人と理論のプロフィール』日本経済新聞社, 1985年11月12日1版1刷.1986年5月15日4刷.pp.190-207.

756　塩野谷祐一「シュムペーター」, 日本経済新聞社編『現代経済学ガイド』pp.175-189.

757　田中悟「Schumpeter的競争と競争政策―動態的な競争政策原理をめぐって」「関西学院 経済学研究」18, 1985年11月30日.pp.117-130.

758　ナガイ・ケイ「ガルブレイスとシュムペーター」『八面六ぴのガルブレイス』富士書房, 1985年12月10日.pp.165-168.

759　越後和典『競争と独占―産業組織論批判―』ミネルヴァ書房, 1985年12月25日第1刷.204+16p.

760　賀村進一「シュムペーターのマルクス経済学批判について」「帝京経済学研究」第19巻第1・2合併号, 1985年12月27日.pp.261-284.

1986年

761 藤竹暁「大衆論③ヨーゼフ・シュムペーターの民主政治 「方法」としての民主主義論が意味するもの」「青年心理」第55号, 1986年1月1日.pp.124-138.

762 熊谷尚夫「経済学100年—マルクス, シュムペーター, ケインズ」『現代資本主義の理論と政策』創文社, 1986年1月15日第1刷.pp.273-281.

763 河野善隆「シュムペーター・ヴィジョンとその理論的枠組み」「長崎県立国際経済大学論集」第19巻第3号, 1986年2月15日.pp.277-312.

764 吉尾博和「シュムペーター研究序説—体制転形論を中心として—」「亜細亜大学大学院経済学研究論集」第10号, 1986年2月15日.pp.50-70.

765 塩野谷祐一「シュンペーターと純粋経済学」「一橋大学研究年報経済学研究」27, 1986年2月20日.pp.3-122.

766 藤竹暁「大衆論④ヨーゼフ・シュムペーターの民主政治 大衆民主政治における人間性」「青年心理」第56号, 1986年3月1日.pp.138-152.

767 金指基「ヴィーコ, ベルクソンとシュンペーター」「商学集志」第55巻第4号, 1986年3月20日.pp.1-14.

768 藤竹暁「大衆論⑤シュムペーターが描いた指導者—政治的指導をめぐる競争的闘争」「青年心理」第57号, 1986年5月1日.pp.135-149.

769 神谷慶治編『想い出の東畑精一先生』農村更生協会, 1986年5月6日発行.3+2+162p.

770 「東畑精一先生を偲ぶ会」摘要 農村更生協会, 1986年7月.49p.

771 根井雅弘「シュムペーター思想形成におけるマーシャルの重要性について」「経済論叢」第138巻第1・2号, 1986年8月1日.pp.82-99. 「シュムペーターとマーシャル」『現代経済学の生誕』名古屋大学出版会, 1992年11月20日初版第1刷.pp.32-56.

772 W. H. ジョンストン「ヨーゼフ・シュンペーター—帝国の遺産を継承できなくなった相続人—」, 井上修一, 岩切正介, 林部圭一訳『ウィーン精神ハープスブルク帝国の思想と社会 1848—1938 I』みすず書房, 1986年8月22日発行.pp.126-129.

773 亀畑義彦『現代経済変動理論の史的展開』泉文堂, 1986年9月20日第1刷.2+6+312p.

774 金指基「社会科学の発展とその伝統—ヴィーコとシュンペーター」, 経済社会学会編『戦後日本の社会と経済 経済社会学会年報VIII』時潮社, 1986年9月25日.pp.81-91.

775 金指基「シュムペーターとその初期の思想形成の一端」, 上杉他編『近代財政経済の理論とその展開』評論社, 1986年10月.pp.535-566.

776 八木紀一郎「オーストリアにおける貨幣的経済論の胎動—ミーゼス, シュムペーター, ヒルファーディング—」「思想」748号, 1986年10月5日.pp.87-110. 『オーストリア経済思想史研究』pp.163-191.

777 パウル—ハインツ・ケステルス, 長尾史郎訳「ジョセフ・アロイス・シュンペーター」『世界を変えた12人の経済学者』TBSブリタニカ, 1986年10月10日初版.1987年12月28日初版第3刷.pp.215-237.

778 米川紀生「Joseph Alois Schumpeter経済学の基盤」「法経論叢」第4巻第1号, 1986年11月30日.pp.1-40.

1987年

779 山之内光躬「財政政策における政府—ケインズ・シュムペーター・ブキャナン—」, 早稲田大学社会科学部学会編『科学と現実 早稲田大学社会科学部創設二〇周年記念論文集』早稲田大学社会科学部学会, 1987年2月15日.pp.129-159.

780 金指基「シュンペーター『資本主義・社会主義・民主主義』」「経済セミナー」通巻第388号, 1987年5月1日.pp.55-58.

781 青木泰樹『シュムペーター理論の展開構造』御茶の水書房, 1987年5月25日第1刷.8+273p.

782 金指基『シュンペーター研究』日本評論社, 1987年5月30日第1版第1刷.10+380p.

783 今井賢一「シュムペーター・ポリシーで日本産業の再構築を カギを握る新企業者精神の創造」「エコノミスト」臨時増刊号, 第65巻第36号通巻2748号, 1987年8月31日.pp.24-32.『情報ネットワーク社会の展開』筑摩書房, 1990年1月15日初版第1刷.1990年3月5日初版第3刷.pp.106-127.

784 永友育雄「発展波動説の立場—シュンペーター学説の精神—」「甲南経済学論集」第28巻第2号, 1987年9月25日.pp.59-77.

785 吉尾博和「シュムペーターの体制転形論—資本主義の生理と病理」, 経済社会学会編『情報と社会システム経済社会学会年報IX』時潮社, 1987年9月25日.pp.155-168.

786 根井雅弘「《研究ノート》人間シュムペーターの一断面—Christian Seidlの論稿をめぐって—」「経済論叢」第140巻第3・4号, 1987年10月1日.pp.100-109.

787 内田忠寿, カラントンにおける経済発展論の図式と性格—シュンペーター発展論の魁(さきがけ)—『経済学説と精神史の間 プラトンからミルへ』東海大学出版会, 1987年10月20日.第1刷発行.pp.116-130.

788 塩野谷祐一「国際シュンペーター学会の設立と第一回会議」「経済学史学会年報」第25号, 1987年11月13日.p.117.

789 米川紀生「新たに発見されたJ・A・Schumpeter自筆草稿『資本主義・社会主義・民主主義』」「法経論叢」第5巻第1号, 1987年11月30日.pp.51-75.

790 賀村進一「シュムペーター経済学の一断面」「帝京経済学研究」第21巻第1・2合併号, 1987年12月27日.pp.265-284.

1988年

791 塩野谷祐一「シュンペーターの経済思想〔1〕—ワルラマとマルクス—」「かんぽ資金」第117号, 1988年2月1日.pp.32-34.

792 塩野谷祐一「シュンペーターの経済思想〔2〕—ケインズとシュンペーター—」「かんぽ資金」第118号, 1988年3月1日.pp.40-42.

793 米川紀生「新発見のJ・A・Schumpeter自筆草稿」「法経論叢」第5巻第2号, 1988年3月20日.pp.1-81.

794 金指基「シュンペーター体系の基本的性質について」「商学集志」第57巻第3・4号合併号, 1988年3月25日.pp.1-16.

795 塩野谷祐一「杉村広蔵とシュンペーター」「一橋大学社会科学古典資料センター年報」No. 8, 1988年3月31日.pp.4-9.

796 塩野谷祐一「シュンペーターの経済思想〔3〕—経済学方法論—」「かんぽ資金」第119号, 1988年4月1日.pp.41-43.

797 八木紀一郎『オーストリア経済思想史研究—中欧ハプスブルク帝国と経済学者—』名古屋大学出版会, 1988年4月15日初版第1刷.7+289p.

798 吉尾博和「シュムペーターの経済思想と資本主義の進化—社会進化の生理過程と病理現象—」「八千代国際大学紀要 国際研究論集」第1巻第1・2合併号, 1988年4月15日.pp.168-191.

799 京極高宣「シュンペーター ゼミナール・経済思想と福祉システムII」「月刊福祉」第71巻第5号, 1988年5月1日.pp.68-73.

800 塩野谷祐一「シュンペーターの経済思想〔4〕—経済発展の理論—」「かんぽ資金」第120号, 1988年5月1日.pp.42-44.

801 塩野谷祐一「シュンペーターの経済思想〔5〕—資本主義の将来—」「かんぽ資金」第121号, 1988年6月1日.pp.32-34.

802 安井琢磨『私の歩んだ経済学の道』創価大学経済学会, 1988年6月30日.25p.

803 塩野谷祐一「シュンペーターの経済思想〔6〕—綜合的社会科学—」「かんぽ資金」第122号, 1988年7月1日.pp.41-43.

804 ディーター・シュナイダー, 森昭夫訳「企業者職能による経営経済学の新構築」「会計」第134巻第2号, 1988年8月17日.pp.119-136.

805 金指基『現代資本主義の発展と変動—シュンペーターの世界—』八千代出版, 1988年9月20日初版.7+191p.

806 金指基「現代資本主義とその分析方法」「商学集志」第58巻第1号, 1988年9月20日.pp.1-15.

807 米川紀生「資料紹介 J・A・Schumpeterの財政政策構想」「法経論叢」第6巻第1号, 1988年10月1日.pp.27-61.

808 村上直樹「技術革新, 企業規模, および自動車排気ガス規制—「シュムペーター仮設」の再検討—」「経済研究」第39巻第4号, 1988年10月14日.pp.325-335.

809 塩野谷祐一「第2回国際シュンペーター学会」「経済学史学会年報」第26号, 1988年11月15日.pp.111-112.

810 塩野谷祐一「シュンペーター・シュモラー・ウェーバー—歴史認識の方法論—」「一橋論叢」第100巻第6号, 1988年12月1日.pp.1-23.

811 賀村進一「シュムペーターの帝国主義論についての一考察」「帝京経済研究」第22巻第1・2号合併号, 1988年12月20日.pp.253-273.

812 森嶋通夫『サッチャー時代のイギリス—その政治, 経済, 教育—』岩波書店, 1988年12月20日第1刷.1991年2月25日第10刷.3+232p.

813 浦城晋一・木南章「J・A・シュンペーター “Capitalism, Socialism and Democracy”のマニュスクリプトの存在と由来—とくに東畑精一との関連において—」「三重大学生物資源学部紀要」第1号, 1988年12月24日.pp.39-49.

1989年

814　金子逸郎「イノベーション理論と企業家」「明大商学論叢」第71巻第2号, 1989年1月25日.pp.67-89.

815　藤田幸雄「シュムペーター「新結合と信用」の一考察―信用の機能と本質―」, 金融学会編「金融学会報告」67, 1989年1月30日.pp.31-39.

816　林康二「シュンペーターとワルラス Schumpeter and Walras」「専修大学大学院紀要 専修社会科学論集」第4号, 1989年3月31日.pp.35-68.

817　ジャック・ライヴリー著, 櫻井陽二/外池力訳『デモクラシーとは何か』芦書房, 1989年4月10日初版第1刷.250p.

818　トム・B. ボットモア著, 小澤光利訳『近代資本主義の諸理論 マルクス・ウェーバー・シュムペーター・ハイエク』亜紀書房, 1989年4月20日第1版第1刷.1989年7月16日第2刷.4+169+14p.

819　吉岡恒明「シュンペーターと現代経済―国際J・A・シュンペーター学会における研究動向―」「専修大学社会科学研究所月報」No. 309, 1989年4月20日.pp.1-27.

820　根井雅弘「経済学古典の再発見・シュムペーター「理論経済学の本質と主要内容」純粋経済学の擁護」「経済セミナー」通巻413号, 1989年6月1日.pp.10-11.

821　根井雅弘「マーシャルの権威への挑戦―シュムペーターの場合―」『マーシャルからケインズへ―経済学における権威と反逆―』名古屋大学出版会, 1989年6月10日初版第1刷.1990年4月10日初版第2刷.pp.155-170.

822　浦城晋一「研究紹介 シュンペーターの手稿草稿『資本主義・社会主義・民主主義』の研究」「学園だより」No. 102, 1989年6月10日.p.14.

823　小谷義次「シュムペーター, J. A. 経済発展の理論」,「シュムペーター, J. A. 景気循環―資本主義過程の理論的・歴史的・統計的分析」,「シュムペーター, J. A. 資本主義・社会主義・民主主義, 1942年」, 大阪経済法科大学経済研究所編『経済学名著106選』青木書店, 1989年7月1日第1版第1刷.pp.86-87, 88-89, 90-91.

824　白杉庄一郎「シュムペーターの景気循環論」, 一井昭編『白杉庄一郎 価格の理論・景気循環論』中央大学出版部, 1989年7月30日初版第1刷.pp.211-243.

825　根井雅弘「資本主義の二つのヴィジョン ケインズとシュムペーター(上)」「エコノミスト」第67巻第32号, 通巻2856号, 1989年8月1日.pp.28-33. 『ケインズから現代へ 20世紀経済学の系譜』日本評論社, 1990年1月10日第1版第1刷.pp.21-38.

826　根井雅弘「独り歩きした「有効需要」vs. 「「供給重視」 ケインズとシュムペーター(下)」「エコノミスト」第67巻第33号通巻2857号, 1989年8月8日.pp.28-33. 『ケインズから現代へ』pp.39-55.

827　根井雅弘「シュムペーター『経済発展の理論』」, 佐和隆光編『現代経済学の名著』中央公論社, 1989年8月25日発行.pp.13-22.

828　金指基「普遍的社会科学の試み」「商学集志」第59巻第1･2･3合併号, 1989年10月1日.pp.163-180.

829　ロバート.L. ハイルブローナー, 八木甫監訳松原隆一郎, 浮田聡, 奥井智之, 堀岡治男訳「シュンペーターのヴィジョン」『入門経済思想史 世俗の思想家たち』HBJ出版局, 1989年10

月6日第1刷.pp.347-375.

830　米川紀生「大蔵大臣としてのJoseph A. Schumpeterの理論と行動」「法経論叢」第7巻第1号, 1989年11月10日.pp.55-85.

831　阿部隆是「シュンペーターとドラッカーの類似性」「山梨学院大学商学論集」第12号, 1989年11月25日.pp.1-14.

832　R. クームズ/P. サビオッティ/V. ウォルシュ共著, 竹内啓/廣松毅監訳『技術革新の経済学』新世社, 1989年12月25日初版.1990年4月10日初版第2刷.10+338p.

1990年

833　吉尾博和「〔研究ノート〕シュムペーターの経済社会学再評価への一視点―ハヌシュ編『進化経済論』を中心に―」「八千代国際大学紀要 国際研究論集」第2巻第4号, 1990年1月15日.pp.88-98.

834　佐藤勝則「オーストリア・ハンガリー関税・貿易政策と対外決済危機―シュンペーター帝国主義論の現実的基盤をめぐって―」, 桑原莞爾, 井上巽, 伊藤昌太編『イギリス資本主義と帝国主義世界』九州大学出版会, 1990年2月20日初版発行.1994年7月30日第2版発行.pp.421-457.

835　宮本光晴「企業者の創造的破壊(J. A. シュンペーター)」,「資本主義の没落(J. A. シュンペーター)」, 佐伯啓思・間宮陽介・宮本光晴『命題コレクション経済学』筑摩書房, 1990年2月25日初版第1刷.pp.70-76, 311-317.

836　米川紀生「BonnにおけるJoseph Alois Schumpeter」「法経論叢」第7巻第2号, 1990年3月1日.pp.55-83.

837　W. カール・ビブン, 斎藤精一郎訳「シュンペーターのイノベーション論」『〔物語・経済学〕誰がケインズを叙したか』日本経済新聞社, 1990年3月30日1版1刷.1990年8月7日7刷.pp.117-123.

838　藤竹暁「シュムペーターと民主政治」『大衆政治の社会学』有斐閣, 1990年3月30日初版第1刷.1991年9月30日初版第2刷.pp.197-226.

839　塩野谷祐一「シュンペーターの「アンナの日記」」「Study Series」No. 21, 1990年3月31日.1+13p.

840　塩野谷祐一「グスタブフォン・シュモラー―ドイツ歴史学派経済学の現代性―」「一橋論叢」第103巻第4号, 1990年4月1日.pp.35-55.

841　金指基「吉田昇三先生とシュンペーターの経済学」, 吉田昇三先生傘寿記念論文集編纂委員会編『経済発展過程の研究―吉田昇三先生傘寿記念―』不二出版, 1990年4月2日第1刷.pp.27-30.

842　河野善隆「シュムペーター理論とイノベーション・プロセス―企業者革新の多様化, 拡散化に関連して―」「長崎県立 国際経済大学論集」第24巻第1号, 1990年8月1日.pp.1-54.

843　林康二「シュンペーターからの享受―日本におけるシュンペーターの影響―」, 寺尾誠編『温故知新―歴史・思想・社会論集―』慶應通信, 1990年10月25日発行.pp.197-219.

844　金指基「〔資料〕シュンペーターについての社会学―シュムペーター年譜―」「商学集志」第60巻第1号, 1990年10月25日.pp.17-38.

845　今井賢一『情報ネットワーク社会の展開』筑摩書房, 1990年11月15日初版第1刷.1990年3月5日初版第3刷.4+4+290p.

846　小西唯雄, 石原敬子「「競争」の概念と競争政策（上）—完全競争, ハイエク, シュムペーターをめぐって—」「公正取引」通巻481号, 1990年11月15日.pp.19-25.

847　小西唯雄, 石原敬子「「競争」の概念と競争政策（下）—完全競争, ハイエク, シュムペーターをめぐって—」「公正取引」通巻482号, 1990年12月15日.pp.24-30.

848　米川紀生「J. A. Schumpeter「『資本主義・社会主義・民主主義』の準備的考察」」「法経論叢」第8巻第1号, 1990年12月20日.pp.1-34.

849　永友育雄「シュンペーター学説考」「甲南経済学論集」第31巻第3号, 1990年12月25日.pp.1-21.

850　賀村進一「シュムペーターの帝国主義生成論に関する一考察」「帝京経済学研究」第24巻第1号, 1990年12月26日.pp.301-321.

1991年

851　小谷義次・置塩信雄・池上淳編『マルクス・ケインズ・シュムペーター 経済学の現代的課題』大月書店, 1991年2月15日第1刷.1991年4月22日第2刷.1991年10月9日第3刷.1993年1月28日第4刷.7+271p.

852　相葉洋一『貨幣と景気循環』相葉洋一君遺稿集刊行実行委員会, 1991年2月16日発行.1+1+258p.

853　金指基「企業者社会学の一研究」「商学集志」第60巻第2・3号合併号, 1991年2月28日.pp.1-24.

854　金指基「《研究ノート》シュンペーターとケインズ—シュンペーターのケインズ宛書翰をめぐって—」「商学集志」第60巻第2・3号合併号, 1991年2月28日.pp.37-44.

855　長谷川啓之「I. カーズナーの企業者活動論—経済発展との関連を中心として」「商学集志」第60巻第4号, 1991年3月25日.pp.1-22.

856　高橋憲一「企業行動理論に関する一考察」, 和光大学経済学部編『マーシャルとその時代』白桃書房, 1991年3月25日.pp.217-236.

857　賀村進一「シュムペーター「諸帝国主義の社会学」第一章「問題」についての一考察」「帝京経済学研究」第24巻第2号, 1991年3月30日.pp.263-281.

858　吉尾博和「シュムペーターの科学観と経済社会学」「八千代国際大学紀要 国際研究論集」第4巻第1号, 1991年4月15日.pp.101-114.

859　川勝平太「日本文明と近代西洋「鎖国」再考」日本放送出版協会, 1991年6月20日第1刷.266p.

860　十川広国『企業家精神と経営戦略』森山書店, 1991年9月20日初版第1刷.4+5+194p.

861　伊達邦春『シュンペーターの経済学』創文社, 1991年10月30日第1刷.8+205p.

862　河野善隆「シュムペーター理論と技術変化の論理」「長崎県立 大学論集」第25巻第2号, 1991年10月31日.pp.1-52.

863　ロバート・L・ハイルブローナー, 八木甫訳「シュンペーターのヴィジョン」『隠された経済思想 資本主義経済の本質を求めて』HBJ出版局, 1991年12月10日第1刷.pp.171-194.

864　米川紀生「増補 Joseph Alois Schumpeter関係文献目録」「法経論叢」第9巻第1号, 1991年12月15日.pp.83-143.

865　林田睦次「「ケインズ」革命の諸定義—L. R. クライン, J. B. シュンペーターの「ケインズ革命」論を中心として」「徳山大学論叢」36, 1991年12月30日.pp.1-25.

1992年

866　若田部昌澄「アダム・スミスと企業者精神—スミスの「動態性」とは何か—」「早稲田政治経済学雑誌」第307・308合併号, 1992年1月1日.pp.325-358.

867　岡田裕之「経済原論の再出発のために政治経済学新原理は可能か(上)—マルクス・シュンペーター問題の現代的解決—」「経営志林」第28巻第4号, 1992年1月30日.pp.33-46.

868　大西広「シュンペーターとマルクス」『資本主義以前の「社会主義」と資本主義以後の社会主義 工業社会の成立とその終焉』大月書店, 1992年2月26日第1刷.1992年4月8日第2刷.pp.147-151.

869　坂本多加雄「「企業者」概念の発見とその伝統的基盤」「創文」330号.1992年3月1日.pp.10-14.

870　伊達邦春『シュンペーター・企業行動・経済変動』早稲田大学出版部, 1992年3月10日初版第1刷.6+319p.

871　川勝平太「シュンペーター体系と日本経済史」, 大石泰彦, 福岡正夫編『経済理論と計量分析 伊達邦春教授古稀記念論文集』早稲田大学出版部, 1992年3月10日初版第1刷.pp.339-356.

872　根岸隆「シュムペーター利子論とマーシャルの均衡概念」, 大石泰彦, 福岡正夫編『経済理論と計量分析』pp.115-142.

873　西川潤「経済発展理論の展開—シュンペーターからペルーへ—」, 大石泰彦, 福岡正夫編『経済理論と計量分析』pp.323-338.

874　大河内暁男『発明行為と技術構想 技術と特許の経営史的位相』東京大学出版会, 1992年3月20日初版.10+213+23p.

875　米川紀生「J. A. Schumpeterに関する三つの回想」「法経論叢」第9巻第2号, 1992年3月24日.pp.121-137.

876　北條勇作「シュンペーターの社会思想像」, 伊達邦春教授古稀記念論文集出版会編『伊達邦春教授古稀記念論文集 経済学の諸問題:理論・分析と思想』八千代出版, 1992年3月26日初版.pp.301-319.

877　林康二「シュンペーター『経済発展の理論』の一考察」「専修大学大学院紀要 専修社会科学論集」第10号, 1992年3月27日.pp.1-33.

878　今井賢一『資本主義のシステム間競争』筑摩書房, 1992年4月5日初版第1刷.1992年6月20日第2刷.8+226p.

879　吉尾博和「シュムペーターにおける社会進化の内生理論—資本主義の内生理論による封建制度の分析—」「八千代国際大学紀要 国際研究論集」第5巻第1号, 1992年4月15日.pp.38-55.

880　R. M. グッドウィン〔著〕, 有賀裕二〔訳〕『カオス経済動学』多賀出版, 1992年6月10日第1版第1刷.9+234p.

881　岡田裕之「経済原論の再出版のために政治経済学新原理は可能か（下）—マルクス—シュンペーター問題の現代的解決—」「経営志林」第29巻第2号, 1992年7月30日.pp.65-86.

882　西村功「日本経済再生の条件—シュンペーター型景気回復への処方箋—」「経済論叢」第150巻第4号, 1992年10月1日.pp.17-28.

883　金指基「シュンペーター研究の過去と未来」「経済学史学会年報」第30号, 1992年11月1日.pp.91-95.

884　根井雅弘「20世紀のエコノミスト連載2 J. A. シュムペーター」「経済セミナー」通巻454号, 1992年11月1日.pp.84-87.

885　根井雅弘「シュムペーターとマーシャル」,「シュムペーター「理論経済学の本質と主要内容」—純粋経済学の擁護」『現代経済学の生誕』名古屋大学出版会, 1992年11月20日初版第1刷.pp.32-56. 194-199.

886　金指基「社会科学における分析と予測—シュンペーター『資本主義・社会主義・民主主義』発刊50周年によせて—」「商学集志」第62巻第3号, 1992年12月15日.pp.37-50.

887　勝又壽良「今こそ「創造的破壊の精神」が甦る時だ 日本経済に必要な本物のシュンペーター」「週刊東洋経済」第5116号, 1992年12月26日.pp.132-137.

888　安孫子誠男「技術 経済パラダイム論の問題像—資本主義像の現在（二）—」「千葉大学教養部研究報告A-25」1992年12月30日.pp.347-430.

1993年

889　池田勝彦「Evolutionary Economicsの最近の発展」「商学論究」第40巻第3号, 1993年1月20日.pp.1-13.

890　河野善隆「シュムペーター理論と継続的技術革新に関する研究（I）」「長崎県立大学論集」第26巻第3号, 1993年2月10日.pp.1-27.

891　伊東光晴, 根井雅弘『シュンペーター—孤高の経済学者—』岩波書店, 1993年3月22日第1刷.6月1日第3刷（5つの事実・事項修正）, 1993年7月5日第4刷.1993年9月1日第5刷.4+216p.

892　井上義朗「シュンペーターからの出発」『市場経済学の源流 マーシャル, ケインズ, ヒックス』中央公論社, 1993年3月25日初版.1993年4月25日再版.pp.3-27.

893　河野善隆「シュムペーター理論と継続的技術革新に関する研究（II）」「長崎県立大学論集」第26巻第4号, 1993年3月31日.pp.1-34.

894　塩野谷祐一「ケインズとシュンペーター」「世界経済評論」通巻452号, 1993年4月1日.p.7.

895　臼井陽一郎「〈研究メモ〉シュンペーターとヴェーバー」「世界経済」第48巻第4号, 1993年4月1日.pp.11-30.

896　金指基「現代に行き続けるシュンペーター経済学 「おもちゃの鉄砲」の理論群を圧倒する魅力」「エコノミスト」第71巻第20号通巻3064号, 1993年5月11日.pp.82-87.

897　N・ジョージェスクーレーゲン, 高橋正立訳「ニコラス・ジョージエスクーレーゲン, 自らを語る1」「みすず」第35巻第5号第386号, 1993年5月15日.pp.2-15.

898　金指基「わが国におけるシュンペーター研究」「商学集志」第63巻第1号, 1993年5月25日.pp.21-53.

899　根井雅弘「シュンペーターの苦悩」「図書」第528号, 1993年6月1日.p.1.

900　週刊新潮「特集 公共投資は景気浮揚させず 脚光浴びる「シュンペーター」理論」「週刊新潮」第38巻第21号通巻1909号, 1993年6月3日.pp.130-134.

901　通商産業省編『創造的革新の時代―中期産業経済展望研究会報告書―』通産資料調査会, 1993年6月15日第1版.11+239p.

902　戸田信正「(大)企業体制の経済学」『経済学四つの視点―経済学入門―』勁草書房, 1993年6月15日第1版第1刷.pp.81-96.

903　森嶋通夫『思想としての近代経済学 NHK人間大学1993年7月―9月期』日本放送出版協会, 1993年7月1日発行.138p.

904　N・ジョージェスクーレーゲン, 高橋正立, 訳「ニコラス・ジョージェスクーレーゲン, 自らを語る3」「みすず」第35巻第7号第388号, 1993年7月15日.pp.85-94.

905　伊東光晴「今こそ日本に必要な創造的破壊 シュンペーターの現代的意味」「週刊東洋経済」第5160号, 1993年7月31日.pp.82-89.

906　河野善隆「シュムペーター理論と継続的技術革新に関する研究(四)」「長崎県立大学論集」第27巻第1号, 1993年8月31日.pp.1-35.

907　米川紀生「大蔵大臣としてのJ. A. Schumpeterの思想と行動」『社会思想史研究』(社会思想史学会年報)通巻第17号, 北樹出版, 1993年9月30日.pp.89-94.

908　根井雅弘「シュンペーターと現代 経済発展から社会的文化発展へ」「日本経済研究センター会報」689号, 1993年10月1日.pp.26-31.

909　加藤秀治郎「シュンペーターの小選挙区論」, 加藤秀治郎編『リーディングス選挙制度と政治思想』芦書房, 1993年10月5日初版第1刷.pp.33-37.

910　渡辺厚代「資源のダイナミクスと企業者機能―シュンペーター理論における―」「経営総合科学」第61号, 1993年10月15日.pp.11-26.

911　八木紀一郎「〔資料紹介〕シュンペーターとヴィーン大学」「経済論叢」別冊 調査と研究第5号, 1993年10月.pp.63-83.

912　林康二「R. L. Allen, Opening Doors, 2 vols Transaction Pub, xxi+348p./R. Swedberg, Joseph A. Schumpeter, Polity Press, 1991, vii+293p.〔書評〕」「経済学史学会年報」第31号, 1993年11月1日.pp.141-142.

913　根井雅弘「シュンペーターと現代」「世界」第588号, 1993年11月1日.pp.194-203.

914　岩井克人・川勝平太「シュムペーターを超えて」「現代思想」第21巻第13号, 1993年12月1日.pp.48-69.

915　米川紀生「翻訳 J. A. Schumpeterの政治活動」「法経論叢」第11巻第1号, 1993年12月15日.pp.27-60.

916　臼井陽一郎「資本主義に関する三つの研究:シュンペーター, ヴェーバー, ゾンバルト」「早稲田経済学研究」第37号, 1993年12月27日.pp.75-99.

III　付　　録

III　付　録

A.　来日時の講演活動

1. 日本におけるシュンペーター

明治11年にフェノロサが、御雇い外国人として東京大学で経済学を講述して以来、わが国の経済学は輸入の学として祖述され、経済学学として展開されてきた。ようやく大正8年4月に法科万能主義の中で経済学部が、東京帝国大学法科大学から分離・独立し、科学としての経済学も一学科として認められた。そこで新設の東京帝国大学経済学部は、教授陣容を拡充するために、ビーダーマン銀行頭取を辞任したり同銀行の破産にも直面した失意の大経済学者シュンペーターを、レーデラーの後任の外国人教師として迎え入れようとした。経済学部長矢作栄蔵の意を受けて河合栄治郎が、留学先のベルリンからこの外国人教師探しの旅を始め、経済学者のヘルクナーやアモンやミーゼスと接触し、1924年12月15日にヴィーンでシュンペーターと直接に面談し交渉した。

彼の日記によれば、その日の夜の「七時半シュンペーターを訪うた。話は大学のことから始めた。氏は解答は十日を与えて呉れと云ったが、自分の現在の境遇を脱しようと思っていた矢先の話で、実に嬉しいと幾度か云った」(1)。12月27日にはシュンペーターが早速受けてきて、翌年1月7日には河合の申し出も大体聞き入れられ、1週間後の1月15日には東京の「教授会がシュンペーターに決定」の電報も来た。しかしながら、迅速な経済学部教授会の決定にもかかわらず、1925年秋になってもシュンペーターから最終決断は得られなかった。そして同年10月21日の教授会での「シュンペーターに関する公使の報告」から、シュンペーターの近状が知られるに及んで彼の招聘は、事実上困難となった。シュンペーター本人が、10月始めベルリンでプロイセン文部省とボン大学の財政学の教授ポストをめぐって交渉していて、10月5日には婚約者アニーに「ボンを征服す」と喜んで打電し、10月15日にはドイツの大学の正教授職を受け入れていた。結局彼は、日本よりもドイツの新婚生活を優先し、最愛の母とアニーの極東行きへの不安とためらいを払拭できなかった。

こうしてシュンペーター招聘は挫折し、わが国での教師シュンペーターは見られなくなった(2)。だが彼自身は、失意の自分を最後まで温かく迎え入れようとした日本への愛着と感謝の念を終生抱き続けた。それを吐露するチャンスが、6年後の日本訪問となって実現する。

シュンペーターは、1930年12月下旬に旧知の荒木光太郎に「今回の来朝は極めてプライベートな日本の風物にあこがれての旅行であって講演等正式の予定はない」(3)と知らせてきたが、実際にはどんな旅でどのような講演であったのだろうか。

シュンペーターは、ハーヴァード大学経済学部客員教授として、ハーヴァードで1930年秋から年末にかけて講義した。そして12月27日にクリーヴランドのアメリカ経済学会に出席してドイツへ帰国する途中にハワイ経由で1931年2月25日午後5時に、中山伊知郎等の出迎えを受けて夕やみせまる横浜港桟橋で秩父丸から日本の地を踏み、直ちに宿泊先の帝国ホテルへ向かった。ホテルに着くやロビーで待ちわびた一経済学徒にシュンペーターは、「当時出版のケインズの貨幣論を読んだか」(4)と質問し、「自分は船中で読んだ」といって「その議論を仕向け」てその学者ぶりを早くも発揮した。ロビーから部屋へ入るや今度は、「教え子一人一人を呼び出して、今何を研究しているのかとか、何かわからぬことはないかとか、更につき進んではサラリーはいくらもらっているか、足りなければやろうかとまでの親切ぶり」[5]を発揮して弟子達をすっかり感動させた。同夜は、ホテルで中山伊知郎等と日本滞在の日程の調整をして終った。

翌日からシュンペーターは、東京近郊の散策を始めるが、先ず本郷弥生町の荒木光太郎の二階建和式の私邸を訪れた。小学生の令嬢明子によると[6]、学校から帰宅したら父の光太郎が、「シュンペーターという大切な方が来られている」から部屋に入らないように言ったが彼女は、シュンペーターが寛畝画伯の大きな絵の掛った床の間に通され、金らんたる金屏風に接して興奮し、西洋間の応接室に移って日本画特に江戸画を荒木夫妻と興味深く鑑賞しているのを垣間見た。彼は帰りは、近くの根津コレクションで古美術を見て回った。なおシュンペーターは、荒木夫妻とは鎌倉見物を東畑精一といっしょに行ない、鎌倉大仏の仏像にほれ込み[7]、近くの鶴岡八幡宮の寺社をめぐっては、「その自然の環境から生じる寺院—感動させる美」を生み出す日本文化を賛美した。

1月28日の厳しい寒さの中をシュンペーターは、わが国において最初の講演をすべく東京商科大学(現一橋大)を訪れ、講演前に大学本館の特別応接室で多くの人々と歓談した。東畑精一の回想では、「あの時の室の寒さはシュンペーターを少しばかりたぢろかせたかもしれなかったが、氏はそれを気にしている当時の教授たちに、「大学は建てものではない」と言ってのけた。そして例えばイタリアのボロニア大学とかその他の例をひいて、その貧弱な大学の建てもののなかで、いかに見事な研究の成果が挙げられたかを物語った。」[8]

いよいよ午前10時30分から兼松講堂[9]で上田貞次郎学長の紹介の後にシュンペーターは、「近代経済学者の科学的武器」という題で2時間にわたり流ちょうな英語で7〜800名の聴衆に語りかけた[10]。講演に感動した学徒には、サインまでするサービスぶりであった。板垣與一は、中山伊知郎に代わって講演後のシュンペーターを帝国ホテルまで送ったが、国立から東京までの1時間20分にわたり電車の中で、講義の内容、歴史学派、方法論争、価値判断論争等についてシュンペーターに次々と質問を発し、一問一問懇切丁寧に答えてもらった。そうしたシュンペーターの教育者魂を板垣は、生涯忘れることができなかった[11]。

同日夜は午後6時から10時まで如水会国際部が、各国公使を招待してシュンペーター歓迎晩さん会を開き、シュンペーターは食後に、「現時の世界恐慌対抗策」という軽いテーブルスピーチをした。彼は、「先ず日本の活発なる発展を賞し、日独関係の常に良好なるを慶賀し、国家間の関係は猶結婚生活の如し。当事者に一定の距離の存する場合、結果概ね可し」、「政治が経済生活の実際を無視するの弊を説き、学問と実業との連絡の緊要を指摘し」、質問に答えて「昔、或る国はその財政立直しのために顧問としてある経済学者を聘した。而して、最も必要なる、然しながら、最も、不人気なる政策は凡て此の外国学者の案として、提出せしめた。現時の如き、経済困難に処する方策は何れも不人気は止むを得ざる所、右某国の利用したScapegoatも亦一方便ならんか」と意味深長なる発言を弄した[12]。晩さん会の座長としてシュンペーターの直ぐとなりに座した一実業家が、最近の経済時事問題を質した時にシュンペーターは、現下の各国政府の財政政策は大体同一の方向に進み、インフレもデフレも度を過ぎると弊害を伴うと指摘し、日本の金解禁については「自分が日本の大蔵大臣なりしなれば旧平価に依らず、通貨の購買力を見たる上「より以下」の相場にて解禁したる」と答えた[13]。

次の日の1月29日は午後からシュンペーターは、わが国実業界の総本山である日本工業倶楽部において、同倶楽部と日本経済連盟の共催で「大不況について」[14]の講演を行なった。団琢磨の紹介の後にシュンペーターは、「不況がいわれるごとにそれを最悪のものとみなす」見方を批判し、目下の不況は立ち直りつつあると言って不況の現状と原因を解き明かした。講演出席者は178名に達する盛況ぶりで、その後の日本工業倶楽部会員有志によるシュンペーターを囲む懇談会には、有賀長文、山本悌二郎、諸井貫一、膳桂之助等の顔が見られた。

1月30日にはシュンペーターは、かつて招聘の件で温かい配慮を示した東京帝国大学経済学部を訪れるが、その前に午前10時半から2時まで山上御殿で小野塚喜平次総長招待の午さん会に招かれ、ひき続いて安田講堂(15)、経済学部研究室、図書館を視察した。そして午後3時から5時まで法文経12番教室で経済学部主催の講演をする。彼は、矢作学部長の挨拶の後に「恐慌の理論」(16)について英語で語り、欧米の最近の恐慌学説を紹介し、景気循環論を展開した。講演終了後直ちに経済学部のシュンペーター歓迎の茶話会が経済学部部研究会議室で行われた。茶話会の前に大学3年生の安井琢磨は、シュンペーターのところへ行って、大学を卒業して本格的に経済学を勉強したいがどういうふうに勉強を始めたらいいか、「何から始めたらいいでしょうか」と助言を求めたのに対して、「経済理論を研究するつもりなら、ワルラスから始めなさい。(17)」と言われた。以後安井は、ワルラスを研究し、一般均衡理論の分析に没頭する。

三日続きの講義から解放されたシュンペーターは、1月31日には数人で日光見物に出かけ、金谷ホテルで一休みした。彼の同伴者は、「車中でもホテルでも、東照宮を見物しているときでも、経済学の議論を戦わされるので頭が疲れた。全くすさまじい理論学者だと思った。…彼の議論は「厳密」経済学といった方がよいような厳しさをもっていて、いい加減な議論をすると、そのようなことは論証できない(unbeweisbar)と一蹴されてしまう。すさまじい理論というほかなかった」(18)と回顧している。

日光から帰るとシュンペーターは、今度は箱根に出かけて富士屋ホテルに投宿し、旅の疲れを熱海ホテルの温泉で癒した。熱海ホテルでは偶然にもわが国の社会政策学の長老金井延と出会い、スタインの思い出を語り合った(19)。このように日光や箱根を旅して歩いている時にもシュンペーターの弟子達は、彼を「パパ パパ」と呼び、先生のシュンペーターは彼等を「マイ・チルドレン」と呼んで麗しい師弟関係を再確認し合った。シュンペーターには子供がいなかったので、「日本に来てはじめてパパといわれたとくすぐったいような嬉しいやうな顔」をしていた(20)。

日本滞在も残り一週間となった2月6日にシュンペーターは、招聘先の神戸商業大学(現神戸大)で最後の日本講演をするために、特急燕号で9時間かけて神戸に向かう。途中車中で「現下の世界的不況とその前途」について、インタヴューに応じた。彼の考えでは、この不景気はいわゆる「景気循環の巨波」が底にあるからであり、今日は不況も漸く底をついた、本年末ごろから回復に入るだろう。銀価の暴落に対しては、金為替本位を採用すべきだ。列国の保護関税政策については彼は、債権国が自由貿易国となるのが本道で、不況期にはいつも戦争の危機が増大するが、財界安定とともに自然に消滅するだろうと答えた(21)。インタヴューを終えて間もなくシュンペーターは、神戸商業大学学長、瀧谷善一、丸谷喜市の出迎えをうけて夜の神戸駅に着いた。そして直ちにトーア・ホテルに投宿し、神戸滞在中のうち合わせを行なった。

翌日の2月7日にシュンペーターは、午後1時から3時まで神戸商業大学講堂で「商業政策の現状」(22)という第1回の講演をする。彼は、世界各国が政治的根拠から目下関税保護政策をとっているが、近い将来は自由貿易が実現され、それには先ず世界の債権国アメリカが自由貿易を実行すれば世界各国もそれに追従するだろうと述べた。講演の後は、場所を同大学の産業研究所に移して、講演をめぐって教授・学生達と質問討論会に入り、活発な質疑応答がなされた。

日曜日にあたる2月8日にはシュンペーターは、神戸を出発して午前11時ごろ京都で高田保馬、柴田敬、小島昌太郎に出迎えられ、専ら柴田の案内で御所、二条院、西本願寺を参観し、将軍塚や西陣の織物工場を見物した。彼は美術の鑑識眼が高く、京洛の美術、特に古画にも一家言を持っていたので、西本願寺の襖の竹の絵を見て大変気に入り、その絵に対しての小僧の説明が間違いであることを指摘した(23)。夜には京都帝国大学経済学部によるシュンペーター歓迎会が、楽友会館(24)で開かれた。そこで彼はマルクス主義に心を寄せる教授連を前にスピーチをし、「私はマルクスの搾取の理論と同じ搾取の理論をもっている。マルクスは搾取に反対したけれども、私は搾取を是認する。なぜなら、搾取がなかったらどうしてあの二条城の美術はできたか[25]」とマルクスの搾取論を皮肉り驚かせた。シュンペーターは、京都を実際に見物することによってますます京都を愛し、『源氏物語』を愛読するようになり、ハーヴァードの学生であった都留重人に後年には「紫式部のような婦人と一晩ゆっくり語りあかしてみたい」と言い、「われわれは、芸術というものをわれわれから疎外して考える。日本人は生活のすみずみにまで芸術を生かしている」と語った[26]。

2月9日の月曜日は午後3時から5時までシュンペーターは、神戸商業大学講堂で「理論経済学の現状」[27]について第2日目の講演をする。彼は、学派を国別、主義別、方法論上より区別して説明し、貨幣理論、国際貿易論の現状を解説した。講演後は前回と同様に同大学産業研究所で教授学生等と質問討論会が開かれた。夜は午後9時までトーア・ホテルで同大学学長によるシュンペーター歓迎晩さん会が、黒瀬市長、ドイツ総領事フットマン、高田保馬等20数名の出席の下に開かれた。晩さん会後も高田は、トーア・ホテルの談話室でとなり合いの椅子にかけてシュンペーターと価格理論について一問一答議論し、続いて翌朝午前11時から1時間かけて再論した。結論を得なかったが、討論を通じて高田は、「理論的なる迫力、分析のあくまでに厳密なること、数学的なるものの考え方」など「こんな鋭い理論家に会ったことがない」[28]とシュンペーターを評価している。

とうとうシュンペーターの日本最後で第3回目の講演が、2月10日に神戸商業大学講堂で午後3時から5時にかけて行われた。その題は、「利子の理論」[29]であった。彼はボエームの利子学説を説明し、自らの利子論を動態利子論として展開した。講演後の例の質問討論会では田中金司、丸谷、高田が次々とシュンペーター利子論について質問し、それをめぐって激論が午後7時まで続いた。その後田中、丸谷、柴田、高田、早川巳代治が加わった晩さんの後、高田は貨幣名目説や貨幣の主観価値論や貨幣数量説に関する柴田の質問を中心に午後10時半までシュンペーターと討論した。

神戸商科大学での三回の講演を全て終え、日本講演を完了したシュンペーターは、2月11日の午前9時15分に神戸を発って田中、柴田の案内で奈良見物に出かけ、奈良ホテルに一泊する。シュンペーターは、奈良では東大寺の大仏と鎌倉大仏を対比したり、その他の寺院の素晴らしさに改めて驚嘆した。一夜明けて2月12日に奈良から帰る途中にシュンペーターは、大阪に立ち寄り、午後2時から大阪放送局で森川太郎の通訳で英語でラジオ放送した。その夜は宮島綱男夫妻の案内で大阪の文楽座の人形芝居「熊谷陣屋」を見物した[30]。

講演と旅行を楽しくすませて帰国するに際しシュンペーターは、2月13日正午前に再び神戸商科大学に挨拶に訪れ、三週間の日本滞在中に日本国民から非常な歓待をうけたことを謝し、「日本は風光明び な許りでなく国民も非常に親切でナイスピープルである。殊に学生が学問に対する態度が非常に真剣である」[31]と語った。同日の午後3時にシュンペーターは、日本での思い出を靖国丸に乗せて、神戸港からホンコンとジャワを経て南洋へと帰国の途についた。涙で見送った高田が、陸路でなおもシュンペーターを追い、靖国丸が門司に立ち寄る翌日の12時半に、かぜ気味のシュンペーターと船上で再会し、2時間にわたり数多の問題を質問し討論しているうちに、「とうとう発船のしらせの銅鑼がなる。私の乗って帰るべきランチが来た。教授〔シュンペーター〕は風邪を引いた身を一しょに甲板に立ってゐる。そして云ふ、今あなたを私から引き離す船が来る。私が機関銃を持ってゐるなら沈めてしまふであらう。…ランチに乗ったが税関の人が乗り込まぬと云ふので、十分も本船をはなれない。その間、しぶきにぬれながら教授は船から私を見下してゐる。寒いから室に入られるやうに呼べば、あなたが見える間見てゐると呼ぶ声がきこえる。ランチはいよいよ離れた。甲板の上からは、いつまでも教授の手にふられてゐる白いハンカチが見える。私のランチは旋回した。かの学会の巨人の姿は全く私の視界から没した。」[32]教師としての、経済学者としての、そして人間としてのシュンペーターが、日本から完全に消え去っていった。

しかしながら、シュンペーターも又、消え去りつつある日本での旅行と講演を2月13日付書簡で、次のように総括している。「私の旅は、一休みするという目的に関する限り失敗です。日本ではわが意に反して友人や学徒が用意した全ゆる類の講演や小旅行を次から次へとこなしたからです。だが、私はそれを大いに楽しみ、日本の同僚や学生ばかりかビジネス・リーダーや政治家にも非常にいい感じを懐いています。後者に関して、ヨーロッパで見られるものと比べてとてもはっきり目立つのは、おそらく日本の政治の貴族的要素だろう。」(33)以後シュンペーターは、1945年に二個の原爆を日本に投下しようとするアメリカ合衆国の決定に狼狽し、それを「愚かな野獣性あるいは野獣的愚かさ」として私的日記に書き留め、愛しの日本と日本文化が破壊されるのを見たくはなかった。「もう一度日本を訪れてじっくりと日本文化を鑑賞する」ことが、シュンペーターの願いであった。

注

(1) 社会思想研究会編『河合栄治郎全集 第二十二巻 日記I』 社会思想社、1969年5月20日, p.167。

(2) 福田徳三は、1926年10月25日付ブレンターノ書簡でシュンペーター招聘の失敗を見ぬいていた。「シュンペーターは我々を裏切った。彼が抜け目ないという先生の予言は、まさに的中しました。」翻刻・翻訳 柳沢まどか「福田徳三—ルーヨ・ブレンターノ書簡 1898-1931年」「一橋大学社会科学古典資料センター Study Series No. 56」2006年3月31日, p.112.

(3) 「帝国大学新聞」1931年1月1日号, P. 2.

(4) 岸本誠二郎「人と学説 シュンペーター」「経済往来」第17巻第10号, 1965年10月1日, P. 75.

(5) シュムペーター 博士の片影(3)「エコノミスト」第9年第4号, 1931年2月15日, p33.

(6) 1990年10月12日付斎藤明子書簡.

(7) 大仏前のシュンペーター. 口絵写真裏を参照。

(8) 東畑精一「由来記」 THE CATALOGUE of Prof. Schumpeter Library. The Hitotsubashi University Library. 一橋大学, 1962年3月1日, p.vii. 「大学は建物ではない」というシュンペーター伝説の由来とその当否は、三上隆三「伝説の種をまく人:シュムペーター」「経済セミナー」通巻363号, 1985年4月1日, pp81-83が詳しい。

(9) 兼松講堂前のシュンペーター。写真前列はシュンペーターを挟んで東畑と中山。中列は板垣。後列は上原専禄、上田辰之助、村松恒一郎。口絵写真裏を参照。

(10) 「一橋新聞」第128号, 1931年2月9日, p.2に講演要旨。

(11) 板垣への1993年2月22日インタヴュー及び書簡。講演要旨と50年後に新発見の講義草稿については、杉山忠平訳「経済学の「危機」—50年前の ……」「別冊経済セミナー シュンペーター再発見」日本評論社, 1983年7月30日, pp.17-26と同資料の考証・解説(pp.27-30)を参照。

(12) シュンペーター博士招待記「如水会々報」第89号, 1931年4月1日, p.71。

(13) 五十嵐覚三「シュムペーター博士を見る」「経済往来」第6巻第3号, 1931年3月1日, p.90。

(14) 講演内容は、日英両語で「日本工業倶楽部会報」第16号,1931年5月25日に載り、代謄写もされている。

(15) 安田講堂前のシュンペーター。写真左より中西寅雄、東畑、河合、シュンペーター、矢作、荒木。口絵写真裏を参照。

(16) その講演速記は、「恐慌の理論」「経済往来」第5巻第3号, 1931年3月1日, pp.23-38。その講演要旨は、「帝国大学新聞」1931年2月2日号, p.3。

(17) 安井琢磨『私の歩んだ経済学の道』創価大学経済学会, 1988年6月10日, p.5。

(18) 岸本誠二郎, 前掲論文, p.75。

(19) シュムペーター 博士の片影(2)「エコノミスト」第9年第4号, 1931年2月15日, p.32。

(20) シュムペーター 博士の片影(3)「エコノミスト」第9年第4号, 1931年2月15日, p.33。

(21) 車中のシュンペーターとインタヴューでの一問一答は、「大阪朝日新聞」1931年2月7日号, p.7。

(22) 講演中のシュンペーターと講演要旨は、「神戸商大新聞」1931年3月15日号, p.1。英語講演は、「国民経済雑誌」第50巻第4号, 1931年4月1日, pp.1-26。

(23) 柴田敬「シュンペーター先生の教え」「別冊経済セミナー シュンペーター再発見」日本評論社, 1983年7月30日, p.32。

(24) シュンペーターを囲んで、右が高田保馬。高田保馬博士追想録刊行会『高田保馬博士の生涯と学説』創文社, 1981年1月25日.口絵

(25)「座談会 人間シュンペーター」での都留重人発言「別冊経済セミナー シュンペーター再発見」日本評論社, 1983年7月30日, p.7。

(26) 都留重人『近代経済学の群像』日本経済新聞社, 1964年9月10日, p201。

(27) 講演の英文要約は、「国民経済雑誌」第50巻第5号、1931年5月1日, pp.1-27。講演の逐語的草稿は、Joseph Schumpeter, Recent Developments of Political Economy (1931) .Kobe University Economic Review No. 28, 1982. pp.2-15. その邦訳は、米川紀生「J. A. Schumpeter 『資本主義・社会主義・民主主義』の準備的考察」「法経論叢」第8巻第1号, 1990年12月20日, pp.11-34.

(28) 高田保馬「シユムペエタア教授の印象」『貧者必勝』千倉書房, 1939年2月18日, p.47。

(29)「神戸商大新聞」1931年2月15日号, p.1.

(30)「シュ教授の文楽見物」「大阪朝日新聞」1931年2月13日号, p.2. 文楽人形を手にした意気揚々のシュンペーターは、Thomas K. McCraw, Prophet of Innovation. Harvard University Press. 2007. p.198.

(31)「神戸商大新聞」1931年2月15日号, p.1.

(32) 高田保馬, 前掲書, pp.50。高田は、手帖に「シユムペエタアはなげきゐむ故国漸く乱れんとす」と書き留める。高田保馬『社会歌雑記』甲文社, 1947年6月10日, p.72.

(33) Ausgewählt und herausgegeben von Ulrich Hedtke und Richard Swedberg, Joseph Alois Schumpeter Briefe/Letters. Mohr Siebeck, Tübingen, 2000. S.186.

2. 写真・記事・講演録

1）写　真

兼松講堂で講演中のシュンペーター
（1931 年 1 月 30 日）（一橋大学附属図書館所蔵）

シュンペーター講演会の盛況（神戸商業大学講堂）
（1931 年 2 月 7 日）（神戸大学社会科学系図書館所蔵所蔵）

京都見物後のシュンペーター、京大楽友会館にて 高田保馬とともに　（1931 年 2 月 7 日）
高田保馬博士追想録刊行会『高田保馬博士の生涯と学説』創文社，昭和 56 年 1 月 25 日，口絵写真
（一橋大学附属図書館所蔵）

2）記 事

世界經濟恐慌の
實相とその恢復期
シユムペター教授に聴く

大阪朝日新聞 1931.2.7

シユ教授の
文樂見物
けふは南洋へ向ふ

來朝中のオーストリアの前大藏大臣、現在ドイツのボン大學經濟學教授ヨセフ・シユンペーター氏は今十三日神戸出帆、經濟事情視察のため南洋方面に向ふこと〻なつたが、日本滞在最終日の十二日大阪へ來り、同夜は宮島綱男氏夫妻の案内で文樂座の人形劇「熊谷陣屋」を見物した

寫眞中央がシユンペーター教授兩側は宮島氏夫妻

大阪朝日新聞 1931.2.13

3）講演録

ヨゼフ・シュムペーター「近代経済学者の科学的武器」

この題下で自分の述べようとする所は今日の経済科学が科学として如何なる地位を有し、またその領域に属する問題を処理するため如何なる理論、換言すれば如何なる科学的の武器を有するかといふことについてである。今日は経済学の領域に属する問題が非常に多いといはれており、しかも新しい問題が続々と出てくる様に思はれる。しかしながら今日我々が取扱つてゐる問題は実は問題それ自身としては決して新しいものではない。欧洲戦争前後のインフレーション及びデフレーションを例にとつて見てもこれらの問題は既にキリスト以前においても存在してゐたもので我々の信ずる様に決して近代に限られる現象ではない。ただこれを取扱ふ所の方法即ちこれを処理する所の武器といふものこそは近代の産物なのである。例へばもし何人かゞ、アダム・スミスの「国富論」を読むならば少しの科学的な素養なくしても決して困難ではない。然しながら例へばリカルドの書物は極めて理解するに困難である。

その理由は丁度この時代に経済学が科学として発達し始めたからである。即ち十九世紀の初頭に至つて科学的の思想はその発達の一定の段階に達し、それ以後は経済現象を理解するためには、まづこの科学的の武器即ち理論を学ぶことが必要となつたのである。

科学的の思考方法、あるひは事物を観察するに当つて用ひる所の武器とは、如何に事物を分せきしまた如何に事物を理解するかを教へる所のものである。か様な意味における理論、即ち科学的の理論は、これを研究者の有する個々の目的意志と混同してはならない。即ち科学は決して我々が何をなすべきかといふ目的を教へるものでなくて、単に事物を理解する道具にすぎないのである。例を社会主義にとつていへば、マルクスを信じても社会主義者でない人もあり社会主義者であつてマルクスを信じない人もある。

一般に社会主義者たると否とを問はずその事象分析に用ひる方法は殆ど同一である。マルクスの理論において真理であることは、また他の理論においても真理であり前者において誤りであるものはもちろん、他においても誤りである たゞ 現象の理解においては等しくてもこの理解を応用する方面においては異るのであり、個々からこれらの見解の相違が生ずるのである。今一つの例を以てこれを立証するに自分とケーンズとは貨幣理論の理解について殆ど異る所がない。しかもケーンズ氏は英国の金本位法を以てナンセンスであるとし自分はそれはよいものと思ふ。この見解の相違は単に気持の相違であつて事象そのものゝ理解においては少しも異る所がないのである。そこでこれらの混同から離れて静かに経済学の領界を振りかへると今日の学界においては我々が豫想する以上に、科学的の武器即ち理論上の見解の一致がある。いはゆる学派の論争なるものは少しの相違をも、本質上の相違の如く論じ立てゝゐるけれども、然し如何に現状を記述するかの問題自身については、従つてその手段即ち理論そのものゝ理解については根本的の相違は思ひの外に少いのである。

根本的の相違といふ点についてしば〳〵例にとられる労働価値説と限界利用説を考へてみよ。昔はこの二説は全く相異るものとして何れが正しいかゞ理論の中心となつてゐた。然しながら労働価値説のいふ所が果して如何なるものであるか。又労働価値説は如何なる前提の下に成立し得るかを考察するならば我々は容易にそれが限界利用理論の一つの特殊の場合であることを証明することが出来る。即ち両者は互に排斥するものでなく単に理論の異る段階を示してゐるにすぎない。唯方法がまちがつてゐたのではなくて単に近代的な方法が古いものよりもより有効であるといふことが証明されたにすぎない。およそ経済思想史の発達はかくの如き科学的武器の精錬の過程を示してゐるものである。

経済的理論といふものはかくて思想の武器の一大倉庫といふことが出来る。たゞ、然しながら経済上の事象は歴史的にこれを見れば常に速かに変化してゐる。即ち経済学においては動態的な要素がきはめて重要で経済理論がよつて立つ所の事実は常に甚だしい変化にさらされてゐる。故に経済現象分せきの武器即ち理論は当然経済史の研究によつてそれと互に提携しまたこれによつて、みがゝれなければならぬ、経済史の研究によつてこの武器を豊富にすることは、然しながら単純に歴史的の事実を知ることによつては得られない。経済学を学ぶものは、この意味においてまた歴史的事実の研究においても一定の見解を有たなければならぬ。

例へば、ある歴史家によればローマではオーガスタスの時代から紀元前二〇〇年頃まで、金が常に流出してゐたといふことをいつてゐる。彼はその原因としてローマが輸入超過に陥つてゐることを指摘し、金の流出をもつて、ローマ滅亡の一つの原因とみなしてゐる。然しながらかくの如きことはナンセンスである もしも、二〇〇年の間金が流出し続けてゐたとするならばローマにおける物価は下落し続けてゐたはずであるが、事実は決して然らず。ローマは輸入に劣らず、多大の輸出を有してゐたもので当時のローマは、故に可成りバランスのとれた貿易状態にあつたといへるのである

歴史上の事物を取扱ふ場合には一般にかくの如き注意が必要であつて、従つて歴史家といふものも我々が歴史を必要とすると同じく経済学を必要としてゐる。この事実は特にアメリカにおいて著るしく見られる所であつて実証的な歴史的な研究が経済的の領域において十分な成功を収めるためにはその歴史家は当然一部分経済学者であり、他方当然統計学者であらねばならぬ

然らばかくの如くして発達し来つた経済学の水準はもつとも手近においてはどこにこれを求め得られるか。いふまでもなくそれはマーシヤルの著述に求められる。マーシヤルの著述は既に一部分は古い。然しながらこの著述こそは今日の理論の一般的の地位をうかがふためにもつとも適当なものであつて、その理論の特色は単に理論的であるばかりでなく、その理論が常に実際上の適用といふことを考へて構成されてゐるといふ点である。勿論理論家としては、我々はマーシヤルを越えて進まねばならないが実際的な概念を理解するには例へば彼の純地代、消費者余剰といふやうなものは大変有用なものである。

経済学の諸理論は、実に結局においては事物を数字に又数量的に説明し得るのでなければ、ほとんど価値がない。この意味において近代の経済学においては統計学と経済論を綜合してこれから一つの科学的の武器を作りだすことが行はれてゐる。たとへばムーアの研究はこの一つの試みを示すものである。

ムーアの研究は先づ最初の試みとしてマーシヤルが理論的に構成した需要曲線を統計に確立することから試みられてゐる。マーシヤルの需要曲線は通常知られてゐる様に価格と需要量との関係が低降的な曲線として考へられてゐる。然しながら之を実際に統計的の数字を以て跡けづるには種々な困難に遭遇する。例へば統計的研究が扱ふ年数が一定の期間を越えれば曲線は、或ひはその期間における購買力の変動或ひは人々のその商品に対する趣味の変化から根本的にその形を変ずるといふ様なことがあるからである。もつともこれに対しては若干の補修を試みることが出来るので必ずしも、斯くの如き事情があるために、例へばムーア教授の云ふ如くマーシアシルの需要の曲線がことごとく無価値となるものではない。ムーアの洗鉄に就いての研究は需要曲線のこの根本的の変動を充分に研究してゐない欠点がある。

然しながらかくの如き欠点は、いはゞかゝる初期の試みに付随的なもので、これがために統計的方法と理論の歩みよりが害せられるものではない。自分は経済理論と統計的方法とは必ず近き将来において一つのものとなるべきことを信ずるものである。即ち統計的方法は経済学に適当なる形に改造せられねばならず、又経済理論は統計の数字に適用する様に改良せられねばならぬ。

このことは極めて困難である。けだし我々は丁度、事物を転覆せしめながら何人かゞ歩いてゐる様な研究室で研究してゐる化学者と同じ地位にあるからである。この何人かといふのは経済学にとつては経済的事物の進行を乱しつゝある政治的事件を意味するに外ならない。けれどもしかし我々の科学の教へる所は実験によつて法則の発見に努めつゝある所の自然科学の教へる所と少しも変りがない。我々は我々の研究の素材たる経済生活から一定の経済法則を見出すことに努めてゐるものである。然しながら斯の如き経済法則は直に、事業の政策乃至高商の実際をより合理的にすることに役立つものとはいへない。科学はかくの如き目的をもつものではなく単にその一定の目的に対する手段を教へるものに外ならないのである。そしてこの方法としての理論は歴史的乃至統計的方法と相提携せねばならない。これは進行の時代が必ず果すべき重大な仕事である。

この試みについては今後もなほ幾多の失敗を経験せねばならぬかも知れぬ。然し我々はこれ等の幾多の失敗を通じてのみ成功への道を進み得るものである。【去月廿八日兼松講堂における講演要旨】
(「一橋新聞」 1931年2月9日号第1面より転載)

昭和六年三月

世界不況に就て

―特に米國の事情を參照したる―

日本經濟聯盟會

日本工業俱樂部

(非賣品)

(2)「世界不況に就いて―特に米国の事情を参照したる―」
(日本工業倶楽部、日本経済連盟共編)

昭和六年一月下旬獨逸「ボン」大學教授「ヨセフ・シュムペーター」博士(Joseph Schumpeter)米國「ハーヴァード」大學の講演を了へ來朝ありたるに際し當兩團體は一月二十九日日本工業倶樂部ニ同博士を招請し一場の講演を聽取したり仍ち本篇は同講演の速記錄英文並に邦譯なり。

昭和六年三月

日本經濟聯盟會
日本工業倶樂部

世界不況に就て

―― 特に米國の事情を參照したる ――

ヨセフ・シユムペーター教授述

會長並に諸君、私は皆樣の御親切なる歡迎を感謝致し度いと存じます。日本に參ります事は私の多年の宿望でありましたが、此度の訪問は愉快なる記憶となつて永遠に私の腦裏に殘るでありませう。今日私は皆樣が御自身で御選擇になつた此講演の題目よりも、もつと面白い問題に就いて御話したかつたのであります。

扨て、不景氣の來る度毎に、我々はそれを未曾有の不景氣であると思ふのが常でありますが、私の考へでは、此度の不景氣と殆んど選ぶところの無い深刻なものが前にも數囘襲來したと思ふのであります。例へば一八七三年及び一八九三年の兩度に襲來したものゝ如きは確に昨今のものと何等選ぶところなく、後者の如きは殊に米國に於て然りとします。然しながら我々が現在直面せる世界的不景氣は一種の特色を有つて居ります。卽ち我等の經濟難局はボルシエヴイズムと稱する友情の無い傍觀者に其成行を窺はれて

— 1 —

(2)「世界不況に就いて―特に米国の事情を参照したる―」
(日本工業倶楽部、日本経済連盟共編 pp.1–19)

居るのであります。我等は我等の經濟組織と全く其趣を異にする經濟組織が、現に露西亞に設立されて居ると云ふ事實と、現下の不景氣が相當の期間繼續するに於ては、各國の人々も自然此組織に望みを屬するに至るであらうと云ふ事を自覺せなければなりませぬ。

加之全世界の目下の情勢は、佛伊間の軋轢、印度に於ける英國の施政難、其他多くの政治的危難によつて益事態が惡化して居るのであります。これに反し一八七三年及び一八九三年には世界は全然平和狀態に在りました。成程そこには苦悶もあれば困惑もあつた事は事實に違ひありませんが、それでも當時の經濟組織は能く是に堪ふる事が出來ました。然し今日に於きましては我々は果して我經濟組織が能く此不況に堪え得るや否やと云ふ點に就いて確言が出來ません。斯かる情勢なるが故に、我人共に此不景氣を憂慮し之を齎したる主因を識らんと欲するのであります。然し我々が其主因の如何なるものなるかを究め得たとしても、我々は不景氣の立直しは出來ないかも知れません。然しながら釋明は少なくとも對策樹立の第一歩であります。

實業家にとつて最も重要な問題は、翌月の景氣を豫知する事と、新規擴張の爲めに準備を始む可きや否やと云ふ事を知ることであります。一九三一年に景氣の恢復を見るも

— 2 —

のと假定し得れば、大會社は將に或は原料、銅、鐵等を仕入れ、或は商品の註文其他の準備を爲すべき絕好の時期であります。然しながら反對に此不景氣が存續するものとすれば、斯る準備をなす者は益窮地に陷るものと云はねばなりません。

實業家が不景氣の考察をなす場合には、丁度其不景氣時代に限り廻り合せたのであつて他の不況時代には見る事の出來ない特殊の事件を目し、以て其不況の眞因となす傾向が濃厚であります。勿論現在の世界的不景氣は、起る必要もなければ又再發の豫想も付かない不幸なる情勢の結果として歷然たる特質を備へて居る事は事實であります。然し此事に就て論ずる前に、私は現下の世界的不況が全然是等特殊事情のみに起因するものでないと云ふ事を簡單に述べさせて頂き度いと思ひます。此度の不景氣には、もつと深い原因が在るのであつて、政治的波瀾とか、生產過剩とか云ふやうに、不景氣の情勢を惡化するやうな外面からの影響が無かつたにしても、早晚起るべき性質のものなのであります。

我々の經驗によつて明かである如く、實業界の景氣は「サイクル」即ち「循環期」と稱せられ、好景氣時代と不景氣時代が互に交代して居ます。此原因は何であるか、何故我產業生活は著實に發展しないか、何故に進歩は不景氣時代に妨げられるか。私は今日此問

— 3 —

題の理論迄も御話しする譯には行きませんが、問題の眞髓だけに觸れ度いと思ひます。申し上げる迄もなく、産業の發展は生産方法及び販賣方法の改善と、新商品の賣出しとに俟たなければなりません。經濟界に波紋を捲起すのは、卽ち此生産方法及び販賣方法の變化と、新商品の進出によるのであつて、此經濟界の混亂が平調に復するのは相當の期間を要します。而して此調整期を我々は不景氣時代と呼ぶのであります。

私は二三の好適例を擧げて此事を證明しようと思ひます。我々の生活樣式に最大更新を齎した物の一つは自動車であります。現世紀の初めに於てフォード氏が、一般需要者の求め得る程度の廉價な自動車の製作に著手したのは、實に恐ろしく困難な事業を始めたと云はざるを得ません。其創業時代に於て彼は其事業に要する資金の調達を得るや否やと云ふ事も判らなければ、又專門的立場から彼の大事業が成功するや否やと云ふ事も見當はつきませんでした。實際に於て彼は最大難關に逢着して居たのであります。卽ち前例もなければ、又模倣すべき他人の經驗の全く存在しない新しい經濟的時局を征服すべき場面に直面しました。而も彼はこれを實行し且つ成功したのであります。米國に於て將た又諸外國に於て、彼の廉價な自動車は大成功を收めました。此成功を目のあたり見た他の會社は、比較的容易に彼に追從模倣する事が出來ました。今日に於ては英佛獨

— 4 —

伊等の諸國に大衆向き自動車製作會社が設立せられ、驚くべき自動車の洪水が絶間なく全世界に向けて流出しつゝあります。實際に於て此種自動車は、最早日常生活の必需品となつて居ます。これが我等の經濟生活に一大革命を來す可きは、見易き道理であります。フォード氏の成功以來、ヂェネラル・モータース、クライスラー、ナツシュ其他の會社が皆廉價の自動車を製作しました。此種自動車を購求する者は、自己の經濟樣式の全部を變更せざるを得ません。從來は衣服とか、飲料とか云ふものに費して居た金を、今はタイヤーとか、ガソリンとか云ふものに振向けねばならぬのであります、自動車の進出により、鐵道の收入は減ずる、沿道の旅館の收入は増すと云つた工合であります。これが皆實業生活の困難を醸すのであつて、實業は總べて或方面は擴張し、或方面は制限して新局面に適應せなければなりませぬ。其結果が遂に不安時代の到來となり、實業家は最後に落付く結果を豫知するを得ず、又執るべき手段をも分らなくなるのであります。そこで我等が不景氣と稱する諸種の徴候が現はれるのであります。それで私の説明が充分に御解りになりましたならば、不景氣と云ふのは、「前の好景氣時代に製作された新らしい商品が、無理に需要口を求めて市場へ進出し、我々の經濟生活が、新しい需要と供給の均衡に適應する時期に過ぎない」といふ事も會得されるでありませう。

— 5 —

— 6 —

もう一つの實例は電氣事業であります。千九百十九年には合衆國に於て、一キロワット時の電力を發生せしむる爲めには、一キログラム半の石炭が必要でありました。今日では同じ電力を右の半分の石炭で發生せしむる事が出來ます。其れが爲め從來電力を用ひては利益にならなかつた多くの仕事に、自然電力を應用する事になるのであります。これは又石炭の需要減退を來す原因にもなるのであります。これが又炭業不振の原因の一部を説明しますが、石炭は我々も知る如く、運輸業や、其他幾多の産業上の用途からも驅逐されつゝあります。此結果が又石炭採鑛事業を、根本から變革せしめ、斯界の投資が無益に終る一方、他の産業は投資を得て擴張されます。これを私は「調整」と稱するのであります。も一つの例は紡績事業であります。米國に於ける綿絲紡績事業に就て觀るに、ニュー・イングランド諸州から南部諸州へ移動の傾向が見えます。然しこれは必らずしも從來ニュー・イングランドで工場を運轉して居た同一會社が南部へ移轉するのだとのみ限りません。新資本家が新紡績工場を設立し、ニュー・イングランド諸州の工場より、安く賣るのであつて、後者は不景氣の有らゆる徵候を呈するのであります。同様にランカシャーの産業は、同一傾向の爲めに衰微して來ました。これは安價な綿絲製品が、日增しに多く印度に於て産出せられるからであります。

— 7 —

然るが故に、進歩其ものが第一に好景氣時代を現出し、次に其結果として不況時代を招きます。然しながら違つた革新や、異なつた種類の産業的及び商業的進歩が、甚だ相違せる方法を以て實業界に影響を及ぼすのであります。例へば新らしい鐵道が敷設されると、其鐵道の貫通する地方の萬事を變化せしめます。即ち新しい産業の勃興も新らしい需要の中心地、各地方間の競爭の新情勢等により、全産業組織が革命化されるのであります。然し此影響は甚だ徐々に來ます。先づ第一に建設であるが、之が中々年數を要するので、綿絲紡績工場等の如く(少なくとも私の國では)今日僅か六ヶ月の間に設立されるもの等とは大に趣を異にします。第二には新産業が起り、新らしい町が出來、其影響を感ずるやうになるのも、中々手間取るのですが、他の變化に於きましては、殆んど即時に其勢力を感ぜしめるのであります、それで好況時代と不況時代とが交互に完全なる秩序を保つて現れる事を期待する事は出來ません。否反對に或種の改革は長期に亘る好況不況を齎し、他の種の改革は短期の好況不況を同時に齎すかも知れません。而して此有らゆる變動は、各自が上向きと下向きの兩變動を有するから、波に喩へる事が出來るのでありますが、皆同時に進行して行くのであります。これは恰も大洋で大波と小波とが同時に起こつたり消えたりするやうなものであります。今のところでは我々は三種の「波」を區別することが出來ます。第一には甚だ長い波があります。それは十八世紀に機械紡績と共に勃興し、一八一一年頃に最高潮に達し一八四二年頃に衰頽しました。第二の長い波は一八七三年頃に最高潮に達し、一八九四年頃に衰頽した。電氣と化學の發明によつて起こつた第三の長い波は、一九一四年から一九二〇年迄の間に高潮に達した。世界大戰の爲めに其頂點が朦朧として居るので、私は明確に何れの年だと指示する事が出來ません。

故に我々は今其大きな波の下向期に面して居るのであるから、こゝ十年位は好景氣よりも不景氣の方が餘計に現はれるといふ事を豫期せなければなりませぬ。

然し科學は七年から十一年間位繼續する別個の「波」の在る事を發見しました。此經濟危急の年代は、一八二五年、一八三七年、一八四七年、一八五七年、一八六六年、一八七三年、一八八四年、一八九六年、一九〇七年であります。若し世界大戰が無かつたならば、同種の不況が、一九一五年にも來たでありませう。此長さは平均大凡十年であります。

第三には、我々は大凡四十個月に亙る、短期循環期を發見しました。此事實を知る事は一九三〇年の猛烈な不景氣の理由の一部を知るに必要な事であります。一九三〇年は

— 8 —

恰も此四十個月循環期の最沈衰期に當つて居たのであります。加之同年は「長波」の下向期でもありました。同年は又十個年循環期の下向期にも當つて居ました。斯の如く我々は今のところ以上三つの「波」を區別し得るのでありますが、一九三〇年には一九〇七年と同様に、此全部が皆不景氣の狀態にあつたのであります。これで一九三〇年度不景氣の酷烈の度合が分り、又一九三一年には幾分の景氣が持直すだらうといふ豫測に、十分の理由のある事を證明します。それは四十個月循環期が再び上騰期にあるからであります。一九三一年と云はず、少なくとも多數循環期中の一つが好況を表示する場合には、有らゆる循環期が相互に不景氣を益深刻化する時代に比較すれば、我々は自然情況は好轉するものと豫期する事が出來ます。然し特殊の事情が事態を惡化せしめなかつたならば、此不景氣は餘程緩和されたであらうと云ふのは、全く事實であります。私は此特殊の事情の内の比較的重要なことに就て述べませう。

先づ第一に、世界到る處に起こつた農業不況は、事態を餘程惡化せしめました。此農業の不況は二つの異なつた原因に基くのであります。一つの原因は單に産業發展の一例證に過ぎません。例へば日本では不況の原因になるやうな事柄で、如何な事が起こつたかと申しますと、比較的新らしい臺灣及び朝鮮地方に米の大量生産が行はれて居たこと

— 9 —

— 10 —

が分ります。此米の大量生産は、日本の増加する人口に食糧を供給するのであるから、結局は日本にとつては一大祝福たるを失はず、又一大偉業であつた事は論を俟ちません。然しながら朝鮮に於て多量の廉價な米を産出すると同時に、日本内地の農家は打撃を蒙るので、適宜の策を講ずる必要を生ずるのであります。

小麥の場合も同樣であります。新しい發明、殊に收穫機械の發明や、合衆國西部諸州の乾燥地帶農耕技術の進歩は、一ブツシエル三十仙の割合で小麥を生産し得るやうになりました。ニユー・イングランド諸州は到底競爭が出來ないから、小麥の生産を全然止めなければなりませぬ。此新情勢に農村が適應する徑路は苦痛甚だしく、實に峻烈であります。ニユー・イングランド地方を自動車で廻つて見ると、家屋は滅茶々々になり、物置や厩は蛇の棲む所となり、此遺棄されたる農村を視ると、實に感慨無量であります。進歩の車輪は容赦なく生産者の體を蹂躪つて行く。而してこれが卽ち進歩が不景氣を齎す徑路なのであります。

然しながら此農業不況は、進歩が無かつたにしても當然起こつたのであります。卽ち世界大戰中に於ける玉蜀黍やパンに對する恐ろしい過度な需要の爲め、合衆國及び其他の國に於ける生産能力が增大されました。其れが爲め今日我々は疑もなく生産過剩に直

— 11 —

面して居ます。ナポレオン戰爭後に於ける英國も丁度同じ狀態でした。一八一五年に平和が恢復すると、玉蜀黍が波蘭や獨逸から來ました。其結果戰爭中耕作されて居た大部分の土地は維持し難くなりました。我々が現在目擊して居る不景氣は同じ現象で、農民階級が甚だ苦痛を感ずるのであります。丁度損失を招きつゝある商賣のやうに、總ての物が清算さるべきもので、其他に救助の途は無いのであります。

第二には大多數の國は、戰前の金貨本位に復歸せんとする金融政策を執つて居るが、これは疑も無く實業界の窮地を惡化せしめたのであります。一部人士は金の産出不充分の故を以て、金の逼迫を稱へる者さへ在ります。然し此論は全く正しいとは稱せられませぬ。將來に於ては金の逼迫があるかも知れませんが、今日に於て世界に存在する金の分量は、或二三の國が必要以上の金を吸收せない限り、四割の金準備の割合で、一九二八年と同樣の物價を維持して行くのに充分であります。

然し二三の國では、其國の通貨單位の購買力の示すよりも高率で貨幣を安定せしめました。大戰以來の不景氣の徵候の大部分は、此政策の結果に外ならぬのであります。一九二五年に於ける英國の金本位法と、これを齎した政策とは、疑もなく一九二七年に英國に出現すべかりし好景氣を抑壓し、英國が目下直面して居る不景氣を惡化せしめたので

あります。

通貨膨脹期が絶頂に達した後の通貨安定其のものが多く不景氣時代を招致するのでありますが、若し通貨單位の購買力より高率で通貨安定を圖れば、經濟界の危機を招きます。卽ち負債償還は困難となり、諸會社の收入は萎縮し、輸入は奬勵され、輸出は困難となります。一例を擧げると、米國品を日本で賣捌する輸入商は、日本の國内物價水準に相當するだけ、餘分の「圓」を得るが、彼は此圓をもつと高率で「弗」に換算するから一定のプレミアムを、稼ぐのであります。同時に輸出はこれに相應じて損失を招くのであります。その結果は餘計な失業者を出す事になります。

然し私はもつとよく說明を致し度いのであります。私は通貨を戰前の平價に安定せしむる政策が、間違つて居ると云ふのではありません。私は只、それは不景氣の原因になると云ふのであります。其れは或は國家の威信等に資する處があり、相當價値があるかも知れません。私は敢て英國や日本の政策を批評しようとするものではありません。私は只其利益が如何なるものであつても、其れには高價の代償を拂はねばならぬと云ふのであります。

も一つの不景氣惡化の原因は、獨逸の支拂ふ賠償金と、聯合國の戰時債務であります。

— 12 —

獨逸には過剰輸出の外には、賠償金を支拂ふに必要なる爲替を買ふべき方法がありません。獨逸が輸出を盛にすればする程、世界の市場を壓迫し、輸入を減ずれば減ずる程、獨逸は貧弱な買主になる譯であります。其れで賠償金支拂の方法として、此二樣の方法の何れを採用しても、必然的に世界市場の困惑を增すのであります。此事實は段々と、米國に於て了解されて來て居ます。

第四の點は、或國の財政政策が甚だ過激で、資本主義制度の根本と相容れざるものがある事であります。其制度其のものは善いかも知れないし、又惡いかも知れない。私は其點を論じて居るのではありません。然しながら經濟的に見て、高率の累進稅は國民の貯蓄と、事業の積立金とを喰ひ込むのであるから、決して永く財政を正規に維持出來るものではありません。從つて此種の過激な政策が續く間は、不景氣は常に好景氣よりも屢々來ませう。而も此過激政策の放棄さるべき機會は全然見當が付かないのであります。高率にして累進的な稅金は又バランスの海外移動を招致します。これは英國と獨逸に於て最も著しい。これを一般に資本の輸出と稱して居るのでありますが、丁度賠償金支拂と同じ結果を齎します。

扨て、御話すると甚だ誤解を招き易い問題でありますが、是非申上げなければならな

— 13 —

い點があります。他でもありません、私は賃銀の上る事に心から賛成します。然し實を申せば、これを云ふのは私の義務であるから申しますが、多くの國に於て賃銀は有らゆる勞働を通じて、勞力に對する報酬として兩立し得ない迄に高くなつて居ります。故に勞働賃銀の水準は、失業と一般不景氣の原因の中に加へなければなりません。英國と獨逸に於て勞銀の低下を許さないのは、勞働組合の政治的壓迫であります。賃銀は勞働の値段である。若し此特殊の値段が低下せなければ、自然に全商品は賣れない事になる。英國と獨逸では賃銀は政治的問題であります。米國に於ては賃銀の適應を阻止するのは政治ではなく、産業家自身の誤謬からであります。米國の事業家は、高い賃銀を拂ふ事は、消費者の購買力を增進するから事業の爲めであると云ふ思想に深く捉はれて居る。從つて彼等自身が高給論者であり賃銀の低落を好まぬ。然しながら、高い賃銀は好景氣の結果ではあるが、決して好景氣の原因ではないといふ事は、明瞭にして置く必要があります。

こゝに當然下らなければならぬ値段で、中々下らないのが一つ在ります。短期金利が大へん安いのは事實であります。紐育に於ける今日の割引歩合は、聯邦準備銀行始まつて以來の最低率であります。然し低率な割引歩合は、普通ならば長期金利を引下げるも

— 14 —

のであるのに、現今では長期金利は未だ中々高い。從つて債券は容易に賣れないのであります。これには二三の理由が在る。資本家が甚だ苦い經驗を嘗めた事があるので、大に警戒して居るのであります。それで債券に對する高金利は、最高率時代に比すれば、實際に於て幾分低下するにはしたが、其れでも未だ下る可き處まで下つて居ません。賃銀は勞働の値段であり、利子は資金の値段であります。兩方が高きに過ぐれば、産業は繁榮しません。

其上重要な商品の中には、其値段が人爲的に釣上げられて居る爲めに、自然的調整を缺ぐものが相當に多い爲めに、不景氣は惡化されるのであります。此例と致しましては、護謨、銅、及びコーヒーを擧ぐれば澤山であります。此人爲的値段の釣上策は、其れが旨く行つても又失敗に終つても、結局經濟的難局を齎します。若し其れが旨く行けば需要が減ずる、失敗すれば不規則な動搖が伴ふので、生産費を精密に計算する事が不可能になります。物品の價格を人爲的に調節する事が賢明な策であるかどうか、大に熟考すべき問題であります。此方法が失敗に歸すれば、事態は此方法を講ぜないよりも、遙かに惡くなるのであります。例へば、護謨栽培者がスチーブンソン法によつて、結局儲けたかどうか私は知りません。コーヒーの値段を加減せんとする企ては、前には數年間旨

— 15 —

く行つた事もあります。然しこれはコーヒー耕作面積の擴張を來し、結局事態は前よりも惡くなつたのであります。

銅の形勢も面白い。米國には一大聯合が行はれて居り、此團體はコンゴーに於ける白耳義銅業者と一つの協定を結ぶ事に成功し、最後に此米國の銅業トラストは、チリーの銅山をも支配するやうになりました。一九二七年から一九二八年にかけて、事實上何等の競爭者もなく、銅價は騰りました。然し此値段では、新鑛山を開く事が有利であつたので、久しからずして破滅的値段の暴落が到來しました。

私は、今迄述べました處によりまして、我々が目擊して居る現象の、大凡九割迄の原因を構成するところの諸原因を列擧したと思ひますが、未だ他にも事態を惡化せしめる原因があります。一九二九年には紐育の株式取引所に、あの有名な大瓦落が來ました、普通ならば株式の瓦落は、事業界に重大な影響を及ぼすものではありません。投機家が損失を招くといふ事は、大した結果を齎らさないが、米國で瓦落が起つたのは、誰でも株をやつて居り、誰でも株取引の儲けで生活して居たからであります。必然の結果として、事業界は此需要に適應して居たので、利益が損失に急轉すると、これが需要品賣捌に一大障害を來す事は明かな事であります。

— 16 —

次に月賦販賣制度も亦相當に非難されて居ますが、然しこれは少々大袈裟にし過ぎた感があります。自動車事業界の月賦販賣で、決濟の附かなかつた部分の如何にも少なかつたのは驚く程でありました。然し此月賦販賣政策も、今回の不景氣に何等かの影響を與へて居るかも知れません。物品を月賦で買ふと、買ふ可き金の貯蓄の出來ない內に求め得るから、此制度が無ければ出來ないものを、此制度が在れば當り前よりも早く手に入れる事が出來る。月賦制があるから自動車は一年も早く買へる。だから其年には人爲的需要が實現した譯になる。第一の自動車を月賦で買ひ込むと、持たない時のやうには買へなくなる。こんな風で月賦制は、單に一時的賣上高を增すに過ぎない。若し生產者が此一時的賣行きを永續的のものと誤解したならば、確に將來の賣行について間違つた豫想を抱くやうになりませう。

高率の關稅も貿易の常軌に障害を與へるから、又大に不景氣に關係があります。卽ち此の種の關稅が無ければ起り得ない新產業を起さしめます。而も此種產業の多くは、基礎薄弱に終り經濟難局を招く傾きがあります。私は米國に於ける一九三〇年度の關稅法は、不景氣惡化の一原因であると斷言するに憚らぬのであります。銀價の暴落も亦不景氣助成の一原因たるを失はぬ。然し以上述べた諸原因の重要性は限定されたものに過ぎ

— 17 —

ません。

こゝに於て私は最後に前途の豫想をして見たい、否、一九三一年には不景氣は全く常軌に恢復する迄には到らないが、少なくとも各國に於て、不景氣は幾分好轉すると先に豫想致しました其理由を申上げ度いと思ひます。私が皆樣に提示致しました諸原因を一瞥なさつたならば、其原因の中には自動的に治癒するものも有れば、永續するものも有る事が御解りになりませう。實際既によくなつたものもあります。然し政治が經濟的理論の進むが儘に委して置くや否やといふ事は疑問の餘地があります。そして多分此不景氣惡化の原因は大部分此儘繼續するかも知れません。然しこれ等の理由があつても、我々は諸種の事情が久しからずして好轉するものと豫期する事が出來ます。即ち米國に於ける金利は既に相當長い間安かつた。此低金利は必らず株式市場に影響し、取引を奬勵するのみならず、又建築界の活動を刺戟するでありませう。現に重要商品にあつては、需要恢復の曙光が見えて來ました。實際一個月前には銅市場に活氣の閃が見えました、此活氣は再び崩れましたが、諸般の事物に蘇生の兆が又見えて來ました。ユナイテツド・ステーツ・スチール會社の註文殘高も段々に増えて行きます。而して最も有用なハーバード・インデツキスも不景氣恢復が、かなり近い内に來る事を示して居ます。それですから、

— 18 —

第一には株式市場に、第二には建築及び設備用品の事業に、最後に實業全般に、經濟的活動復活を豫期する事が出來ます。

其他忘れてならない事は、一九三〇年には一般の意氣が大に銷沈したので新らしい註文は殆んど無く、殊に米國に於て甚しかつたといふ事實であります。生産は消費の後から重い脚を運んで居たが、此事自體がそれ相當に恢復の原因になるのであります。私は失職者の數も實質的に減少するだらうし、總べての狀態が、幾らか正常な外觀を呈するだらうと思ふのであります。然し私の此豫測は經濟的立場から觀たものであると云ふ事を御忘れ無いやうに願ひます。私は敢て世界の政治に就て云々しようと思ひませぬ。全然望みの無い事もない將來も、政治的及び社會的不安の爲めに勿論臺無しになるかも知れませぬ。　（完）

— 19 —

THE WORLD DEPRESSION

WITH SPECIAL REFERENCE TO

THE UNITED STATES OF AMERICA

BY

Professor Dr. JOSEPH SCHUMPETER

March 1931

JAPAN ECONOMIC FEDERATION

AND

INDUSTRY CLUB OF JAPAN

TOKYO

(2) "THE WORLD DEPRESSION WITH SPECIAL REFERENCE TO THE UNITED STATES OF AMERICA"
JAPAN ECONOMIC FEDERATION AND INDUSTRY CLUB OF JAPAN TOKYO p.1-14.

THE WORLD DEPRESSION
WITH SPECIAL REFERENCE TO
THE UNITED STATES OF AMERICA

Address by Professor Dr. Joseph Schumpeter before the members of the Japan Economic Federation and the Industry Club of Japan.

January 29th, 1931.

Introductory remarks by President Baron Takuma Dan.

Mr. President and Gentlemen,

I want to thank you for your kind welcome. It has been an old wish of mine to come to Japan and I shall always remember my visit with pleasure. I wish, however, I could talk to you about a more pleasant subject than the one you yourselves have chosen.

Whenever we have a depression, we think it is the worst one we have ever had, but there were some depressions before the present one which I do think were about as bad. For instance, the crises of 1873 and 1893, the latter one especially in the United States, were certainly not much milder. But the present world wide depression has one peculiarity, and this consists in the fact that our troubles are watched by an unfriendly onlooker, by Bolshevism. We must realize that an economic system different to ours is actually set up in Russia, and that men in all countries will naturally look to that alternative if our crisis should last a sufficiently long time.

Moreover, the situation all over the world is made much worse by the fact that there are so many political danger points

— 2 —

such as the tension between France and Italy, the trouble England has in India, etc. In 1873 and 1893 the world was entirely at peace. Suffering there was and difficulties were there, yet the system could stand them. Today we cannot be so sure of this, and it is therefore with some anxiety that we ask the question, what are the outstanding factors which have brought about this depression? If we succeed in understanding them, we may yet be unable to cure it, but explanation is at least a first step towards forming a remedial policy.

For the business man, the most important question is what is to be expected of the next months, and whether he ought to begin to prepare for a new era of expansion or not. If we may assume that 1931 will witness a revival, then indeed it is high time for most big concerns to replenish their stocks of raw material, copper, steel, to place orders and so on. If on the other hand the depression should last they will be all the worse off, if they do so.

When a business man looks at a depression, he is always inclined to attribute it to particular events which have come about just this one time and which are peculiar to this depression and to no other. It is, of course, true that our world-depression presents features which really are nothing else but the result of unfortunate circumstances and which need not have happened and cannot be expected to recur. Yet before turning to these I want you first to follow me in a short argument to prove the present world-depression is not entirely due to such special factors. There are deeper causes underlying it and it would have come about in any case, even if no outside influences, such as political troubles, overabundant harvests and so on, had occurred to aggravate the situation.

— 3 —

Business life, as we know from experience, displays alternating periods of prosperity and depression which we call "cycles." What is the cause of this fact, why does not our industrial life simply grow steadily, why is progress interrupted by periods of depression? I cannot go into the theory of the subject, but I want to give you the gist of the matter. Industrial progress consists of course in the improvement of productive and commercial method and in the introduction of new commodities. It is this change in method and this introduction of new commodities, what creates disturbances which take time to be absorbed into the normal state of economic affairs, and these times of adjustment we call depressions.

I will show this by giving a few characteristic examples. One of the greatest innovations in our life has been caused by the motor car. When at the beginning of this century Mr. Ford undertook to produce cheap motor cars, within the reach of vast masses of consumers, he did something tremendously difficult. He did not know whether he would find financial support, whether technically his huge enterprise would work, in fact he was faced with that most difficult task, which consists in mastering an entirely new situation, for which there was no precedent and where nothing could be copied from experience of other people. He did it and he succeeded. In America and many other countries his cheap motor car has had a tremendous success. With this success before their eyes other concerns found it comparatively easy to do the same. Today in Germany, in Italy, in France, in England there are a number of concerns making motor cars for mass consumption, and a tremendous stream of motor cars pours out continuously all over the world, these motors have become now really a necessity of every day life. But it is

— 4 —

easy to see that this must cause quite a revolution in economic life. After Mr. Ford was successful, General Motors, Chrysler, Nash and others produced cheaper cars. The people who buy these motor cars, change their whole way of life. They now consume tyres and gasoline instead of, perhaps, clothes and wine. The takings of the railroads fall off, and the revenue of inns on the roads increases. All this means disturbances in business life, which must adapt itself to a new condition, expanding in some directions, restricting in others. The result is a period of uncertainty in which business men do not know yet what the ultimate consequences will be and how they are to act. Hence those symptoms, which make up what we call a depression, and if I have made myself clear you will understand when I say that a depression is only a period in which the new things created in the previous period of prosperity are forcing their way into consumption and in which economic life adapts itself to a new equilibrium. Of course since 1921 we have had many such changes.

Another example is the electric industry. In 1919, in the United States, 1-1/2 kg. of coal was necessary to produce 1 kilowatt hour of power. Now electric energy is produced by about half of that. This naturally has the effect that electric energy can be employed for many purposes for which it was not profitable to use it before. It also has the effect that the demand for coal falls off. This partly explains the depression in the coal trade, which as we know is also being displaced in many other lines, in shipping, in many industries and so on. Now this in turn alters the whole position of coal mining, where many investments prove useless, while other industries invest and expand. This is what I mean by "adjustment."

— 5 —

Another example is the textile industry. In the cotton industry in the United States we observe migration from New England to the Southern States. Now this does not necessarily mean that the same concerns which used to operate mills in New England move to the South, but new people open up new cotton mills down there, undersell the industry of the New England States, so that naturally the latter will display all the symptoms of a depression. Similarly, the industry of Lancashire has lost ground because of the same tendency, because cheaper cotton goods are now being produced to an increasing extent, in India.

Progress itself, therefore, creates first the period of prosperity and secondly as a consequence of it the period of depression. But different innovations and different kinds of industrial and commercial progress act in very different ways on business life. For instance, the building of a new railroad changes everything in the country through which it goes. It revolutionizes the whole industrial structure, by creating new industries, new centres of consumption, new conditions of competition between different places. But this influence comes about very slowly. First, it must be built, which takes years whilst a cotton mill, at least in my own country, can now be set it up in six months. Secondly, the new industries or towns can come into existence, and make their influence felt, only by slow degrees, whilst other changes exert their influence almost immediately. Therefore, we shall not expect to find that periods of prosperity and periods of depression succeed each other with perfect regularity. On the contrary, some improvements may cause long time prosperities and depressions, whilst others may simultaneously cause short ones. And all these movements, each of which consists of an up grade and a down grade movement and may therefore be compared to a

— 6 —

wave, will go on together at the same time, just as on the Ocean big waves and small waves rise and fall at the same time. So far, we have been able to distinguish three kinds of "waves." There is, first, a very long one. It rose in the 18th century with the rise of the mechanical spinning and weaving; it culminates about 1811 and comes down in 1842. The second reaches its peak in 1873 and comes down in 1894. The third long wave, the wave of the great inventions in electricity and chemistry, culminated between 1914 and 1920. I cannot say exactly in what year, because the peak is blurred by the World War.

Hence, we are now in the down grade of a big wave, and we must expect for another ten years that depressions will be more marked than prosperity.

But science had discovered another wave which lasts from 7 to 11 years. The dates of the crises are 1825, 1837, 1847, 1857, 1866, 1873, 1884, 1896, 1907, and perhaps there would have been one in 1915 if the World War had not prevented it. The average duration is about 10 years.

Third, we have discovered a short cycle of about 40 months length. Now, all this is important to know because it partly explains the severity of the depression in 1930. That year has been the trough of a 40-months cycle. It was moreover, on the down grade of a long wave. And it was also on the down grade of a 10-years cycle. So the three cycles, which we are so far able to distinguish, have all been in the depression phase 1930, just as they were in 1907. This explains the severity of the depression and justifies the prophecy that 1931 will witness a substantial improvement, for the 40-months cycle will be on the up grade again in 1931, and whenever one at least of the cycles displays prosperity, conditions can naturally be expected to be

— 7 —

better as compared with a state of things in which the depressions of all the cycles intensify each other. Yet it is quite true that the depression would have been much milder if other circumstances had not aggravated it. We will mention the more important of them.

In the first place, the agrarian depression everywhere in the world, makes matters much worse than they otherwise would be. This agrarian depression is accounted for by two different things. One cause is simply another example of industrial progress. For instance, what has happened in Japan is that the comparatively new countries of Formosa and Korea, have been cultivating rice on a large scale. In the long run this is a great blessing to Japan as it will help to feed her increasing population, and of course it was a great achievement. But as you produce in Korea so much cheaper rice, the grower in Japan proper suffers, and readjustments will be necessary.

The case with wheat is similar. New inventions especially in harvesting-machines and the progress of the technique of farming in the arid regions of the west of the United States has made it possible to produce wheat at 30 cents a bushel. New England cannot compete and will have to drop wheat growing. This process of adaptation is serious, full of suffering. Few things have impressed me so much as these derelict farms, which one sees when motoring through New England—the houses falling to pieces, fences dropping down, barns and stables inhabited by snakes. The wheels of progress go over the bodies of the producers. And this is how progress produces depression.

However, there would be an agriculture depression even if there had not been any improvements. The reason is that the panic demand for corn and bread during the war extended

— 8 —

productive capacity in the United States and elsewhere, and we have now an undoubtedly overgrown production. It was the same in England after the Napoleonic wars. When peace was reestablished in 1815 and corn came in from Poland and Germany, a large part of the land which had been taken into cultivation during the war, became untenable. It is a similar phenomenon that we are witnessing now. The agrarian classes will suffer a great deal. The whole thing will have to be liquidated, just as losing businesses are liquidated, and there is no help for it.

Secondly, the monetary policy of most countries trying to reestablish pre-war gold standards, has undoubtedly added to the difficulties of the business situation. Some people even speak of a stringency of gold owing to insufficient gold production. This however is not quite correct. Perhaps there will be stringency of gold at some future time, but at present the world's monetary stock of gold would be sufficient to keep up the price level of 1928 on the basis of a 40 per cent gold reserve, at least if some countries did not absorb more gold than they want.

But some countries have stabilized their currency at a point higher than that indicated by the purchasing power of their monetary units. This policy is responsible for a great part of the depressive symptoms ever since the war. The English Gold Standard Act of 1925 and the policy which led up to it undoubtedly weighted down the prosperity which she would have had in 1927, and aggravated the depression she is having now.

Already the mere fact of stabilization following on the top of a period of inflation may and often does create a depression, but if you stabilize at a value higher than the purchasing power of your monetary unit, you produce a crisis: Debts are more difficult to pay, receipts of concerns dwindle, imports are en-

— 9 —

couraged and exports made more difficult. The importer who sells say an American commodity in Japan gets as many yen as correspond to your internal price level, but he can change these yen into dollars at a higher rate and so gets a premium, whilst exports are correspondingly penalized. The consequence is more unemployment than there otherwise would be.

But let me be quite explicit. I do not say the policy of stabilizing any currency at pre-war parity is wrong, I only say it causes a depression; it may be conducive to national prestige and all that, and so may be quite worth while. I do not presume to criticize either the English or the Japanese policy, I only say that whatever the advantages may be, they are dearly bought.

Another aggravating factor is the German reparations and the interallied debts. Germany has no other means to buy the exchange necessary for the payments but an export surplus. If she exports more, her exports weigh on the world markets, and if she imports less she is a worse buyer than she would otherwise be. And either of these ways to meet the reparation claims must necessarily add to the difficulties of the world markets. This is being more and more understood in America.

The fourth point is that the fiscal policy of some countries is so very radical, as to be incompatible with the necessities of the capitalist system. That policy may in itself be good or bad, I am not criticising it, but economically a highly progressive taxation cuts into savings and reserves and makes it impossible for the financial mechanism to function normally. As long as this radical policy persists, and I do not see any chance of its being abandoned, we shall always have more depressions and less prosperity than we should otherwise have. High and progressive taxation also leads to the transference of balances,

— 10 —

especially from England and Germany, to other countries. This is usually called export of capital, and it acts exactly as reparation payments do.

There is one point, which must be mentioned although in mentioning it, it is hardly possible to avoid misunderstanding. I welcome with all my heart any rise in wages, yet it is incumbent upon me, if I am to speak the truth, to say that in many countries wages are higher than is compatible with the full employment of all laborers, so that the level of wages must be listed among the causes both of unemployment and of the depression generally. In England and Germany it is the political pressure of the trade unions which does not allow wages to go down. Wages are the price of labor. If this particular price does not go down, naturally the whole of the commodity will not be sold. In England and Germany wages are a political matter. In America it is not politics but an error of the industrialist himself which prevents the adaptation of wages. The American business man is so imbued with the idea that paying high wages helps industry by increasing the purchasing power of consumers, that he is himself in favor of high wages and does not like to cut them down. But it ought to be clear that high wages can be the result of prosperity, but never its cause.

There is another price which won't go down so much as it ought to. It is true that the interest rate on short time money is very low. The discount rate in New York is the lowest in the history of the Federal Reserve Banking system, but whilst normally the lower discount rate creates cheap long time rates, interest on long time loans is very high still, and bonds are difficult to sell. There are several reasons for this. Capitalists have had such bad experiences that they are cautious. So the higher rate of

— 11 —

interest on bonds has indeed been a little reduced as compared with the peak but not anything like as much as would be necessary. Wages are the price of labor, interest is the price of capital. If both are too high, industry cannot prosper.

The depression is made worse, furthermore, by the fact that quite a number of prices of important commodities have been artificially regulated and therefore lack adjustment. I need only quote rubber, copper, coffee. These regulations of price create difficulties, both if they work and if they break down. If they work, consumption is curtailed, if they break down, irregular movements follow which make it impossible to calculate costs with precision. It is a matter to ponder over, whether it is a wise policy to regulate prices. If the thing breaks down the situation is much worse than it would otherwise have been. I don't know whether for instance the rubber plantations have been in the long run benefited by the Stephenson Act. The pleasure of higher rubber price was short. The attempt to regulate the price of coffee has previously worked for years. But it brought about a further extension of the area of coffee plantations, in the end things are worse than before.

The copper situation is interesting. There is the great American combine; furthermore it succeeded in making an agreement with the Belgian interests of the Congo, and finally the American copper trust also controlled the copper mines of Chile. In 1927–8 there was practically no competition and the price went up. But at this price it was profitable to open new mines, and it did not take long for a catastrophic slump to come about.

I think that I have enumerated the factors of the situation which will account for let us say about 90 per cent of the phenomena which we observe. Yet there are other elements of

— 12 —

the business situations, which aggravate condition. In 1929 there was the famous crash on the New York Stock Exchange. Normally, a crash does not seriously affect business. The fact that speculators lose money has not as a rule very great consequences. But what happened in America was this: Everyone was speculating and as everyone speculated so everyone lived on the gains he or she made on the stock exchange. Naturally industry adapted itself to this demand, and when gains turned suddenly into losses it is obvious that this must have seriously interfered with the sale of consumers' goods.

The installment selling has also been blamed. But this is probably an exaggeration. It is astonishing how small a percentage of the installment payments in the motor car industry have failed to be met. Yet the practice of installment selling may have something to do with this crisis. If you buy a thing on installments you can buy it before you have saved up the money, therefore you can buy it earlier than you would if there were no installment plan. Motor cars could be bought a year earlier because of the installment plan, and an artificial demand was displayed during that year. After you have bought your first automobile on installments you do not go on buying more of them than you otherwise would. Hence the installment plan increases sales only temporarily. Now if producers mistake this temporary demand for a lasting one, this will certainly lead to erroneous expectations as to future sales.

High tariffs too have much to do with the depression owing to the fact that they impede the normal channels of trade. They create industries which would otherwise not have been created and which are likely to remain weak and to create difficulties. I have no hesitation in saying that the American Tariff Act of

— 13 —

1930, was one aggravating cause of the situation. The drop in silver is another. But all these factors are only of limited importance.

Let me sum up and make a prediction, or rather give you the reasons for the prediction which I have made, that in 1931 things will get better in almost all countries, although not yet entirely to normal. If you look through the list of factors which I have put before you you will find that there are some troubles which will automatically remedy themselves and others which will last. There are a few which have already got better. But a doubt may be permitted, whether politics will allow economic reason to have its way and perhaps most of these "aggravating circumstances" will remain as they are. Yet in spite of this we may expect things to get better soon. The rate of interest in America has now been down for quite a time, and this must have some encouraging influence on the stock exchange activity. It will have the effect of stimulating building activity. We see already little signs of a reviving demand for basic commodities. So there was about two months ago a little spurt in the copper market; it relapsed but things are showing signs of life. The unfilled orders of the United States Steel Corporation are increasing. And the Harvard Index, which is the most useful one, points to revival being fairly close at hand. We can expect therefore a revival of economic activity, first on the stock exchange then in the industries of construction and equipment, and finally, in business in general.

You must not forget, too, that during 1930, especially in the United States, discouragement was so great that hardly any orders were placed. Production has been lagging behind consumption. This itself will cause a modest revival. I think the

— 14 —

number of unemployed will be materially reduced and that things will acquire a somewhat more normal look. But it should be borne in mind that this prediction is an economic one. I do not presume to judge the politics of the world and political and social unrest may of course spoil what may be otherwise a not unpromising future.

（23）

恐慌の理論

ジェー・エー・シュムペーター

獨逸ボン大學教授、前墺國大藏大臣ジエー・エー・シュムペーター博士一九三一年一月卅日東京帝國大學に於ける講演

學長、同僚諸教授並びに學生諸君私は先づ第一に諸君に話掛くる機會を得たことを心から喜んで居ることを申上げ度い。實際私は久しく之を望んで居た。そして今そう出來るのを喜んで居る、私の希望から云へば諸君に近づくためには數回の講演をせねばならないのだが、不幸私は僅か三週間しか此の美はしき貴國に過し得ない、三週間日本に來る人があればその人は又少しは景勝の地や日本の舊蹟を見たいと思ふことを諸君は認めてくださることと思ふ。私は勿論箱根山、日光其他名勝の地を見物せねばならぬ。

私は此の二時間に私が希ふ程ではなくても何か少し諸君に役立つことを爲し遂げて見たいと衷心希ふのである。

我々は茲に論題として、經濟學が爲し得又はなし得ない種々の研究を見通すのに本當に役立つ問題を選んだ、即ち恐慌理論に於ては我々は實際にあらゆる統計的方法及あらゆる歴史的知識を用ひ

（3）「恐慌の理論」

（「経済往来」第5巻第3号 1931. 3. 1, pp. 23–38. 一橋大学附属図書館所蔵）

（24）

なければならないのである。それ故恐慌の研究こそ諸君が單に此の問題のみを理解する許りでなく更に經濟學一般をも理解し得るが如き問題の一である。

諸君の爲めに私は此の問題の研究に關する二三の示唆を與へることから始めよう。勿論御承知の通り恐慌に關しては驚くべき澤山の文獻がある。私は既に此の問題を研究して居られる方々に斯く初歩的な話をすることをお詫びし度い。然し單純なことから始めて次第に複雜に詳説するに至らしめやう。先づ二つの有名な書物を擧げよう。

ミッチェルは彼の『景氣循環論』（Wesley C. Mitchell; Business Cycles. Vol. I. The Problem and its setting. I.ed. 1927）に於てアメリカのあらゆる資料を踏査して居る、これは有益な書物である。彼は優秀な人ではあるが厳格に云へば本書は厳密なものではない。然し非常に良い手引を與へてくれる。自ら思考せんと欲する人にとつては全くは同意し難い様な書物から始めるのは非常にいゝことだ。何故なら反駁と批評とによつて自己の考を發展させることが最も容易な方法だからだ。

第二にピグー教授の書物「産業波動論」（A. C. Pigou; Industrial Fluctuasions. 1927）は經濟學上の深さを持つ點に於て全く優れたものである。ピグー教授はあの部厚な書物を書く驚くべき才能を持つて居るので讀み難いと思ふであらうが、然し唯に恐慌理論のみでなく貨幣及信用、其他全く多くの問題に關する彼の見解に於て常に得る處があらう。

言ふ迄もなく資料は全く驚くほど多い。然し今日では諸君は前代の人々より遙かに好都合の狀態に置かれて居る。資料は多いが然し諸君の爲に非常に手際よくまとめられてある、そして諸君が用ひ度いと思ふ統計的調査が手近にある。即ちハーバード大學の諸統計や、スタンダード、ビヂネス・コンパニーの統計や或は米國商務省の經濟時事狀態の調査等には多くの資料がある。若し之等の資料の源泉をとれば米國に關する必要なるものの約九〇パーセントを得られる。他の諸國に於ては遙かに不自由であるが獨逸に於ては一九二五年以來大張りの有益な資料を蒐集する機關（Institut für Konjunkturforschung）が出來た。

以上を以てしては諸君は非常に簡單な評釋だと考へられるだらう。然り。我々は恐慌を單に大戰後の期

間に於ける事實を基礎としてのみ研究することは出來ない。何んとなればそれは倚未だ世界戰爭の影響の下にあつて多くの點に於て正常ではないのだから。若し問題を理解しようとせば大戰爭前の時期を究めなければならぬ。アメリカには一九一九年以後に就ては四〇條の統計數列があるが、大體に於て僅かにその中の三分の一のみが、一九〇三年迄溯り得、又極く少數のもののみ一八七五年に溯り得るに過ぎぬ。そして段々溯れば後には僅かに一般物價及價格水準の指數の一數列のみが殘るに過ぎぬ、而して之は英國及米國では一七九〇年頃に溯り得る。

今や十四世紀に溯る價格數列を我々に與へようとする大事業がアメリカの出資によつてスペインで發見せられて整理の緒について居る。之は叢澈なものであらうが、私は之が現はれる迄に死んで埋葬されるであらう、然しそれは諸君には役立つだらうと思ふ。

私は恐慌問題を討究するには諸君は手本に自由に扱ひ得るあらゆる手段を利用しなければならぬと話した。諸君はある程度迄經濟統計家たり經濟歴史家たらねばならぬ。斯様なことを云へば、それは洵に平凡に響いて、何か例を擧げなければ人を納得せしめ得ないであらう。私の非常に感謝する人々より成るハーバード經濟調査委員會（Harvard Committee on Economic Research）は當初總ての理論を打棄てゝ單純に非常の統計數列を蒐集した。それから之等の數列の何れが周期的に上下に動き、何れが動かないかを見出さうと試みた。そして、有名な三つの曲線バロメーターを作り上げた。

第一に投機（スペキュレーション）曲線、次に商業（ビジネス）曲線（之は現在では單に商業取引を弗で表はした總額と物價指數とのみより成る）最後に金融（マネー）曲線である。統計數列に於ては金利は最後に動くことを發見するだらう。何となれば好景氣が始まると多數の自由な流動信用が現はれる。そして總てのものは利率が騰貴するより先に進行する。從て金融曲線も亦三者の中最後に來る。之を見てハーバード委員會は金融曲線が降ると投機曲線が昇る、そして兩者の相關關係は非常に密接であると云ふ。即ち彼等は景氣の恢復期の前には金利が低いから恐らくは此の低い金利が景氣恢復の原因だらうといふのである。そして實に彼等は斯様な理論に從いて利率を以て斯かる現象の原因だと看做さうと努めつゝある。然し兩者の間に相關關係があると云ふことを以て始

（25）

(26)

むるとも、それは右の證明にはならない。蒸々金利が沈滯期に下降し、そして其後間もなく上昇期が來るに相違ないと云ふことは容易に理解し得よう。從つて金融曲線が下降して投機曲線が上昇することが分るだらう。然し前者は後者の原因ではない。

諸君は理論的知識を以て理論上豫期する樣な連續關係を引き出し、而してそれを事實と比較することを試みなければならぬ。然し、今や諸君は單純なる理論家たるを得ないので宜しく統計數列を取扱ふことを知らねばならぬ。

さて、諸君が理論上のアパラタスを得るについて助言を與へることは私には左程困難ではないが、然し諸君の目的に必要な統計的方法に關する良い手引について語るのには非常に困惑する。スカム、及ベドン教授のハーバード大學で教授用に用ひて居る書物はその一つである。之はハーバード流の方法を研究するには良い手引である然しそれは充分なものではない。此のハーバード流の方法は非常に良い助けになる。本書の載す材料はハーバード方法の開始せられし一九一九年以來のものを以てしてゐるが、今では本書も古くなつた。

さて私はハーバードの機關の統計の時間數列の分拆方法が如何なるものかを明かにしたい。彼等は此の數列が構成されてゐる諸項目を述べて居る。その各項目は第一に季節的に、第二に景氣循環の影響によつて第三に傾向の影響によつて、次に第四に不規則な影響によつて變化する。私は今季節的變動の問題に入るだけの時間を持たない。その問題は現在では全く充分には取扱はれてはゐないが、それを評論する必要なき樣に整つて居るものと假定しよう。

私は更に經濟生活を攪亂する地震、戰爭の如き不規則なものを除外しなければならぬといふことを自明のことゝして置く。我々は恰も斯くの如きものが起らなかつたものとして吾々の問題を取扱はねばならぬ。統計的數字には常に不規則なるものが存在するだらう。そこで如何にしてそれを取除くことが出來るかといふ問題が起る。私は今迄に如何なる滿足なる方法をも見出し得なかつたことを告白しなければならぬ。或る點に不規則なるものが作用したことが分れば私はその點を潔よく切取りその數字を捨てゝしまふ。例を擧げん

(27)

に、大戰が勃發した時にフランスの外國爲替が低下するだらうと豫期し得る。獨乙でも同樣だ。ところがフランスの外國爲替は低下せなんだ。何故と云ふに所謂米國が爲替相場の後押(backed the exchange)をやつたから。即ち米國は一九一九年迄フランス銀行に爲替相場を維持するだけの信用を與へたのである。然し一九一九年以后は此の援助は撤去され、從つてフランスの爲替相場は激落した。かくて一九一五年から一九一九年に至る時期に於ては不規則即ち茲に述べた Backing 後押が作用して居たことが分る。從つて私は此の間の數字を切捨てる。然し若しより不明瞭な不規則が作用して居るとすれば今や仕方がない。然し尚ほ一つの可能性がある之れ即ち我々は景氣循環の問題に立ち入る前に或る程度迄歷史家にならねばならぬと言つた所以である。我々は調査する時代の產業史を研究しなければならぬ。產業史には非常に良いものがある。我我はその國の歷史のみならず屢々產業の歷史を研究しなければならぬ。一九一九年以前の獨乙の歷史を書くには大化學工業トラストの歷史を知らずしては不可能である。我々は或程度迄歷史家たり統計家たらねばならぬ、そして全くそうなるのは比較的容易だ。何となれば現今では各種の統計及歷史に關する良い小教科書がある、從つて必要なる智識を得ることはさう厄介なことではない。諸君は比較的早く且つ容易に了解し得る。

扨ハーバードの數列は季節的變化並に循環及傾向をも與へて居る。而して此の全體の中最も疑問とする點は傾向の問題である。ハーバードの人々は簡單に經濟生活は時の力によつて變化すると云ふ、即ち彼等は傾向は現實の事實だと考える。或はそうかも知れぬ。然し私は將してそうだと言ふことを明かにして居ない。彼等の爲したことは材料に基いて曲線を組立てる事だつた。さて諸君、世には曲線の構成について餘り知らない人が多いのである。アメリカ、及獨逸の學生によつて諸君を判斷すれば茲で諸君に私が望む程には理解して貰ふことは難しい。

曲線の構成は次の如きものより成る。即ち若し諸君は此の樣な(黑板に畫く)統計的材料があれば此の黑板上の曲線圖表を貫いて所謂「分割部分の自乘の總和」(Sum Squares of division) が最少になる樣に線を引くのである。

（28）

諸君は常に曲線を畫くことも出來るし又直線を得ることも出來る。直線を作つたが爲めにそれらの材料によつて表現されたる一の資料があると考えてはならない。直線に表はすのは材料自體でなくて是を取扱ふ諸君の業である。圖表に何等の意味なき直線を畫くことも出來るのだ、若し斯くの如きをばその傾向(トレンド)と呼ぶならばそれは存在しない或る物に名前を與えたのに外ならぬことになる。諸君は唯だ統計的操作を行ふのみで、若しも此の場合に結果するものがあればそれは取扱ふ問題に關する理論如何に基いてゐる。

經濟的意味を持つ傾向線に關する私の考について唯僅かの間にヒントを與へるかどうかを危ぶむが茲に極く簡單に示さう。尤も此の點は以下に述べる議論には影響はない一七九一年から一九一四年に至る即ち約一二五年間の英國の物價指數の數列をとつて見よう。先づ之等を圖に表はす。之れを單純に二ケ年の移動平均をとつて表はす、次に第三年を累ね、平均を移動せしめ、かくして全體が平滑になる迄續ける。只今の場合、第十三級移動平均が平滑な曲線に表はれることだけを言つて置かう。そこで諸君は、統計的素材から作つた一つの曲線を得る。而して之は一般物價が一二五年間に如何に動いたかと言ふ觀念を與えることになる。然らば此の場合傾向は何てあるか。

私の說は斯うだ、あの曲線を見、轉向點が如何なるものかを數學的に見出し、而して之等の點を結ぶ。それは斯の如きものだ。（黑板に畫く）。そこで諸君自身によつて作られたのではなくて歷史自身によつて資料として提出された一の意味を持つ線を得る。そこで黑板上に見らるゝ通り下降する一種の傾向を得る。之は勿論單純なる曲線たるを要さない、然し之は經濟的意味を持つ曲線である。それは此の不揃な圖表の中の正常點を結んだものである。

此の傾向(トレンド)分析の問題は非常に重要なものであるから私はその問題の數理を最もよく書いた著作を擧げ度い。それはノルバート、ウイナー君(Norbert Wiener)の書物——標題は、(Generalised Harmonic Analysis)——である、然しこれには言ふ迄もなく多くの數學が必要である。以上私の欲したことは唯諸君にわづらはしいことであつたらう。以上は即ち事物は動いて居るといふことを示すことであり、我々は皆學ばねばならぬといふこと及唯入口に居るに過ぎないといふことを示すにあつた。

私は諸君は斯の如き方法を理解する意味に於て理論家であり、統計家であり、歷史家たらねばならぬといふ話に轉じよう。

今若し實業家が經濟恐慌を見れば彼は現實に存在する恐慌を說明する特種の事情を指摘するに相違ない實業家が今日の世界の狀態を見れば彼は農業不況、デフレーション政策、或は賠償支拂等多くの歸せらるべき原因を列擧するだらう。そして彼は恐らくより深い物があるといふ事實には氣が付かないだらう。彼は總ての產業的變動を私が不規則と呼ぶ所のものに歸せしむる傾向がある。彼は若し不規則がなかつたならば事物はスムースに續いて行つたゞらうと考へる、之等の不規則に就ては私が昨日工業俱樂部で實業家に話したことである。今日は科學的聽衆の前に居るので不規則は略して問題の理論に入り度いと思ふ。そして今以上述べた樣な不規則が經濟生活を混亂せしめないと云ふ重大な假定をする。

經濟學の發展の極く初期に於て人々は恐慌の現象を觀た。最初の大きな資本主義的恐慌の一は一七二一年の南海泡沫(サウス・シー・バブル)企業のそれてある。この恐慌は最初人々が失策をしたが爲めに起つたもので、必然的に起るべきものではない災難だと云ふ風に看做された。然し十八世紀の終り及び十九世紀の初めには恐慌か相續いて起つた。それによつて、その現象の裡には災難といふことによつては說明し得べからざる或る規則的なものがある、即ち經濟制度の裡には時々經濟の進行の中斷を起す何物かゞあるといふことが經濟學者達に次第に分つて來始めた。最も單純な理論即ちマルクスの消費過少又は生產過剩の理論が展開されたのは此の時代てあつた。

當時の最も重要な科學的業績はフランスの經濟學者ゼー・ビー・セイ（J. B. Jay）の一般的過剩生產といふが如きものは在り得ないと云ふ理論の承認であつた。今日でも尙ほ此の特種な理論の說明に努めるのに甘んぜんとする人々もある。今過剩生產說をとつて考へる。恐慌が既に起つた場合には實業家は、彼等の商品の販賣に困難を見出す。そして彼等は餘り多く生產し過ぎたと云ふ。生產過剩說は、誰れでもが恐慌時に於て販賣し得ない商品があると言ふ印象を業々しき言葉て表はしたものに外ならない。

（29）

經濟學の進步が遲いので此の古い理論が今尙多くの優秀なる著述家に支持されてゐると考えるのは誠に

悲しむべきだ。（例、アフタリオン Albert Aftalion: Leskrises périodiques de surdropuktion. 2 tomes 1913)）

然し十九世紀に於て恐慌の現象の分折に第二の進歩があつた。第二の進歩は、その名を何の景氣循環研究史に於ても常に敬意を以て記さるべきフランス人――ジユグラー（Clément Juglar · D·s Crises commercielles et de leu· r·tour périodique. 2. éd. 1889）に歸せられた。彼は發見を爲した。それは單に統計上の發見であつたが然し、理論にとつても非常に重要なるものなるが明となつた。此の發見とは前代の人々が恐慌と呼んだ處のものは、隔離された出來事ではなくて、恐慌はより深い所に在る波狀運動の中の單なる一要素に過ぎず、進化の曲線に於ける一點に過ぎないといふことであつた。それは繁榮より沈滯に入る轉回點に外ならない。そして周知の如く繁榮と沈滯との間の交替こそ眞實の現象である。

前代の人々は何故に絶えず經濟の中斷に遭ふかといふことを尋ねた。現在の人は何故に經濟的進化は平垣なる直線を爲して進まずして繁榮と沈滯を表はす波狀線を爲して行くかを尋ねる。恐慌の問題は循環の問題に變じた。

此の發見は總て其後の研究の出發點であつた。二十五年前私が恐慌の現象に就いて考え初めた時、私は單純に此の發見から出發した。繁榮と沈滯との間の箇條書きから出發した。私が説明せんと欲するのも之である。其後私は次第に他の影響を受けた。私と共に多くの人々が經濟生活か唯一の波動に從ふことが眞なりや否やに疑問を持つに至つた。そして他の重要なる發見が爲された。之は數人の著者に歸せられる。私はウオルフ（Wolff）、コンドラチイエフ（Kondratieff）及び私の大學の同僚シユピートフ（A. Spiethoff）の名を擧げよう。之等の著者は或る時には前述せるヂユグラーの場合よりも比較的長き繁榮の時期があり、又他の場合には比較的長き沈滯期があることを見出した。換言すれば遙かに長い期間を持つた他の波狀運動が發見された。

最初に擧げたヂユグラーの景氣循環の波は正に約十一年（七年乃至十一年）間程繼續する。私が茲に長い波動と呼ぶものは之れよりも遙かに長い。即ち第一に波動は一七九〇年に始り一八一四年に頂點に達し、一八四二年に最低に降下する。次いで一八七三年に頂點に達する第二の大なる波動が起り一八九四年に最低點に降下する。最後の循環は一八九四年に始まり一九一四年に頂點に達し現在迄下降しつゝある。以上の事實は何を意味するか。經濟生活は唯一種の變動に從ふのではなくて二種の變動に從ふことを知る。例で示すと斯ふてある。今靜かなる池を假定しよう、大きな石を投げれば波が起る。そこで此の波が繼續せる間に小石を投げる。さすれば大きな波の間に小波がある。正に之れと趣が同じてある。

一九二三年にキチン（Ktchin in Review of Statistics 1923）の書いた論文が出た。その中で彼は僅々に四十ケ月繼續する第三の波動が存在することを明かにした、否、最も蓋然的のものたらしめた。そして私が私自身の理論を實證しようと試みた時私は少くとも價格の取引に於ては約二十二ケ年の循環があることを發見した。そして私がそれを爲し遂げた後既にそのことが爲し遂げられて居たのを（ワードウエル Wardwell によつて――この研究は未だ出版されてゐない）發見した。之が所謂大循環と呼ばれるものである。

我々は統計的に經濟界は外部からの混亂がなくても繼續的に進行しない、樹木の成長の樣には成長せずして、經濟界は波狀を畫いて進行し、そして更にそれは單に一つの波動ではなくて少くとも以上に述べた四つの波が相併びて進行することを觀察する。之をアメリカに適用するに四十ケ月の波は次の如き方法で起つて居る、即ち一九〇三年、一九〇六年、一九〇九年、一九一一年、一九一四年、そこで波に凹所が起り續いて世界戰爭が來る、一九二一年から此の小周期は再び一九二三年、一九二七年及び明かに一九三〇年に起つて居る。之は粗雜に云へば四十ケ月週期である。また我々は此の資料に於て十ケ年の周期を、即ち一八六六年、一八七三年、一八八四年、一八九三年、一九〇〇年、一九〇七年、及び恐らく一九一四年に於ても見る、然し云ふ迄もなく續いて世界戰爭が起つた。一九三〇年は沈滯期であつて周知の如く最も深刻なものであつた。何故か、それは總て以上に述べた循環の波が下降期にあるからてある。若し何處かに周期的波動があるとすれば、或る場合には一が上昇し他が下降しそして互に中和しようとする。總ての波が下降する場合には大きな谷になり又上昇する場合には大好況となる。そこで今私は恐慌の最近の最も重要なる構成に達す

（32）

る。曰く。

一、何故に經濟の中斷が起るか。

二、何故に發展が繼續的に進行しないか。

三、茲で取扱ひ得る問題とは全く離れるが別に眞の問題がある。即ち經濟生活に見らるゝ異なる波動の間の干渉を如何に敍述し如何に說明するかといふことである。

私は諸君に辯解しなければならぬ樣に思ふ。日本の同僚及び學生諸君に講演する機會を得て、私は一種の科學的挨拶として最も新しき方面（即ち 右の第三問）を話す責任を負ふ樣に思ふ。が遺憾ながら今はその點を捨てゝ古い問題に歸らう。そして殘りの時間を單に一つの點に就て長期の波狀運動に歸る以外は專ら約七年乃至十一年に起る所のジュグラーの周期を說明するとに問題を限定しよう。此の說明はジュグラー自身によつて非常に平易にせられた。彼は簡勁にして重要なる文句を書いた。即ち沈滯の自然的原因は繁榮であると。此の言葉には多くのものを含んで居る。私はそれを說明したい。近時我々は常に好況期を幸福なる社會福利の時期として又不況期を不幸なる禍難の時期として見て居た。此の印象は、第一に實業家は取引が惡化しやすきが爲に又破產が頻出するが爲に不安を感ずる事實に因る。また大衆は失業によつて不幸であり大藏大臣は歲入の萎縮するが爲に不幸であると云ふによるのである。然し尙嚴密に見れば不景氣の際に比較的多量に消費されるのを見出す。從つて我々は正常的に消費は增加し且不景氣の時期は決して困窮の時期ではないと言ひ得る。

好景氣の時期に起る事はそれが如何にあらうとも確かに平衡の攪亂であり、不況は經濟生活が好況時に爲し遂げられた新生活に適應せんとする時期である。好況期は本質的に平衡の攪亂である。不況は好況への反動に外ならない。而して此の深淵なる眞理はジュグラーに歸せられる。勿論我々は今此の說明を之以上進めることは出來ない。ミッチェルの如く、好況は不況に依存し不況は好況に依存する。と云ふのは、循環論的推理以外の何の理由をも供しない。然し不況を以て好況時に起るものによる平衡の攪亂の賜物だと說明することは正しい。

（33）

御承知の如く、斯の如き說明は澤山ある。而して諸君の中此の問題に多少不慣れの人々に對して私は私自身の見解によつて自然に明かなる若干言を發したい。何故に此の如き循環的な繁榮期從つて又沈滯期が起るのか、その理由を求めるのは困難ではない、それは外ならぬ經濟的進步自體に在る。經濟生活は三つの異なる理由によつて變化する。孤立せる國民を假定し、且つ外部よりの影響によつて何事も起らないと假定すれば、經濟生活は年々恐慌を現はす事はない、然し變化はするだらう。人口の增加も實際平衡を攪亂するものであるが繼續的に起るから或る時期に經濟生活に入り來る勞働者の數は何時でも比較的少く從つてその人口は激しい攪亂を與へずに吸收される。

蓄積についても同樣である。これは繼續的な流となり、投資を求め、そして絕えず吸收され、攪亂を起し得ないものである。

第三の理由こそ攪亂を起す、それは生產方法の變化である。即ち人口の增加しつゝある國民はより多く働き、貯蓄する國民は資本を增加する。併し經濟生活の表面を最も力强く變化せしむるものは、我々が生產手段を用ひる方法を變ずる事實であり、產業組織、商業上の慣習、消費の慣習を變更する事實である。例へばその一例は十八世紀に於ける紡績機の移入であり、最近の事例は自動車の移入である。商業上の慣習の變化の事例はインドゴムをブラジルからのみならずジャバ及びマレー諸國の栽殖農場から購入することである。常に經濟財が變革された方法で作られ始めると、それは生產及消費に限なく影響を與へる。斯かる方法によつて世界の諸國民は次第に富裕になつたのである。

然らば、斯の如き變革が何故何時でも繼續的に導入されないのであるか、又何故之等の變革が平衡狀態に激しき動搖を與へる原因となるかを尋ねるだらう。その理由は私によればかうである。即ち若し新しき發明とか變革が絕えず導入されるとすれば、即ち每月同數の發明が連續して實際界に用ひられると恐らくは沈滯がなくなるだらう。何となれば斯樣な小さな動搖は恰も增加する人口が絕えず吸收されつゝある如く絕えず吸收され得ようからである。然し何故に產業の進步は斷續亂入的に行はれるか。

一例を以て答へよう。一九〇四年以前にあつては、何人も自動車が大量消費の財貨にならうとは思はなか

(84)

つた。事實一九〇四年以前の大多數の人々は私の兩親の老いたる抱え御者と全く同一の意見だつたと思ふ。當時彼は馬車の馬を驚かす外何の取柄もない自動車の流行は間もなくすたれるだらうと豫想すると語つた。年々數百萬の自動車が賣れるといふ此の驚くべき可能性のある事は何人も知らなかつた。

フォード一人のみは別の考へをもつてゐた。彼は安價な自動車を製造する爲に巨大な工場を建てた。始めはその自動車たるや誰も見ようともしない様な不格好な物であつた。米國に一の笑話がある。一人の友人が他の友人に自動車を持つてゐるかと尋ねた。するとその友人は「否、然し私は一臺のフォードを持つてゐる」と答へるのである。さて商業上の天才的な手際によつてフォードは、斯様な自動車の有する可能性を見、競爭者のなき新しき財貨を作り出した。彼は自動車を低廉に販賣した。併も彼は競爭者なくして賣ることが出來た。そして御承知の如く世界で最も富める人となつた。然し一度フォード氏が工場を始め、そして他の人々は之が成功を見れば、それを模倣することは容易だ。ゼネラルモータースはシボレーを作り出した。イタリー、ドイツ、フランス、イギリスに於て諸會社は安い車たるシトロエン、ホイペット、フイアト、その他を製出し始めた。之等の人々は皆フォードの大成功を收めた途に從ふべく亂入した。若しフォード氏のみが自動車を製造したとすれば之は僅かに小さき動搖にすぎなかつたであらう。然し米國其他の國々に於て之等の人々が皆フォード氏に倣つたので素晴しい産業が産み出され成長した アメリカ人は彼等の所得の約十五パーセントを自動車に費してゐるのである、以上の驚くべき事實は一つの大なる混亂を意味する。而して茲に諸君は恐慌の説明を得るのである。

新しき生産方法は遂行し難い。それは全く異る種類の危險即ち新しき事をなす危險及び未だ試みられたる事なき行程を踏み行くの危險を感ぜしむる。事實上此の新しき行程では十中九は失敗する。併し一人が成功すれば人々はそれに殺到する。之が何故進歩が突然にやつて來るかといふことの説明である。それは經濟生活に於てのみならず至る所に行なはれる。アメリカの統計學者に新産業生長史を研究したプレスコット氏(Prescott)がある。彼は第一に苦鬪を、次に一人の成功を、次いで國民一般が此の成功を吸收し行きて最後に落付くてふ事實を見出した。自動車に於て然り、電氣裝置に於て然り、化學工業に於て然りである。

(85)

普鐵道が大きな動搖を作つた。之が私が諸君に恐慌問題を理解する爲に經濟史を學ぶ事を希望すると云つた理由である。諸君は經濟循環の最初の頃に於てはそれは鐵道、鋼鐵等の新産業によつて總て支配されてゐる事實を見出すだらう。獨逸では電氣及化學工業によつた。新しき産業を導き出し繁榮を作り、又繁榮の後に沈滯を作るものは此の産業の進歩である。併しその機構を説明する爲には更に一歩を進む事を願はう。私が更に説き始めようとする次の段階は信用に關するものである。

簡單にする爲に假定を作らう。上昇又は繁榮は現實にある様に實際上沈滯期からは出發しないものと假定しよう。(それは若し沈滯期から説き出すと茲に既に理論的敍述の明確さを汚す攪亂要素が既に存してゐたことを容認したことになるから。)そして一の平衡狀態から起る繁榮期を觀察するものと假定しよう。平衡狀態に於ては蓄積は非常に少ない。その理由は單純である。事實、蓄積に關する統計を見れば蓄積の大部分は繁榮より生ずるを知る。また利潤は變革より生ずる。靜止平衡狀態に於ては發明もないだらう。然らば新規産業は如何にして資本を供給されるか。

若し私が上に試みた假定の下に於て一人の假定されたフォードを考へ彼が工場を建て初めたとしても、誰も彼に資本を貸すものはなかつたであらう。こゝに英國の文獻に於て信用創造(credit creation)と呼ばれる現象こそその手段となる。それは未だ豫め商品の生産なくして然も支拂手形たるものであるを意味する。銀行に行つて貸付を求むれば信用が與へられる。即ち銀行は其の人の勘定としての其の要求額の信用を設定する。それは他の人々の貯蓄から生じ得ることもあるが、然し此の創造された信用によつてこそ彼は自動車を作ることを得る、即ち銀行は新しき信用額だけを世に生み加へた。そして借り手たる假定されたフォードは右の創造された信用から小切手を振出して支拂をなすことが出來る。以上の如くであるならば茲に繁榮期に於て物價水準は騰貴するわけである。何故か。蓋しそれは生産物の量は增加しないのに從前からの支拂手形に加へるに新に創造された信用が加はり、支拂手段が增加するからである。我々の假想したフォード氏は工場を建てる。未だ賣るべき生産物を有して居ない。然し新に創造された信用によりて得られた購買力を有して居る。所が財貨の量は依然として舊の如し。從つて物價水準は騰貴する。之が我々が繁榮期に於て

（38）

常に見る價格水準上昇の說明である。

さて以上の基本的現象につゞいて更に考へらるべき現象がある。

價格水準が常に繁榮期に騰貴するから、我々は單に理論のみならず、二三統計上の重要點をも加へやう。さて若し價格水準が自然に上昇するならば一般の實業家は喜ぶ。彼等は利潤を得る。之は實は見掛けの利潤に過ぎないのだが、誰でも彼等は繁榮して居ると思つて居る。商品の增加なくして信用の增加することが、インフレーションである。然し實業家は彼等の負債を支拂ふことが出來、又誰でも欲するものをより多く買ふことが出來て幸福だと思ふ。若し商人が一層速かに賣らんとすれば彼は銀行に尙多く信用を求め、それを得、卸賣商人により多く注文を發するだらう。かくて繁榮は右のフォードの場合に建てられた工場から、その波を展げて全產業に飛躍し行き、商品の消費率は自然に全經濟生活に於て擴大し、遂には何人も總て之等の進化が最初二三の新企業に基くものたることを知らない樣になる。

從つて私は右の基本的現象に附隨し且つ其の結果として起る之等の現象を二次的波動と稱する。二次的波動は多くの人が知るものである。さて上に素直に述べた私の基本的現象に對する見解を人々が受け入れないとすれば、それは主として二次的波動か、それを生み來せる基本的波動より遙かに顯著だといふ事實より生ずるのに外ならぬ。

從つて私の見解に依れば繁榮期を特徵付けるものは實に生產能力の生產にある。多くの人々が云ひ又屢考へる樣に、產業上の目的或は機械のための建物がどしどし立てられる事は其の一般的擴張とかではない。

次に假定されたフォード氏が彼の建物を完成し、之に機械を据え付け、生產を始め、そして低廉な小自働車を不斷に市場に流出せしめる。此處に於てか小フォード達が續々飛出す。然らば信用制度は此の場合何を意味するかを觀よう。フォード氏は販賣する。而して販賣し得たが爲に大なる收入を得る。そこで之を銀行に預金し、之によつて負債を銷却する。（私は話を簡單にするためにフォード氏を例にとつたのであるが、事實はフォード氏は銀行信用を以て仕事をしたのではない。）企業が始まれば利潤が流れ込む。然し負債を銷却することは支拂手段の消滅を意味する、然らば此處に何が起るか。新商品が市場に入り來る間はそは增加せる信用との間に均衡を保つに足らう、然るに要求拂信用が消滅する時には支拂手段が減少するが爲にそれと元の價格水準との間の平衡は破れる。

かくて「國民配當分（社會產物）」は增加したが支拂手段の量は減じた、換言すれば我々は繁榮期にインフレーションを見、沈滯期にデフレーションを見た。而してデフレーションは自動的に——即ち政策等によりて動かされる所なく——現はれるのだから、私は之を、自動的又は自己的（セルフ）デフレーションと呼んだ。仍つて私は理論的理由に依つて價格水準は沈滯期に下降すると豫言しなければならぬ。また此の自動的デフレーションには更に信用額のみならず其の利子まで返却されるのであるから、デフレーションの程度は一層强まるのである。故に一般に云へば、金の發見等が起らなければ何世紀かの長い間には一般物價水準は下降すべきであり且つ事實左樣であつた。（云ふ迄もなく金の發見等が價格水準を上昇せしめたのであるが）

以上は經濟生活自體從つて又信用制度の側からの理論である。我々は三種の統計數列を實證として持つ。物價の數列 生產の物理量 の數列及び個々の價格より成る數列之れである。又以上を結合せる數列がある。私は充分其點に入ることが出來ないが二三の事例を與へよう。さて理論的に繁榮期に價格水準を驅り立てるものが信用曲線なりと云ふこと及 價格水準を下降せしむるものがデフレーションなりといふ事が眞であるならば、事實に於ても價格水準は繁榮期に上昇し沈滯期に下降するのを見なければならぬ。

ワーキング（Working in Journal of American Statistical Association）はアメリカに於て生產の物理量が一八五一年以來毎年三パーセント宛增加したといふ古い發見に論據を置いて次の如く推理した。即ち若し價格水準が、不變であるとすれば支拂手段は亦毎年三パーセントづゝ增加しなければならなかつたであらうと。彼は要求拂預金（demand deposit）が支拂手段の毎年三パーセントづゝの增加を比較して何程の高低があるかを觀察した。そしてそれが繁榮期に高く沈滯期に低いと云ふことを示した。そして例へば今日の不景氣を一九三〇年より始まるとするは誤であり、一九二八年よりとすべきであると爲した。若し諸君に示した私の理論が正しいとすれば物價は要求拂預金の需要の高低と一致して正常線の上下に騰落すると云はなければならぬ。そして價格は事實さうなつて居る。

（37）

（38）

其他ピグーの著書に於ける諸種の統計及カール・スナイダー（Carl Snyder）の生產の物理量に關する諸種の統計等に其他の實證を發見し得よう。

また合衆國に於ける建築契約の統計數列がある。之は僅かに一九二〇年以後の分のみ產業用及住宅用建築の區別を爲すに止まる。即ち過去には遡らぬが然しそれでも尙今日の統計を補助するに役立つのである。

尙ほ其他吾人の述べた理論か正しいならば、然らば建築及機械製造に、必要な銑鐵の消費額が繁榮期には增加し沈滯期には減少せねばならぬ。吾人は獨逸の銑鐵の消費額即ち總生產額プラス輸入額マイナス輸出額は繁榮期の非常に早い頃に增加し、沈滯期には極めて特徵ある減少を示すことを知る。（シュピートホーフの研究を見よ）

上述の理論に依れば、殆ど總ての所得、特に經濟的利潤及び賃銀は繁榮期に於いて上昇すべく又實質賃銀は沈滯期に騰貴すべき筈である。私は獨逸で一八一二年より一九一二年に至る間の此の研究を得ることが出來た。繁榮期に於ては貨幣賃銀が騰貴し、沈滯期に於ては實質賃銀が騰貴するから、賃銀の總額は繁榮期に於ても沈滯期に於ても共に增加する。沈滯期は苦難の時であるとの印象は此の論證から全く支持されない。私は實質及貨幣の双方の賃銀總額について云つて居るのである。

最后に私の希望は愉快な整つた講義をすることであつた。それには餘り時間が短かすぎた。然し私は諸君に二三のヒントを與え諸君が私の說を取り入れるにしても取らぬにしても問題を提起したいと思つたのである。大切なことは諸君の進む途の何等かの助けになつたかどうかといふことである。

私は諸君に會つて非常に喜んだこと又再び諸君にお話することが出來ないのを悲しんで居ることを申し上げて置き度い。（了）

附記　本稿はシュ氏の東大に於る講演速記である。本誌があらゆる努力を爲して著者の云ふ所の眞意を傳へんとしたが、何分著者自身の校閲の到着に間に合はなかつた爲に萬一の誤解なきやを惧る。若し然る場合には次號に於て氏の訂正並に註釋を揭載する積りである。

The Present State of International Commercial Policy

Lecture delivered at the Kobe University of Commerce

by

Dr. Joseph Schumpeter

Professor of Economics in the University of Bonn (Germany)

I.

While government's *talk* about commercial cooperation, tariff unions and tariff truces, they *practice* protectionism. While international commissions discuss the abolishing of barriers, these barriers become higher every day. While nations profess to act on the most-favored-nation clause, they try their best to evade it by such devices as for instance that over-refining of tariff-schedules, which permits to differentiate between *countries* while seeming to differentiate between *qualities of commodities*.And the same politician who likes to make a speech of international good will at the dinner of some chamber of commerce, will be exerting himself at the same time to secure from his government additional protection for some industry on other. This situation is paradoxical and it almost looks insincere. It seems to be very similar to the attitude of politicians with respect to limitations of armaments and other related questions:always *talking* peace and at the same time *preparing* war.

And there is, in fact, much insincerity about the present situation. Nevertheless, it would be unjust not to admit that what looks insincerity, is often nothing else but perplexity in a situation of unprecedented difficulty. Nor would it be just to define the situation, as some economists seem inclined to do, as a struggle between economic reason and political prejudice. For although there is a lot of political, and especially nationalistic, prejudice in the commercial policy of almost all nations, yet it is also true that economic conditions themselves do not admit of clear-cut action either in the direction of Free Trade or in any other.

In order to understand this, we must realize two things:First, that commercial policy is not, and cannot be, a mere matter of economic reason. Secondly, that Free Trade and Protection are neither of them eternal truths, which could be established by general economic arguments and which would then hold good for all times, places and conditions.

Politicians are as a rule very bad economists and very ignorant of the teachings of science. But even if every politician were a most competent economist, he would still be faced by the fact, that in commercial as in other matters, the will of nations is not merely influenced by considerations of economic advantage. Nations take pride in their independence and greatness. Hence it may flatters them to have as many as possible of their articles of consumption produced at home, especially those which like ships, was material, machines and others, are rightly or wrongly supposed to be of special national importance. They are prepared to pay for the gratification of this pride, for their "autarky", and as far as this is the case it will be of no avail for the economist to point out that a policy conductive to such independence may be harmful economically. Moreover, there are other non-economic considerations. So for instance, many people think that a numerous and healthy peasantry is a national asset. It may be true that the peasants method of production is a backward one and that, economically speaking, it would be advantageous if it disappeared. But if the fate of the peasantry is bound up with that method of production——it not always is ——and if you want to keep your peasantry, you will have to act in defiance of some of the economic rules of commercial policy. Besides, there is the pressure of the groups immediately interested in Protection. Whatever we may think of the soundness of protective policy if looked at from the standpoint of the economic advantage of *all* classes of society, it is certain that every single industry, taken by itself, profits by a protective duty on the commodity which it produces. This is not so evident as it seems to be. For on the one hand, the advantage to the workmen and to the capitalists of the protected industry is doubtful as protection is likely to reduce real wages and the real income of the capitalist, but the manufacturer or entrepreneur himself certainly profits. Even to him there may be compensating disadvantages. But he *sees* his advantage, which is obvious, and *overlooks* his disadvantage, which is less obvious, and so he urges the politician on to protection, a pressure the politician is not as a rule in a position to withstand, even if he wanted to. Finally, there is another consideration. Tariffs produce a shift in the purchasing power of the incomes of different classes:No duty falls with equal weight on everybody but every duty hits some people more than others. At the same time, this consequence of tariffs is hardly ever clearly grasped by the public. Hence a tariff may be the means to effect a shift in purchasing power to the advantage or disadvantage of some class without encountering such resistance as would another measure towards the same end, a tax for instance. Now this may be an important motive for politicians to declare themselves in favour of protection. Take the instance of England. English wages are probably too high at present in the sense, that they produce unemployment. At the same time, workmen and their trade-unions resist any cut in wages. If protective tariffs were introduced, then the object of lowering wages would be attained, for real wages would undoubtedly be lowered by import duties on articles of mass-consumption. And this could be achieved without that dangerous struggle incident to a process of directly lowering wages, there would even be some support from the workmen themselves for a protective policy, because some workmen would believe it to be a remedy for unemployment.

Also, politicians may sometimes have no very decided opinion in favour of protection and yet be forced, by considerations of political tactics to adopt it. The American Tariff act of 1930 may perhaps serve as an example:Hardly any competent economist was in favour of it, and it is difficult to see what advantage America can reap from it. But protection was an old point in the programme of the Republican Party. That party always styled itself as the "party of prosperity"and claimed that their protective policy was the right way to assure prosperity. In the minds of American people, high tariffs are, vaguely and irruptionally, associated with prosperity. So it would be very difficult for the Republican Party to drop protection. Having stood for it so long and having told the electorate for such a time what a good thing protection was, the party would feel it was giving up the very essence of its policy and of its political soul, if they gave up protection. They are already in troubles with the other main item of their programme——prohibition. They may have to drop it. If they drop protection too, they may well ask themselves anxiously what will remain for them.

All these things must be taken into consideration if we are to understand what actually happens. But it is not even true, that the economic argument itself points in *one* direction only. For the greater part of the 19. Century almost all competent economists thought that Free Trade was the only right thing and that Protection was nothing but either error or the selfishness of small groups of producers. Now, it is very important to see clearly that there was some justification for this view:Many protectionist arguments are really nothing else but primitive economic errors due to ignorance of both the facts and the laws of economic life. Indeed, a whole list of fallacies in economic reasoning could easily be drawn up, for the benefit of elementary discussion in classes of beginners, from the usual protectionist arguments. In this respect, the Free-Trade-arguments were really much superior and in this sense they were indeed, what they claimed to be, a lasting contribution to economic science. And it is precisely some of the most erroneous protectionist catch-words which have survived and which have gained new authority during and after the War, when so many *old errors* were served up as *new truths*.I need only quote the wide-spread belief, that every export means a gain and every import means a loss to the nation, or that it is always an advantage to produce at home, instead of importing, a commodity which a nation is at all able to produce, and that we ought to rejoice in every national industry created by a protective duty, or that tariffs remedy unemployment, or safeguard the national currency, or that they are necessary to keep up a high standard of wages, or that it is their function to equalize cost of production at home and abroad and to enable the home industry to compete with foreign products on what has been called "fair" terms.

All this is wrong. The last argument for instance, which is so popular in the United States runs directly against the very meaning of international trade. What other reason can there be for importing a commodity from abroad, and why is international trade advantageous if not for the reason that a nation may, importing, get a commodity with less effort that is to say, at less cost, than if it produced it at home? Hence, equalizing costs at home and abroad would, if carried out to its logical consequences, put a stop to importation and exportation and amount to prohibition of international trade. And if we want this, it is much more logical and much simpler to say so and to prohibit imports entirely, instead of creating in the public mind a vague impression that equalizing costs of production at home and abroad only eliminates some "unfairness" from international trade but is not really meant to *present* imports.

Yet, although protectionist arguments can often be proved to be nothing else but errors, it does not follow that protection itself is always wrong. Indeed, few modern economists will hold the free-trade argument so absolutely as the classics did. They will hold rather that every case has to be dealt with individually and that it is impossible to recommend Free-Trade on general gounds, and for all times and places. In order to understand this, a distinction suggests itself, which is in many economic problems essential to clearness of thought:In economic analysis, we have always to deal with a given situation. We may *either* accept it as it is and investigate the consequences of small changes in any single element of it, all the rest of the conditions remaining constant, *or* we can investigate the possibility and consequences of fundamental change in the situation. This distinction is not the same as the distinction between what may be expected to happen in *short* and in *long* periods, which is due to Alfred Marshall. For *short* periods do not give time for *any* change, great or small to produce its full and ultimate effects, while long periods, which would give time enough for this, invariably also include *other* changes which must always come about in any longer stretch of time and blot out what we really want to observe. Therefore, it seems better to draw the distinction simply between economic phenomena looked at from the standpoint of given conditions which are expected to last and phenomena which may be produced by revolutionising those given conditions or data. For shortness'sake, let us call the first class "static"and the second one "dynamic"and let us look at "static"consequences of protection and "dynamic"consequences of protection separately.

Now, it has be shown by *Edgeworth* in his famous paper on International Values, and by many later authors, that it is not true that the "static"argument is all in favour of Free Trade. Indeed, Free-Traders themselves have not always gone as far as this. What they have really held was that Free Trade leads to greatest advantage for all nations *taken together*.And it can easily be shown that the advantage of any *single* nation, taken by itself, may be increased by protective duties and other, interferences with the channels of international trade. If for instance a nation demands for some foreign commodity is very elastic and the supply of this commodity is inelastic, an import duty may benefit this nation as is readily seen by reference to the well-known curves which Marshall has made familiar. It is even possible that protection benefits *both* countries although such cases will be rare. We cannot enter into this subject, but we may state, that the static argument while not *wholly* for Free-Trade, is yet *substantially* so and that cases in which lasting advantage can be reaped from protection, the fundamental conditions being assumed to remain constant, are no more than exceptions.

It is different from the point of view of "dynamics". Everyone knows the argument for protection to infant industries (Erziehungszoll).It is often abused by interested parties, who claim protection which they really mean to be lasting. It involves the danger that industries may be built up which will never be able to stand without artificial support and which, while they *look* like national assets, are really a source of economic loss to the nation as a whole. Finally, this argument is, even where not wrong, apt to be exaggerated, It is absurd to believe that Germany or the United States would not have been able to build up their industries if they had not had Protection. Yet, with all these qualifications, the infant-industry argument has *some* validity. And it is only a special case of a much larger truth:That Protection and other interference with international trade may help to create new things and make it easier for progress in methods of production and industrial organisation to come about. To be sure, Free-Trade has also its "dynamic side".The whip of international competition may so shake up the energy of home industries as to make them conspicuously efficient in some lines, wile others would be with advantage left to other countries. Yet it may fairly be considered an open question which of the two policies is more likely to benefit a given country. Personally I must confess to a belief that the cases of Germany and of the United States prove no more than that strong countries can stand protection without obvious suffering. The United States with their vast territory containing practically all opportunities in an ideal combination, I have always looked upon as an example for *the benefits of Free Trade rather than of Protection.*

But there is yet one element in commercial policy which must be borne in mind and which I should like to call:The Tyranny of the Temporary Situation. By this I mean the fact that whatever we may think of Free Trade as a policy in the long run, we are faced with an industrial organism shaped by Protection, Government Subsidies, Railway Rebates, Tax-Privileges, and which therefore is different from what it would have been if it had been allowed to grow by itself. We may be convinced that we have industries which work at costs so high that we should be better off without them. But we *have* them. And if we leave them to their fate, there will be losses, failures, unemployment, and all this will affect the whole of the industrial life of nations. Germany for example has an overgrown beet-sugar-industry which is overgrown because it had been artificially fostered, and which could not compete now with cane-sugar. The shipping and ship-building trade of all countries, which is one of the worst in the present world-depression, would be much better off, if it had not been the object of so much benevolence from governments.

The textile industry of Czechoslovakia is so great, because it used to supply the 54 millions of inhabitants of what was the old Austro-Hungarian Monarchy. It finds itself now fettered by the tariffs of the new states into which that Monarchy has been split and is left with a home-market of about a dozen millions. Italy has built up, during and after the War, steel and iron industry which could not compete with that of other countries. But all these things are now in existence. Dropping them and reorganising economic organisms on the lines of Free Trade would mean disasters and revolutions even if it were certain that all nations would benefit in the end. Business-men and Politicians equally fear these disasters and revolutions. And so the errors of the past become the tyrants of the present. To remedy the evils of Protection we are driven on to *more* Protection.

II.

All this applies not only to the present state of things but also to international commercial policy before the war. There were, however, two hopeful elements, one of which has vanished now, while the other may vanish any day:By the Underwood-Tariff-Act of 1913, the United States reduced import duties considerably, and England's public opinion was as yet adverse to any protectionist policy. The War brought a revival of nationalist passion and that well-known War-organisation of industry, both of which have prevented normal commercial intercourse between nations for a time after. But these are things of the past by now. Yet the War had other consequences, which still subsist and some of which must be expected to last indefinitely.

There is, first the creation by the peace-treaties of a number of small new states. The effect upon commerce turns less on the thousands of miles of new frontiers created thereby, than on the new nationalism which naturally developed in these states. Their citizens or their politicians are proud of their independence. They insist on doing what they see the great states do. They want to have economic independence too, and so they practice a mercantilism which may be just bearable in big territories but the absurdity of which stands out grotesquely in small ones. Of course this policy has much to do with the world depression, as all these territories used to be supplied from industrial centres, which now suffer from being shut out from them while the citizens of the new states suffer from having to pay dearly for inferior goods.

Secondly, the monetary disorders of the war have for a time disorganised foreign trade. Inflation stimulated exports which drove *some* countries to measures of protection for their industry, and deflation stimulated imports against which the deflating countries tried to protect themselves by tariffs. Everyone knows *how* inflation stimulates *exports*.In order to see how deflation stimulates *imports*, it is only necessary to consider that if a country deflates, the effect on foreign trade must be obviously the same as if the other countries *inflated*.

If we have two countries, say Japan and America, and if Japan deflates and America keeps her Dollar constant at the same time, trade will be affected by this exactly as it would be if Japan kept her Yen constant and America inflated her Dollar.

International payments such as reparations or interallied debts are a third disturbing factor. *Paying* countries will have to export more and import less than they otherwise would. As far they do the former, they became more eager competitors, as far as they do the latter, they become worse clients of the *receiving* countries. This means that periods of prosperity will be less, and periods of depression more, marked in the receiving countries than they otherwise would, and their industries, finding it more difficult to compete, will insist on increased protection. But protection will also commend itself to paying countries because import duties,will contribute towards that restriction of imports necessary to produce that surplus of exports over imports which in turn is necessary in order to put at the disposal of the paying governments sufficient amount of foreign exchange. *Hence reparations will lead to protection all round*. But observe the difference between the two arguments for protection in paying and in receiving countries. The argument for protection in paying countries is correct. It is indeed one of those candid mercantilist errors, which classic doctrine has successfully refuted, to believe that a "favourable Balance of Trade"is an advantage to a country and that it must be enforced by tariff policy. But if country has to make annual payments, for which it does not receive any economic compensation, the case is different. As long as such one-sided payments last, there must be a favourable balance of Trade, or else it will be impossible to effect reparations. And mercantilist policy, which may be an error in every other case, is correctly advocated in this particular one.

On the other hand, there is *no* justification for increased protection in receiving countries. For as reparations necessarily mean increased exports and as the economic meaning of these payments consists furnishing commodities to the receiving country it is obviously absurd to insist on the payments and yet to refuse to admit the commodities, by which alone these payments can be effected. However, the United States have not only tried to "protect"themselves by increased import duties against imports which they create themselves by their policy, but they also have enacted the so-called "flexible clause, "according to which tariffs can further be raised by presidential proclamation, if the Tariff-Commission finds, that foreign costs of production are too low for American manufacturers to compete with. Now consider what this means. As a consequence of reparation payments and in order to make them possible, Germany has to produce cheaply. Therefore, cases must arise, to which the flexible clause will apply. Tariff duties would be raised. And in order to continue the necessary exports, Germany will have to produce still cheaper. Hence, new cases of application of the flexible clause must present themselves. And so on, until the absurdity of the situation becomes clear or, the more probable case, until further reparations become impossible.

Capital-migrations do not act as reparation-payments do because they develop the countries which become debtors. Yet the great shift in the financial relations of nations and continents brought about by the War, is another, the fourth, disturbing factor, which by the displacement of demand consequent upon it, created difficulties, which also lead to increased protection, just as, all disturbances is, to which nations try to make adaptation easier and less violent by import duties. Before the War, the net balance in favour of Europe was about 24 billions of $.To-day, Europe is a debtor to the amount of about of billions. And the United States have changed, within ten years, a position of debtor to the amount of about 16 billions into a position of a creditor to the amount of about 60 billions as against Europe, while increasing their investments in the rest of the world by about 30 billions more. This must affect all channels of trade. And transition to conditions so different will for obvious reasons create demands for protection in the areas affected by it.

There are other disturbing factors, such as the fall of silver which stimulates Chinese exports, especially of silk, but there is besides, fifth, a great historical process, not brought about, but quickened, by the war, a process which can in importance be compared only with such events as the decay of the ancient Egyptian or Persian Monarchies or the fall of the Roman Empire:Industrial Supremacy is being lost to Europe. That position of the Industrial Centres of Western and Central Europe, which every European has been taking for granted for centuries, is obviously going to pieces. While, on the one hand, the production of raw material and food stuffs is carried on in America, Australia, Asia with such advantage as to make European agriculture well-nigh hopeless, there are, on the other hand, native industries growing up everywhere and even in tropical countries. So Indian textiles are displacing the cheap grades of the products of Lancashire, Indian foundries are competing successfully with English one. And there is no doubt that South America will go through a quick and successful industrialisation such as Japan has already embarked upon.

For the industries of Europe and the 250 millions of people, which live in the industrialized parts of Europe, this means an entire change of the conditions of life. Agriculture can only survive by artificial support, which means that there is a deficit which has to be borne in one form or another by the industrial classes. European industry feels instinctively, although it naturally does not like to confess it, that its home-market will be all that is left to them. The industrial states of Europe used to have a net import surplus of foodstuffs and raw materials of nearly eight billions, which they paid for by nearly the same amount of industrial exports and services such as shipping, banking receipts and so on. There was, to fortify this business, the vast amount of foreign investments bringing in its interest and assuring the control of the oversea-industries. All this has partly vanished already, and is partly in the process of vanishing. Hence the struggle to keep home-markets and, as one mean towards this end, protection.

III.

This explains both the present situation of commercial policy and the plans which have been proposed in order to remedy it. Immediately after the War, and when animosities began to subside, there was both among politicians and among specialists of commercial policy a distinct tendency towards *freer*, if not *free*, trade. My impression is that many people really thought that a period of comparatively free trade was at hand, and that it was in this spirit that they entered upon a policy of the most-favoured-nation-clause. Besides, in some countries, where tariffs are drawn up in terms of duties per piece, the lowered purchasing power of gold carried automatically with it a lowering of import duties. If this situation had been clinched at the right moment, it might have been possible to arrive at agreements such as that which has been recently proposed by a French committee:That a convention should be agreed upon to the effect that certain moderate duties should apply to the exports of the member-states, while higher duties should apply to the exports of states who refuse to join. This would have been a great steps towards *freer* trade and a great bar in the way of extremely protectionist countries. But I am afraid it is too late now. The right moment was somewhere about 1925, and it has been lost. Meanwhile, almost all countries, with such exceptions as the Netherlands or Sweden, have gone so far on the way of protection as to have created a vested interest in it, and what hope there was for some understanding at least among European States, has passed away. To be sure, people do realize, that some such convention could better the European situation by bringing about a better division of labour, and thereby a rationalization, of European industries. But politics stands in the way of so desirable an end. Commercial policy is, as I have said at the outset, a part of general policy, and no understanding is possible on commercial matters among states, who will not or cannot agree politically. In this sense it is true that political federation would have to precede economic federation. But if this is true, then the League of Nations is carrying on a hopeless campaign for the “tariff-truce”.

The situation differs of course in different countries. France has, since 1926, returned to that thorough protectionism which always was congenial to her. Italy is strongly mercantilist as it is natural for her to be under a nationalist and militarist government. Germany, after having in 1925 regained her liberty to shape her commercial policy, was not very protectionist at first. But she has drifted since into both agrarian and industrial protectionism, which as said above, is in her case explained by the reparations——although her policy would probably not be much different even without them.

England still keeps to Free Trade. Deviations indeed there are or were, such as the McKenna duties imposed already during the war, the protection granted to key industries (optical instruments, certain chemicals), the safeguarding duties of 1925 or the dye-stuff regulation act of 1920, but all this does not amount to much. Although Germany's exports to England are just of the kind which is likely to be hit by these duties it is yet only about 10% of German exports which suffer by it. These measures have been so moderate, bacause they had to be carried against free-trade opinion, which still predominated in the public mind and among politicians and business-men especially among bankers. Being conceived as measures of relief of a temporary character and in an abnormal situation, they are not really deviations from free-trade policy. Probably John St. Mill himself would admit, that there may be circumstances, in which industries are temporarily threatened, which it would not be wise to leave to their fate, because they are perfectly fit to survive under normal conditions and would have to be built up again if they were destroyed by abnormal events.

But now public opinion is changing, and the question of *really* abandoning free-trade presents itself. Even this is no new phenomenon. Both the sources of the current in favour of Protection are, on the contrary, quite old. The one is the prolonged depression, the other the wish to consolidate the British Empire. As to the first, it was already in the long depression of the eighties of the 19. century that some manufacturers and even workmen came to believe that free-trade was partly responsible for it, and that protecion would be a remedy. And ever since there has been some favour shown to the battle-cry: "Tariff reform means work for all". This movement allied itself later on to nationalistic ideas about the Empire, and both were carried *near* to success by the powerful personality of Joseph Chamberlain. Both were defeated in 1906, but both are before the country again to-day. It is interesting to see that the nature of both problems has not changed. It is just as true to-day as it was in the eighties of the 19. century, that depression is not due to free trade and that not much relief can be expected from protection:Unemployment is worst in some indusries, where is hardly any foreign competition, as for instance in the coal trade, or in industries, like shipping, where no safeguarding by tariffs is possible. Protection would not alter the fact, that coal is being replaced by oil or water power, and the demand for coal reduced by a better technique which economizes it. Nor could protection prevent the industrialisation of India and the Dominions. And already the Balfour committee found, that the foreign tariffs most injurious to British Trade are really those imposed by other parts of the Empire. The Safeguarding-of-industries-act was no success. Neither would systematic protection be, especially if extended to half-finished products, the cheapness of which in England is the basis of some of her industries.

The economic value of the Empire-idea is not much greater. It would amount to "Preference".But England already enjoys preferential treatment, and it does not help her. So for instance, Australia grants preference to English goods of from 35-40% of the ordinary duties and yet England's share of the Australian trade has gone back ever since pre-war times. The colonies in the proper sense of the word, with a population of about 50 millions, might be more rigorously reserved for English products than they are. But although this may be of importance in the future, the immediate effect could not be great, owing to the poverty of those countries.

England's Trade develops more favourably, and seems to have more chances, in the rest of the world than in the Empire itself. And of course there is moreover the difficulty that England would have in order to reciprocate further concessions by Dominions, to introduce duties on food-stuffs and raw materials.

Nevertheless I believe that England is nearer to embarking upon a protectionist policy than she ever was in the last hundred years. The fact which makes me think so is, that not only some trade-unions, and many individual workers are becoming protectionist but that there are even signs of a change of opinion among Liberals who so far have been uncompromising advocates of free-trade. If the liberal party, small though it is, comes round to protection, there will be an end of free-trade. Therefore, all nations interested in England as an export market for their goods, would act wisely if they tried to conciliate England by timely concessions. This would strengthen free-trade opinion in England, and perhaps prevent England from taking up pretection. Soon it may be too late, and then concessions to England will have to be made for a small part of what it would now be possible to retain. It is obvious that any change in the commercial policy of England will powerfully influence the attitude of Belgium, the Netherlands, Danmark, Sweden and other smaller states, so that the whole of Europe may be riding on a wave of mercantilism before long, a mercantilism which by hampering international division of labour and keeping alive backward methods of production, must be injurious to all.

Hence it does not seem that there is much hope of cooperation. But there is one force which tends towards cooperation among European, and other states, and that is the policy of the United States, which is universally resented as strongly as debtors dare to resent anything which their creditor does. We have already repeatedly touched upon the subject, and can confine ourselves to a few remarks. The American tariff-policy embodied in the Underwood-Act of 1913 was shortlived. Very soon America returned to her traditional policy. The Fordney-McCumber Act raised duties to an average of 35%.And by the Hawley-Smoot-Act of 1930 they were raised again and now average 41%.Some items were new, especially those on leather, boots, cement and timber. Some were raised considerably, as those on agricultural products, pig-iron, woollen goods, rayon-silk and sugar. Others were raised moderately, such as those on cotton goods, glass, porcelain. I have said already, that in order to understand this measure, we must look to the political situation, especially to the position of the Republican party. But it is also a good example for the truth that protection invariably leads to more protection. If one industry obtains a protective duty, this is obviously an advantage for the firms of which this industry consists, and a damage to those who consume its products. If the protected commodity is itself a producers' good, a raw material, a machine on a half-finished product, then the protective duty is a damage to the industries which buy it. Of course, both advantage and damage arise from the fact that the import duty changes the relative value of the protected commodity as against other commodities. Every single act of protection, while it *seems* to be directed against the foreigner, is *in reality* directed just as much or more against the rest of home-industries. Now if these other home-industries also obtain protection, then relative values will be changed again, and the advantage reaped by the industry which got protection first, is, according to circumstaces *lessened, annihilated* or even *turned into disadvantage*.Hence the paradoxical result, that a tariff which would be so constructed as to "protect" all industries equally, would really "protect" none of them. This truth businessmen do not understand, but they feel it. And so they want not so much protection simply, but *more* protection than other home-industries get. Every rise in any duty is therefore sufficient motives for other industries to ask for a rise of *their* duties in turn. Hence that race of industries for as much protection as they can get, which we observe always when a new tariff-bill is in the making, and hence that tendency of protectionism to run to extremes.

This tariff has intensified depression in the world at large, and it has injured the people in America more than appears on the surface. Americans usually comfort themselves by pointing to the fact, that foreign trade form only a very small part of the total volume of their business. This is true, while in Italy imports equal 20% of the National Income, in France 23. 7%, in Germany 25%, in England 31%, in Switzerland 46%, they are just under 5% in the United States. But this is so, *because* there is this exorbitant tariff, which prevents the American workman from consumption of cheaper foreign goods, which could benefit him much more than high money-wages.

IV.

Summing up, we may say that partly for good and partly for bad reasons, practically the whole world has taken to protectionism, and that this tendency will be intensified rather than softened in the immediate future. I have often been asked, whether international cartels or understandings in some other form, from industry to industry may not be expected to improve this state of things. To some extent they certainly have that tendency. But first we must not overrate the importance of what has been achieved. Understandings such as have been arrived at in the steel industry or, of late, about oil, or such organisations as the international export-cartel in copper, or, different again, the explosives-trust, or the European union of producers of bottle-glass, or the concern for the exploitation of the Owen-process, or the swedish match combine——they are all of them either exceptions due to very peculiar conditions or temporary devices brought about by severe depression. Secondly, we must not forget that even if international cartels became the rule, free interchange of commodities would gain but little. If, say, the steel-industry of all countries of Europe or even of the world came to an understanding about dividing up markets, this would kill competition just as effectively as prohibitive tariffs do. The objection to tariffs is precisely that they hamper competition and that continuous readjustment of industry, which we call industrial progress. And this is just what international cartels do too. If industries of different countries agree not to compete with each other and to respect each others hunting grounds, this implies just as much the danger that they will go to sleep and enjoy their safe profits as protection does. Besides, this policy will not even do away with protection. For as the industry of every country knows that the understanding has to be renewed after a certain time and as it also know that negotitations may fail, it is to their interest to have a protective duty to fall back upon.

Under these circumstances we shall understand it, if all the endeavours of Geneva have been nearly unavailing so far. Inspired by the best intentions and relying on the most authoritative scientific opinions, these endeavours are thwarted partly by the necessities of an unhappy situation and partly by the tricks of politicians. Three years ago the World-Economic-Conference expressed unanimously the ardent wish of all those who took part in it, to inaugurate a new era during which the fetters of international commerce should be untied. Statesmen applauded, but did the contrary. Not discouraged by this, those men persevered and a modest suceess was achieved by the agreement of March 24, 1930, which indeed failed to condemn increases in duties but at least tried to make them more difficult. Even this much has not been carried out, and one has the impression that politicians are laughing at the idealists who think it worth their while to work for so unpractical objects. Such successes as have been achieved, as the international treaty abolishing export-prohibitions and the one reducing export duties on hides and bones, are of no practical importance. It is true that sometimes a more hopeful note is sounded. At a conference of representatives of Bulgaria, Estonia, Hungary, Lithuania, Poland, Roumania, Czechoslovakia and Yugoslavia, held in Warsaw at the beginning of last year, it was agreed, that an effort should be made to secure from those European states which import agricultural products a preferential treatment for such products of European origin. This of course implies, although nothing was said about it, that these states would agree in their turn to preferential treatment of industrial products of European origin. But nothing has come, or is likely to come, from this.

Yet, although little or nothing is to be expected from the wisdom of politicians, something may be expected in some more distant future from the force of facts. And these facts are likely to be brought home to America first of all. The United States are increasingly developing an export-interest. In some industries, their gigantic productive apparatus already now cannot be fully utilised without access to the worlds market. This is conspicuously the case in the motor car industry, but other industries will follow. And then manufacturers and politicians will discover that it is impossible to export without importing correspondingly. Moreover, the United States are a creditor country now, and will increasingly become so in future. A creditor country's policy is free trade. And this too they will discover sooner or later. No change in public opinion shows itself as yet. But public opinion in the United States is a very peculiar thing, and quite different in its ways from the public opinion of other countries. Americans are very slow to change their views. They stick to old views much more than other nations. But when they do change, they do so with a rush, and they trample on what they have held sacred for long years. This, I predict, will happen on the subjects of commercial policy. And then a tremendous weight will be thrown in the scall of free-trade.

Besides, not only the worlds depression will pass, but also those special depressions in agriculture, coal mining, textiles and so on. What is *overproduction* one day, is *underproduction* the other day, and then, if not all, at least some of the most powerful motives for protection will be weakened. Empire-preference in England may come about, but it will probably take a mild form and even be useful in creating a new power to fight the worst excesses of protection. An understanding between France and Germany, which is at least not impossible, would be a great help.The small eastern states of Europe may see the absurdity of their mercantilism. And therefore we may have some hope of seeing achieved an end, which would mean a great blessing to humanity in general. The pity is, that such ends are never realized as soon as thy become possible economically, but that they have to be forced on nations by needlessly hard struggles and by bitter experience. (「国民経済雑誌」第50巻第4号, 1931年4月1日. pp.1(481)-26(506)より転載)

「商業政策の現状」

現在世界の各国は一様に関税による保護政策を採つてゐるが、これは経済上の理由からやつてゐるのではなくて実は政治的の根拠から行つてゐるのである、しからば自由貿易はもはや実現しないかといふに今直に可能であるとは思はれない。しかし近い将来には必ずやヨリ自由な合理的な貿易が実現するに至るであらう、そしてそれは先づ米国から実行するであらうと思はれる、その理由の一つは現在アメリカは世界の債権国となつてゐるから、これを回収するには高率の保護関税を撤廃して、他国から輸入される商品を以て受け取らなければならぬ必要に迫られてゐるからである、第二の理由はアメリカは生産力の増大に伴つて自国で之れを消費することが不可能となるから、他国にその市場を見出す必要があり、従つて他国の関税の低きことを望むは必定であるから、このために自ら進んで関税を低下するであらうと思はれる、かくしてアメリカは先づ自ら進んでより自由な貿易主義をとり、全世界に向つても之を勧告するであらうから、他国も亦之に従ふであらうと思はれる。(「神戸商大新聞」1931年2月15日号, p.1より転載)

Professor *Joseph* A. Schumpeter, The Present State of Economics OR On Systems, Schools and Methods

Prefatory Note

The following pages present a summary of a lecture delivered by the author at the Commercial University of Kobe on the 9th of February of the current year. Much matter has been left out, which while necessary or useful in a spoken address, would be out of place in a written essay. Instead, some points have been inserted which it was not possible to touch in the lecture. The author hopes that in its new form this paper may be of some interest to Japanese colleagues and students, to whom he has great pleasure to submit it. Of course they cannot expect much that is new in a survey of this kind. But they may like to have before them the view of one economist, who even in the present chaos of conflicting standpoints believes that there are not many systems of economics, but that there is only one economic science, which is based on experience, and deals with the data of this experience just as any other science does.

I.

It sounds like a paradox when I say, that Scientific Thought in its infancy is more comprehensive than in its manhood. Yet it is so. When men begin to think about the phenomena around them, they at first aim at explaining *everything,* at penetrating the nature and essence of things, and at building up an organon of truth spreading from philosophical bases and metaphysical beliefs to definite doctrines about practical action. Such an organon of truth is called a System. It is *both* philosophy *and* science, and claims to give to its disciples the absolute light of truth while all other Systems, which may exist, must logically appear as absolute darkness. But when successive generations, in the lapse of centuries laboriously heaping thought upon thought, come to look critically at those imposing systems, they discover sooner or later that their edifices are not so homogeneous as they thought. They discover two things:First, that Truth is of two kinds, one of which consists of Belief, Vision, Revelation, which may be ardently held by, and be very evident to the disciple, but which is yet unreprovable by logical proceeding, while the other kind consists in statements about the empirical relations of the things which we observe. Secondly, the human mind discovers, that it is faced with different problems when discussing how things *are* and when discussing how things *ought to be.*If you knowenough about your phenomena, you can prove and verify certain statements about their relations to each other. But no amount of knowledge of empirical data, will be itself enable you to prove or verify anything about Ideals, Ends-in-themselves and so on, except in the sense, that Sociology may help you to understand why certain Ideals are, at certain times and places, held sacred by certain people.

When these two discoveries are once made, Science emerges. And Philosophy, which at first is all-comprehensive, becomes a distinct Empire of Thought. essentially different from Science, but still wedded to the teaching of what ought to be, to the teaching of Ideals and

Ends. Science itself, after having parted company with Philosophy, develops on its own lines.Its scope is much reduced, its splendour dimmed, it is, for ever after, nothing else but a storehouse of methods to describe, measure and connect facts, as given by experience and as amenable to empirical verification. It becomes infinitely more efficient for the exploration of the world of experience. But it loses all those fascinating implications about the innermost Nature of Things, the speculation about which is so dear to the human heart. Having *no* such implications, it becomes, on the one hand, *independent* of Philosophy and, on the other hand, *compatible* with every Philosophy. It is important to grasp this point. Whilst philosophers often fail to recognise it, scientists not less often draw a wrong conclusion from it. Having fought hard for the autonomy of Science, they often think that they have achieved more than autonomy, namely that they have annihilated speculative philosophy. Nothing could be more erroneous. Science cannot be guided by the Philosopher, and such things as the law of gravitation are entirely independent of the philosophical views of the physicist who teaches it. But no more can philosophical thought be guided by empirical science, or be either proved to be wrong or proved to be right by its methods. Both lie on different banks of a river, over which these is no bridge. And neither ought, in its labours, allow itself to be fettered by views useful or true for the one, but in their logical nature inapplicable to the other.

In my own country, my teaching is associated with the tendency to sever the bonds between economics and either general, or social, philosophy. And I accept this. I do believe this tendency to aim at the beneficial separation of an unhappy marriage. But the critical implication is, that my tendency towards *"Entphilosophierung der Ökonomie"*proceeds from any hostility against Philosophy. And this I do not accept, and I am anxious that Japanese colleagues should not fall into the same error about the true meaning of that tendency. I wish to see philosophy cultivated and developed. I should consider an age uncivilized which would not take interest in philosophical problems. All I want is that we should cease to mix up what is kept distinct in all other fields of human knowledge. And in view of some recent tendencies, especially in Germany, I must add, though with much regret:I do not wish scientific incapacity to shield itself behind philosophical phrases.

II.

To return to my argument:It is when those discoveries are made that "Systems"crumble into pieces like Temples may crumble in an earthquake. The founder of a System claims to teach, at the same time and as a harmonious whole, Philosophy, Science and Action(or Ideal).Much as we may regret it, we must face the fact, that no such claim is warranted any more. And to me it seems more dignified and manful to face this fact than to try to revive bygone states of the human mind, just as it is more dignified and manful to face the facts of the present social and economic conditions, although we may not like them, than to cry for the conditions of, say, Feudal Times.

Platos teaching was a “System” in this sense. It attempted to teach metaphysics, science, action, all by the same logical processes. And all through the middle ages and right up to the end of the 18 century it was the same mental attitude which prevailed. Even the founders, and early masters, of modern science, while preparing the ground for the edifice of modern thought, still adhered to the old one. Descartes for example, troubled himself about the Nature of the Universe, about metaphysics first of all, and probably looked upon his experiments and discoveries in physics and mathematics as parts of , and as subservient to, a comprehensive whole of homogeneous knowledge, of a philosophy. The same is true of Leibniz or Newton, and even much later generations display this tendency. But the important point is that they do not let their scientific work be influenced by it. And philosophers, on their part, have largely ceased to dogmatize on matters of physical science, and probably do not wish to repeat such things as Hegel's “proof” that there could be no more than seven planets.

But it is not so with economics. Here the belief in some close connection between philosophy and science still prevails in the minds of many eminent men. And discussion of our problems still suffers from the fact that some economists try to defend by philosophic argument what they cannot defend by scientific proof. Lest anyone should reply, that this is quite right because economics deals with human action and human action presents of necessity philosophic aspects, I want to submit that the distinction between philosophy and science which I tried to-draw above, is quite independent of the subject we have to do with. That distinction rests on logical grounds, which hold good whatever the nature of the facts of a science may be. There are plenty of differences, no doubt, between “natural” and “social” sciences. But this is not one of them. We deal with facts of economic experience such as that rice gets cheaper when there is more of it, and there is no *more* philosophical connotation to this than there is to the equation expressing the way in which a pendulum moves. We try to connect and to explain our economic facts by an *apparatus of concepts and theorems* constructed for the purpose and, although very different from the apparatus of physical sciences, quite as “unphilosophical” as it.

This apparatus of concepts and theorems is what we call” theoretical economics”.It has often been mistaken to be a set of *doctrines* ,while it is, as Marshall stated as early as 1885, an *engine of analysis* or a *set of tools to* grip our facts with. It has often been—and sometimes still is—mistaken to be “speculative”, while it really rests on observation of common economic facts, facts which are so common as not to require any conscious effort of collecting them. It has, finally, often been mistaken to imply materialistic, naturalistic, mechanistic analogies or prejudices, because its concepts are in their nature quantitative and because its theorems have some share of the exactness of the theorems of physics. And this last misunderstanding I believe to be the most unjustifiable of all. But unjustifiable as it is, it has a strong appeal to all who prefer foggy ideas to clear ones and who feel unable to live in the rugged mountains of scientific truth.

III.

It follows that "Systems" are a thing of the past, and that any attempt at system-building in our own day must be looked upon as an attempt to revive the ways of thinking of bygone ages. The word "system" will lose its meaning for us as it has lost it for other sciences and it will acquire that other meaning which it has in such connections as "a systematic treatise", "a system of equations" and so on. But this means, at the same time, that there is no more room for different "schools". Of course, there, is *one* meaning to the word "school", which is incident to the very life of science: groups of disciples gather round some teacher or some institution. By being interested in similar problems, by being taught similar ways of handling them, by exchanging and assimilating their views and results, they acquire a sort of mental familylikeness. And, let me add, they all have a stake in the fortunes of their group, with which individual success is bound up for every member. The history of Science is a fascinating study which unveils to us the ways of the human mind. And it has a neighbouring field of research, which is developing slowly and is perhaps more fascinating still. It may be called the *Sociology of Science*, and consists of the study of Science as a social phenomenon, for example of how the scientific profession developed, from what social groups its members come, how their social origin and position influences upon their work and so on. In this study, the phenomenon of grouping, which we call scientific schools, is of primary importance. How such schools arise and decay, how and why they fight each other and how their success or defeat determines the directions in which scientific endeavour moves, all this explains to a considerable degree why we have just the sort of science which we do actually have and why it is that not other lines of thought, just as promising in themselves, have been followed. Schools in this sense will probably always exist, for they are intimately linked up with the fundamental sociological phenomenon of Leadership.

But now I mean a different phenomenon. Schools such as the ones just mentioned, always stand on common ground. They differ in details of results, in the values they attach to different lines of advance, in the way they use one concept or theorem more, than another. Yet their *scientific worlds* are the same. In economics, to mention only a few, there are to-day schools in *this sense* which everyone knows: The Marshall-School, the school of Lausanne, which of course includes most Italian economists, the school of Vienna, the schools of Clark, Taussig, Mitchell, Moore in America, groups which gathered round Cassel or Wicksell in Sweden, the Pierson-School in Holland, the schools of Schmoller, Brentano, Knapp and others in Germany. We shall have presently something to say about their relations to each other. But just now we mean schools of a different kind, namely schools, which do not stand on the common ground of scientific thinking but expressly refuse to step on this common ground, and profess to differ radically from every other group in existence as to fundamentals: for example, as to the meaning of science, or even of knowledge in general. As a rule this is only possible by falling back on extra-scientific standpoints, such as philosophical or political ones. That is, why I have linked up the discussion of "schools" in this sense with the discussion of "systems" in a similar sense. The "Universalistic" school of Professor Spann may serve as an example. After the War, the wounded pride of the nation, smarting under defeat and a humiliating peace, very naturally produced, among other consequences, also a violent outburst of nationalistic feelings among a minority of Germans, both in Germany itself and in Austria. This feeling allied itself with a current of half-religious conservatism, which arose after *this* world was just as it did after the Napoleonic worlds war one hundred years ago. This has nothing to do with science. But it will rally young men around the flag of a teacher, who espouses both these causes. And this is what happened. Universalism itself is neither new nor fruitful. It goes back to a scholastic controversy in the middle ages, as shown by Professor Pribram of Frankfurt who is really the man who revived it, but who is far as possible removed from either Nationalism or Religious Conservatism. And it hardly embodies more than a common-place, from which no single new contribution to scientific knowledge has come so far. But as it fights Individualism and Rationalism, or seems to do so, it is applauded while those states of feeling last. I am sometimes credited with the saying, that there are *no schools in economics*. By this I mean, that there are now no differences as to fundamental standpoints among serious economists. I do not deny the existence of schools in the sense which we have first defined. And I do not deny the existence of schools in the sense, for which Universalism is an example. Only, in the first case, I hold that the differences are much less important than fervent disciples like to mate out. And in the second case I deny, that the phenomenon comes within the realm of science.

IV.

But are there not *scientific* schools differing fundamentally from all the rest of economists? Professor von Gottl and his followers may be quoted as an example. He certainly does not response any humours of the moment and yet he separates himself all along the line from almost all economists who ever existed. Yes, but the importance of his doing so will depend on the success, with which the general views, which he has so far developed, will produce concrete solutions of concrete problem. This is the criterion:Science is nothing but an engine for discovering a certain kind of truth. And any general view or standpoint is valueless as a contribution to science, if it does not help us to do so, however interesting or beautiful it may be in other respects. Take as an example to illustrate my meaning, Professor von Gottl's "Allzusammenhang". This is, if I understand him, the view that in economic, and generally in social, life everything is so connected with everything else that it means killing the soul of things, if we isolate any group of phenomena. Very true. Everyone admits it. It is just as true for the physical world around us. That is why scientific truth is never the whole truth. And this is also the reason why we have, and want, philosophy, religion and art. Of course the cock painted by an artist is something very different from, and superior to, the analysis of the same cock by a zoologist. But the zoologist can do nothing with the artists vision. Science exists because it is useful for some purposes to decompose phenomena. It is to this device that we owe scientific achievement, and there is no sense in looking down on it with contempt because it decompose the richness of reality and deals with miserables fragments at a time. And indeed, if we try to make the "Allzusammenhang" work, we quickly see, that what is really fruitful in it, has long ago been expressed by the system of interdependent quantities due to Léon Walras.

I want to urge the economists of Japan to stand firmly on the ground of empirical science and not to be led astray from the only path which ever led to scientific achievement, by antiscientific attitudes however brilliant they may be. As soon as we make up our minds to judge the performances of our time by *scientific* standards, and by scientific standards *alone*, it will be easier for us to distinguish between good and bad work. To-day, many of us look upon the works of an economist as they would look upon the works of a philosopher. We have an immense respect for "standpoints" and are quite ready to grant to any writer the right of holding any views whatever. This is the right way of feeling towards a philosopher. For in every philosophy there must necessarily be unprovable points, and in this sense every philosophy is a personal message from the author, which carries its own standards in itself. It may appeal to us or not, but we cannot simply call it "right" or "wrong". It is different in science. Science has its general, if limited standards and every proposition, which claims to be scientific, can in a definite sense be proved to be right or wrong. Our half-philosophical way of thinking sometimes makes us forget this. So for example, many people in England and elsewhere admire the works of Mr. Hobson. Now, as far as his opposition to Marshallian economics is concerned, his whole critique of marginal analysis turns on a misunderstanding of its nature and meaning. It is impossible to say, that he is within his rights in denying its validity and that here we have simply another standpoint, just as good as any others and just as much entitled to respect as any other. For we can *prove* his mistake, which consists in his failure to grasp the meaning of theorems about infinitesimal increments and as soon as we recognize this, there is an end of it, and there is no use to register the existence of a "new school" and to philosophize about It.

I could go on indefinitely in giving similar examples. I will add one more. An eminent man, whose great personal force has done very much to revive the interest in economic theory in Germany, Prof. Oppenheimer, has tried to base a whole "system" on the Monopoly of Land, which he took to be fundamental fact of our social organisation explaining well-nigh all the essential features of it. Now there is no such thing as a Monopoly of Land (Bodenmonopol). This has been proved many times, and as soon as it is recognized, naturally the system collapses and there is no sense any more in speaking of a school of economic thought, which differs fundamentally from others by holding that there is such a monopoly. It is this habit we have of coordinating, on an equal footing, truth and error, which accounts for the impression in the public mind, that there is any number of economic "systems" and "schools", all differing fundamentally but all having equal claims to attention, and that economics is therefore in a chaotic state. People, then, speak of a "crisis in economics", and very naturally suspect, that the *whole* of the present teaching will have to be cast aside if we are to get a really valuable science of economic life. If I am not mistaken, we are ourselves to blame for this impression, which so much impairs the authority of our science.

V.

Of course, it is quite wrong to make the divison of economists into schools turn on the difference in their views as to politics and social ideals. This abuse is quite frequent. Many historians of Economic Thought divide economists up in Liberals, Reformers, Socialists and so on. It should be obvious to anyone who is at all interested in knowledge for its own sake and possessed of a scientific attitude of mind, that this principle of division is entirely un-scientific. Adam Smith may be entitled to a place in the history of Free-Trade, but his *scientific* place is no more linked up with that than with, say, his personal taste in art. His scientific contribution would be just as important as it is, if he had lived in a protectionist age and had expounded arguments *for protection* in his chapters on practical political questions. Marx as a scientist has much more affinity to Ricardo, than to any socialist writer. Léon Walras was personally a socialist. And so I would go on giving examples for the fact that there is no necessary connection between a man's theoretic views and his social ideals or political preferences. If we divide up economic writers according to these, we are sure to combine people into groups, who have scientifically nothing to do with each other, and to separate people, who are close relations in the realm of science.

But what is the reason for this? We shall have the answer, if we remember again, that there is, logically, an impassable gulf between our knowledge and our wishes, likings or ideals. What we *want* is one thing, what we *know* is another thing. I may wish to live eternally, yet I know I am going to die, and there is no contradiction between this knowledge and this wish. One can be socialist without being a Marxist. It sounds paradoxical that one could also be a Marxist without being a Socialist. Yet it is true. In order to convince us of it, it is only necessary to point to any one of the salient features of the Marxist teaching. Marx taught the economic or materialistic interpretation of history. A Marxist must believe in it and also in that element of it which consists in the prediction, that the economic process will necessarily bring about socialism. But if a man *believes* this, he yet not *like* it. We may be with his whole soul averse to socialism while believing that socialism is inevitable. Or, take another instance, Marx taught the exploitation-theory of interest. A Marxist must accept it, or he is no Marxist. But he need not therefore disapprove of interest. He may very well think it essential to culture. The other day, I have been deeply impressed, when visiting Kyotoy by the artistic wonders of the ancient palace of the Shoguns. It is pretty clear, that the means which paid for this palace and for all the splendid works of art which adorn it, was raised by methods which any Marxist would have to call "exploitation". If so, I can personally only say, that I heartily approve of so much of exploitation as was necessary to call into existence that dream of beauty.

In logic, therefore, the scientific standing ground ought to be the same for men of all parties, for adherents of all ideals. They will, of course, draw different practical conclusions from the same scientific results. That does not matter. But there is no truth which is only true, say, for the socialist, there is no error which is only error for, say, the anti-socialist, and there is no scientific method which would belong to one party and be unscientific for any other party. Now, one of the most hopeful signs of our time is, that this is coming to be recognised more and more. True that there are still those, who will in any discussion take flight into those philosophic or other "fundamental" standpoints, where scientific argument cannot follow them. True also, that there exists an orthodox Marxist sect, In Germany and in Russia, which still holds aloof from the common ground of science, and which is really a school in the full sense of the word, similar to a medieval school of theologians. This school, the Neo-marxist, commands adherents of great eminence, especially in its Vienna section, such as O. Bauer, R. Hilferding, M. Adler. R. Luxemburg and F. Sternberg are other notable exponents. But it is pathetic to see how they squander valuable force on bolstering up positions, which have naturally become obsolete and would not now be defended by Marx himself, how they shut their eyes to whatever is being done outside the Sacred Creed, how they sterilize their talents by turning over and over again old doctrines and shibboleths while the world around them presents fresh outlooks and problems every day. But this is not the way any more of the modern socialist, who has been trained in economics. His arguments are forged in the same workshop as the arguments of anyone else. To give an instance, we have had in recent years a controversy in Germany about the level of wages and the consequences of unemployment benefit. The leader on the one side was Professor Cassel, the leader on the other side Professor Lederer. Of course this conclusions differed. But their arguments were of the same scientific material. And it is this what matters. The modern socialist will of course pay respect to the great shadow of Marx. It is right and decent that he should do so. But he will no longer condemn his cause to be defended by obsolete weapons. He will learn from Marx, but he will not copy him, nor confine himself to interpreting him. Professor Lederer may serve as an example. One of the greatest of his merits consists precisely in that he is leading German Socialists gently away from the deserts of a half-religions cult of Marx, and on to more promising fields, without hurting their feelings and without any shock to the tradition, which it is of course difficult for a social party to break of suddenly.

VI.

I therefore believe it to be quite unreasonable to make the distinction of "schools" turn on political aims of economics. But it is of course much less unreasonable to make it turn on "methods".This distinction presented itself with full force to our scientific world at the time of the famous controversy on method between Schmoller and Menger, historians and theorists ("Methodenstreit"), and it was quite justified then. For, although the theorists took from the first the line that history had its place in social science and that it was excesses only what they wanted to fight, historians either expressly or by implication claimed that historical research was the *only* admissible method, a position which was held partly on positivistic and partly on Dilthey's principles. So for time, a "historical school"came into existence, definitely at war with what they considered as a revival of classic economics. But comparatively soon this changed, and what looked like *alternatives*, subsided into *cooperation*.The "Methodenstreit" has produced quite a literature on questions of method. In spite of many valuable contributions I regret that so much time and strength has been, and still is being, expended on this subject. In Germany, from one fourth to one third of all the articles appearing in scientific magazines, is "methodological" in character. Now, of course we must discuss methods. But methods in another sense. Fruitful and necessary is discussion on, say, the Pearsonian method of correlation-measurement, or on the methods of trend-elimination or on measuring inequality of incomes and so on. But this is not what our "methodologists" do. They discuss such questions as whether economics is a historical science, on what the relative merits of induction or deduction are, in short generalities which are well-nigh valueless for the practical work before us and which might safely be left to logicians and philosophers, whose fields we have been invading instead of giving our energy to our own problems. Yet we must understand why we fell into this deviation. The historical school has the merit of having partly done partly inspired, a vast amount of historical work of detail, which has lighted up things for us and which we should not like to miss, but on the contrary we must keep on to cultivate. But it so entirely mistook the meaning of theoretical work as to cease to teach and even to understand it. So the theoretical tradition broke off, and when later German economists, having discovered their error, wished to get back to theory, they did not knew how to do. it. They thought it was a sort of philosophy or methodology and they started to philosophize and to discuss scientific "methods". And it is only recently, that real theoretic work is taken up again on serious and promising lines. This, by the way, also explains, how during the time, when serious critique was in abeyance, all those "schools" like Universalism and so on, have been able to make so considerable an impression, which would have been impossible in England. But much as we may regret the loss of time and force entailed by all, this, the result was nevertheless a respectable one. The place and the limits of historical research in our science have finally been defined with such clearness, that all quarrel has ceased about it. Henceforth historians and theorists will be able to cooperate peacefully, and it will seem just as absurd to think of them as antagonists, as it would, seem absurd to every same person to speak of a fundamental antagonism between a professor of experimental physics and his theoretical colleague. There is no experimentalist "school" in physics. *All* physics is experimental in *one* sense. And in *another* sense *all* physics in theoretical, and there is no "school" of theoretic physics which would wish to replace experiment by theory. Of course, some people feel more inclined, and are better fitter by nature or acquirement, to do theoretical, and others to do experimental work. It is human that each of these should rate higher what they do themselves. But this is all. And it is all that remains in economics of what has seemed to an order generation to be an antagonism of principle.

This settlement of an old controversy is indeed a great step forward. It has not yet produced its full results. It is not enough that historians and theorists should recognize the rights of each others pursuits, but they should cooperate just as theorists and experimentalists do in physics. The theorist should shape his theories so as to be of use in the analysis of historical facts, and the economic historian should understand, and make use of, the tools of theory. We are as yet far from this ideal but are beginning to realize it. Again, I think I may call it one of the hopeful signs of our time, that there is, as I know from experience, an increasing tendency among economic historians to consult the theorists about the questions which they are to investigate and the ways in which to connect cause and effect in their narratives, and among theorists, to consult historians about facts and developments.

In calling that controversy settled, I have left out of account a very regrettable revival of it in America. There, the old errors of the Historical School, have been served up again, but without being linked to positive work like those errors were in Germany, by the "Institutionalists".Institutionalism has caused a great commotion on the surface, but it has not produced any new results as the Historical School did. It is still being discussed, and in the recent discussion of it at the meeting of the American Economic Association in Cleveland in 1930. I have been referred to as the "arch-enemy" of Institutionalism. I plead guilty to the charge, but I want to make it quite clear what it is I object to. If Institutionalism went quietly to work on the programme which seems to be implied in its name, that is to say if institutionalists produced studies about social institutions, such as the family, private property and so on, I should not only not *objet*, but *welcome*.But they do nothing of the sort. Instead, they criticize without understanding, what has been done and is being done, and they replace positive achievement by ambitious programmes. Whatever of value has been written by any member of that group, could have been written by any other economist and does not imply any fundamental change in method and outlook. I reproach to the most famous of institutionalists, to Th. Veblen, *bad workmanship* and *insufficient scientific equipment*, which made him take old err for new truth. But this whole movement is passing away. And that eminent economist, who for some time showed some favour to it, Wesley C. Mitchell, has by his most recent work proved that he is willing to lead towards reconciliation.

Of course, all this applies equally to the relation of theorists and statisticians. As soon as the great development of economic statistics had led to some statisticians specializing in it, these statisticians at once displayed a tendency to set themselves up as economists and, as it is usual in our field, founders of a new economic science, which alone was founded on exact fact and compared with which everything else was antiquated speculation and so on. And they proceeded to chart frequency-curves, to calculate standard deviations and coefficients of correlation, to fit trends, and they called that scientific results. This tendency is by no means overcome by now. But I believe it will be overcome soon for the simple reason that the application of formal statistics without reference to the theory of the subject-matter so quickly leads to obviously absurd consequences that its devotees are likely to lose the taste for it soon. Already cooperation is beginning to work. And I want to express my belief that it will indeed bring about a new era of our science. Theory will have to be remodelled so as to be better equipped to the requirements of statistical analysis, and new statistical methods will have to be created, the results of which will carry economic meaning. By the work of H. L. Moore and his followers we are already well advanced on this road. And one only needs to look up the works of modern theorists, of Professor Pigou for example, in order to see how much they keep before their minds the goal *of welding into one statistics and economics.* Wide vistas open up here. Economics, always and of necessity a *quantitatibe science* , is on the verge of becoming a numerical science. What a pity if, instead of working together in the fresh atmosphere of scientific sun-rise, we should employ ourselves in fighting out method-logical or philosophical questions!

VII.

If, then, there is no Historical School any more, if there is no room for a Statistical School, if it is futile to set up Schools according to political aims or ideals of economists or according to the philosophical views they may happen to have, and if, finally, there is very little scientific meaning to all those Schools which are constantly advertising for a new era in economics—I conclude, that it is time to put an end to all the talk about schools in the sense of bodies of doctrine repudiating on principle the common basis of scientific work. It is time to recognize this common basis, to leave philosophy to the philosopher, and to go to work on the wide possibilities which are opening up before us. Much phraseology, dear to many of us, will have to be relinquished, for science has no symbols for confused ideas. But we shall enjoy instead all the pleasure incident to scientific conquest, and all the beauty incident to the forms of rigorous thought.

However, it is now necessary to ask the question, whether differences within scientific opinion itself are not too great to allow us to consider economics as *one* homogeneous field, where people work towards common ends and from common starting points. In other words: Even if we discard all those "schools" which we hold to have no title to attention within the realm of empirical science, have we not ourselves been forced to admit, that there are schools within our empirical science which disagree fundamentally? Do so not constantly hear of "marginalism" and "neo-classicism" and so on, and are there not "schools" in the sense of claiming possession of truth denied to all other similar schools? I admit that it looks like it, because human vanity makes us *inclined* to stress points of difference, and *adverse* to recognize points of agreement. But I hold that it *looks* like it only, and that below the surface there is as much fundamental agreement between economists as there is among scientists in any other field.

To show this would take a volume. We will confine ourselves to one point, taking it from the fundamentals of general economic theory. What is the position of the theory of Marginal Utility to-day? Is it the badge of one "school", or of several schools which thereby disagree fundamentally with others? Of course it is *not.* The discovery of Jevons, Menger and Walras was substantially the same. Most people will admit so much, and they will also admit, that what difference there is between those three at all, consists only in differences in technique and in details. And the work of the Great Swedish economist Wicksell shows, that it is possible to build on the foundations of both the so-called Vienna-school and the Lausanne-school, at the same time. It is only the uninitiated who, seeing the mathematics of the one, and the unmathematical exposition of the other, concludes that what looks so dfferent, must differ in substance too.

But it is less universally recognized, that the teaching of the Austrian and of the Lausanne theory, fundamentally identical as it is, also fundamentally the same as Marshalls. Marshall himself would not have admitted it, as shown by the ungenerous review he wrote when Jevons' work appeared. He stressed so much the continuity of science as to make his teaching appear much more Ricardian than it was. However, if you divert it of its language and put it into the pitiless light of equations, you find that its fundamental structural idea is marginal utility and marginal productivity, and nothing else. You could leave out of Marshalls great work all the concepts which taste of Ricardo, without missing anything which is essential. And as a matter of fact, disciples of Marshall and disciples of the great Austrian leaders, have no longer the feeling of crossing a frontier when they discuss with each other. In America, Walras' message was first received and developed by Irving Fisher. And Clarks theory is, though less satisfactory, essentially the same, as everyone can see who will take the trouble of reading what Walras says on marginal productivity. How much less important differences are than we think, is also shown by the example of that great teacher, whom History will rank as one of the greatest of economists, Professor Taussig. He is no "marginalist", it seems. But he defines wages as the "discounted marginal product of labour". And whoever so defines them, *is a "marginalist", however we may call him.*If should be noted too, that the work of H. L. Moore and his followers proceeds on Walrasian lines. And there is a tendency now among authors, who were no friends to theory some years ago, to connect the results of their work with the fundamental principle of the great Frenchman:I may mention for instance Professors Mitchell and Mills.

Yet it has become the habit of many people to contrast Walras sharply with Pareto and Cassel. Are not they at least leaders of a new "school"? To answer the question as to Pareto, it is sufficient to remind us that the concept of equilibrium is just as much due to Walras as the concept of marginal utility is itself. And that concept is the basis of Paretos work. Undoubtdely Pareto has much improved and generalised the teaching of Walras, as every capable discipal naturally improves the store of scientific truth which is handed to him. But he has committed the wrong of making appear as fundamental innovation what was progress on the same lines only. And the public has been told that we are now blessed with a new school. This is not true, and still less it is true in the case of Cassel. Cassel, too, is a pupil of Walras. He simplified Walras' theory so as to make it accessible to many who would be lost with Walras himself. This was a great service to the progress of our science. But he tried to vest with a pretence of originality what was due to Walras. He did so, for example, by pretending to eliminate marginal utility, while he only gave it another name. This name in fact, was used by Walras already, who instead of "utilité marginale" sometimes speaks of "rarété".Well, "rarété " is the French word for Cassel concept of "Knappheit"or scarcity. But if we tear off the veil of differing technique and phraseology from the essence of the theoretical thought of our time, an unexpected harmony appears.

Of course, there are plenty of differences on single problems. Very important ones, such as the problem of interest, are among them. We also differ in our ways of handling things, some of us stressing the distinction between statics and dynamics, while some of us think much less of its usefulness. Differences of this kind must always exist. They are the very life of science, and without them progress would disappear. Now ideas have to be fought for, and our whole teaching must be in a constant process of revolution and evolution for ever. But this is another thing, and perfectly compatible with the statement that at any given time both starting points and goals of all competent workers are substantially the same. And I repeat:There are no "schools"among serious economist to-day, except in the sence of personal preferences for certain problems or methods. We have *one* science of economics just as we have *one* science of electricity.

What has been said about the fundamentals of general theory could be proved to be true also of everyone of the branches of applied economics, such as money, banking, international trade, labour economics ("Sozialpolitik"in German), public finance and so on. The general theorist of to-day usually keeps less in touch with all those branches than the classical writers did, and a vast amount of facts and arguments has been allowed to grow up which has little or no contact with theory. It is perhaps the foremost task of the next generation to enrich theory by these facts and problems and, on the other hand, to bring the principles of theory to bear on them. Yet, wherever the task has been taken in hand already, that common ground and substantial agreement shows up at once. The literature on money has just been enriched by Mr. Keynes' important work. And reading it, one is struck by the fact that there is hardly anything in it with which most competent theorists could not be expected to agree heartily. Or take the work on International Trade by the great economist of Harvard:It is a standard work which focusses the attention of all competent workers in that field, and it will serve as a common starting point for quite a time to come. Or take Professor Pigous Economics of Welfare which is theoretical Code for Labor economics or "Sozialpolitik".It is an arsenal of theoretic tools, and there is little disposition to quarrel with any of its fundamental features. So everywhere economists are drawing together and trying to unite their efforts in the building of the science of the future. Let us not lag behind. Let us take up the tools we have and attack real problems instead of sitting down and musing over philosophical or political connotations of our terms—this we better leave to those who cannot keep the pace. (「国民経済雑誌」第50巻第5号, 1931年5月1日. pp.1(679)-27(705)より転載)

1931年講演稿(「政治経済学の最近の発展」)(1)

I

この小論で私は, 経済科学の現状を見渡そう——鳥瞰図を描こう——とするつもりである。いかに不完全とはいえ, 私が取り扱おうとする問題は,

　　我々がどこに立っているか

我々がどこから来るのか
我々がどこへ行くのか
我々の方法が将来どうなるだろうか

ということである。

こうした見渡しでは, 皆さんに多くの新しい事実を語りはしないでしょう。日本の学者と学徒は, 他の国々で科学の問題で生じているものについて非常によく知らされているので, 私は皆さんに何か全く新しいことを付け加えることができないと述べてきました。私が皆さんに興味をもたせようとすることは, 科学の現状がその分野で1つの作用をあてにしているその方法を示すこと——それが1つの特別な性質の眼鏡で調査される時に現われるその方法を皆さんに示すこと——である。それを観察する私の方法が, 別のものにも気に入られる一理がある, と言うつもりはありません。

経済学の範囲は非常に広い。もちろん, 我が科学は, 問題が展開するにつれて広くなる。一人の人が経済学を把握することは, ますます困難になる。だが, ある意味では経済学の範囲は, 社会学が進歩したために30年前よりも制限されている。我々は, 社会学を大いに非難しなければならないとしても, 社会学は上出来の方法で多くの分野で進歩してきた。その結果, 経済学者のかつて取り扱った多くの主題が現に存在し, こうした主題がその姉妹科学(2)に任されうるということになっている。

例えば, 誰でも経済的主題を取り扱おうとしたり, どんな教師も経済学を講義しようとしたりすれば, 私有財産, 相続権, その他のそうした経済的制度を取り扱わざるをえないのだと考えるのは, まったく当然のことである。しかし, 今日では我々は, 実際的目的のために必要である限り, そうした主題を取り扱いさえすればよい。 というのも, そうした主題が, 今では社会学の明確な部分をなしているからである。社会学者による私有財産と相続権についての優れた諸著作がある。そうした制度が, 国家にとってどういう意味があるのか, そうした制度が発展したり衰えたりするその理由を, 諸論文から詳しく調べられる。経済学者は, 昔の世代と同じようにそうした問題に悩む必要はない。

社会科学は, ますます一つの科学ではなくなっている。かつては自然科学は, 一つの科学と見なされたけれども, もはやそうではないのである。理論物理学者や化学者や生物学者は, 実践的科学者とは異なった思想癖を身につけた全く異なった人々である。我々は, 理論的仕事と経験的仕事とを分離して以前の仕事の素晴らしさの多くを減じるのを残念に思うかもしれない。それは見渡しの広さを減じ, その仕事を狭くし, それを美学的により美しくはさせないのである。その埋め合せの利点は, それが効率を増すということである。近代科学者は, 専門化するほかに手がない。経済学者も又, そうせざるをえない。かくして, この意味での問題の範囲が, 過去にそうであったよりも制限されるのである。

II

私は, 経済学を一科学と見なすという自白から始めねばならない。私がこのことを主張するのを必要だと考えるのは, 異常だと思われるかも知れないが, 我々のうちの多くの人々は, 経済学者が自己の信念を自からの信条から引き出すと考える。その他の人々は, 経済学の哲学が個人的なものであると考える。このことこそ, 私が明らかにしようとする点である。つまり, 経済学は, その他の科学とちょうど同じように一科学である。その目的は, その他の科学と同様に, 我々が観察する諸現象の間に機能的関連をうち立てることである。

経験科学は, 経済的な諸事実を取り扱う。我々はそうした事実を単純化し整序する結果, そうした事実の間の諸関係が現れてくるのである。ある神秘的方法でこうした関係が, 真理と呼ばれる知識に対する人間の心の渇望を充たす。それは, 例えば宗教的啓示や直観力のように, 永遠の真理ではない。

それは，単に諸現象の合理的相互関係に過ぎない。それで全てである。このような方法で観察すれば，私は一自然科学が包含する全ゆるものを経済学が持っていると考える。

経済学が，一つの社会科学であるということと，経済学について精神的態度の上で多くの相異が存在するということが，自然諸科学にとっては普通である方法を用いることを妨げるものではない。方法についての先験的判断は，妥当ではないのである。ある方法は，あてはまらないかも知れない。が，実験の結果だけが，我々に知らされうるに過ぎない。論理の一般的規則以外には，科学的真理の発見に対して予想された規則はないのである。適切な方法を追求することこそ，科学の最も素晴らしい局面である。それは，一種の知的冒険であり，そこではある時にはこの方法が，そしてある時にはその他の方法が，有益で効果的である。どんな方法でも，全ゆる問題に役に立つというものではない。あらゆる方法には，それぞれの場所がある。こうした理由のために私は，方法論争を非常に軽蔑するのである。

私は，理論と経験法との間の区別を認識論的につけない。定理と統計的規則性との間に根本的な相異はない。両者は，異なった事実から明確な技術によって引き出される経験法である。理論家が論理的推論を用いることを怠ったり，統計家が理論的道具を用いようとしないのはばかげている。両者は，実質的には同じ経験的基盤を持っている。彼等は，異なった観察に基づくが故に，異なって見えるに過ぎないのである。

専門家は，ある特殊な分野に対して特別な才能を選びかつ持っているが故に，専門家であるのかも知れない。理論家がそれを好み，理論化が社会科学の最も素敵な局面であると考え，ほかの何事をも軽く軽蔑するが故に，理論家であるのかも知れない。こうしたことがそうであるのは，当然でありもっともである。もしも我々みんなが，知識の重要性，特に我が科学の知識，我々の個人的に貢献できるもの，を過大評価しなかったならば，科学が発展したであろうとは，私は考えない。人生で何かをする——偉大な科学的発見をし，戦いに勝利し，偉大な政治家になる——ためには，我々は自分のしたいものの重要性を過大評価しなければならない。もしも我々があまりに哲学的な方法で，あるいはあまりに幅広い見地から事態を観察するならば，何世紀も経つにつれて，あたかもほとんど実際には問題にならないかのようにして，それは現われるでしょう。

III

我が科学の状態を見渡すにあたっては，学派と呼ばれるものの間の相違を示すのが普通である。そうすることは，なるほど便利であり，しばらくの間こうした実践に多くは従ってきた。が，私自身は同じやり方に従うよりはむしろ，それに賛成しないということを皆さんにお話しした方がよい。全ゆる科学の始めの頃は，教えられうるもの，知らされるもの，為されうるものは，非常に制限されている。そして，一科学の始めの頃は，達成されうる全ゆるものが非常に重大に見える。

それから体系構築の時代又は時期がある。科学の教師達は，喜んで一つの体系，知られているはずのものを具体化すると彼等が考える一般的真理の一本体，と呼ぶものを築き上げる。その他の全ゆるものは，特に他の教師達の体系は，邪悪で誤謬である。この体系構築は，科学が成年に達する時に終わる。それが成年に達すると，間もなく一般的な体系の見地が考えられるほど重要ではないということが発見される。

例えば，近代心理学は，人間の霊魂についての問題を問わない。それは，専門化された諸現象を取り扱う。霊魂の概念は，哲学者に任される。かくして，従って特殊な問題に役に立つ実際的仕事が，ますます表面化する。 一般的な体系構築は，背後に退く。 全ゆる問題がそれ自身の技術を要求するということを，我々は今や発見した，あるいはそうでなければ発見するはずだっただろうと思う。問題が, 方法を強いるのである。我々は, 問題を解くにあたって適切な方法を用いることを避けることができない。まず問題に接近することもなく, それを理解することもなしに, 続行する方法の先入見を作ろうとしても, 無駄である。

皆さんが御存知の通り, 18世紀の初めには, 全ゆる経済学者は自からの分析を個人から始めた。19世紀の経済学者も, 個人的見地をとった。しかしながら, 個人から始めるのが全く間違いであるということこそ, 方法論的普遍主義の信条である。この見解では, 個人は単に社会的存在の所産に過ぎない。それ故, たった一人の人間から出発するのは間違いである。我々は, 全ゆる個人が自分の成長する社会的影響によって作られるということを知っている。この意味では, 彼は社会的存在又は階級の所産であり, それ故に自由な行為者ではない。このことは, 確かにそうである。だが, それがただの言葉にちがいないところでは, この一般的形態で述べられる限り, それは全く興味のないものである。

個人対階級の関連は, 我々がその考えから具体的な知識をうち立てることができる時に興味があるにすぎない。私が大いに反対するのは, 信条としての普遍主義を単に説教することによって, 我々が知識を前進させるのではないということである。社会学又は政治的生活のいくつかの問題で, 我々は社会的全体から出発する他に手がない。その他の場合, 例えば市場現象や近代産業のたいていの問題のような場合には, 個人から出発する以外には手がない。

ある問題群では普遍主義が, 別の問題群では個人主義が, 指示される方法である。それ故に, 我々は, 個人主義的でも普遍主義的でもないはずである。それは便宜の問題である。方法論的個人主義も方法論的普遍主義も, 永遠の真理ではない。両者とも, ある時には有益で, 他の時には進歩を妨げる方策にすぎない。それ故に私は, 教義の関係のある本体である体系の存在を信じない。私は, 学派の存在を信じない。

IV

私はたいていの経済学部門での全ゆる有能な研究者が, 表面に現われる以上にお互に同意しあっていると思う。経済学で問題なのは, 当該科学に於いて有能な研究者の間に同意があるはずがないということではない。普通の医者や数学者や歴史家は, 普通程度に有能であるけれども, 経済的問題について話す人々が普通程度に有能でないということこそ問題なのである。我々が経済学について持っている真理の量は, それほど一般的には認められてはいないし, そうした真理はその他の科学に於けると同様に近づきやすいものでもない。

新しい数学的方法が確立される時には, それが全ゆる他の数学者の財産になる。しかし, 新しい経済的方法が確立される時には, それは共有財にはならないのである。経済的世界の大部分は, 非常にまずく訓練されていて天賦の才もほとんどないので, 問題を適切に議論させたり受け入れさせたりあるいは否認させたりするには長い時間がかかるのである。それが全体的真理である。それ故, 私が学派について語るべきだとか, 私がちょうど議論してきた意味で学派が存在すべきだとは, 私は考えない。

学派とは何か。言葉の最初できわめて無邪気な意味では, あらゆる大学と制度に於いては, 生徒は著名な教師に自然と群がる。こうした学生達は, 同じ方法について教えられる。彼等は, 同じようなやり方で問題を取り扱う習慣をつける。彼等は, 思考と著作上である共通の癖を用いるのみならず, 共通の術語をも用いる。このことは必然的であり, あらゆる科学に存在する。

学派は又, 何か他のものを意味する。例えば, フランス, ドイツ又はイタリア学派のように, 我々は, 国と結びついた学派と少なくとも一致したいく人かの人々を区別する。科学には国境はないのであるから, この分類は本当は全く無駄である。ドイツの理論家とフランスの理論家は, 彼等のいずれかが隣りの事務所での同僚と同じであるよりもはるかに共通点が多いかも知れない。

経済学者のフランス学派について言うことは，過去の歴史に於いてある場合について言いうるに過ぎない。18世紀の中頃に，重農主義学派がパリで起こり，フランスで大成功を博した。そして始めは，その他のどこに於いてもそうではなかった。それは，特にたまたまフランスの現象であった。後に学派全体は，消滅した。我々は，その他の国で重農主義を実際見い出す。だが，重要な貢献をする著名な重農主義者は皆んな，フランス出身であった。それ故，我々はそれをフランス学派と呼ぶのである。

イギリスの古典学派は，1776年（Adam Smith『諸国民の富』）から1848年（J. S.Mill『政治経済学の諸原理』）まで溯る。イギリスの経済学者達は，あるグループを作り上げた。そのメンバーはお互に知り合い，お互に密接な交際をもった。その意味で彼等を一学派として言々することは，可能である。しかし，我々が学派と国家とを同一視できるのは，ごく稀な場合である。しかもこのことは，想像されうる経済学史を書こうとするのにほとんど最悪の方法である。

V

学派の別の意味は，政治的信条か社会的信条によって経済学者を分離することである。ある人々は，重商主義，自由主義，あるいは社会主義学派等々について言々する。これらのグループを観察するそうしたやり方は，問題を受け入れ易くする。科学的見渡に関して意見の一致した重商主義者，自由主義者，又は社会主義者は，決していなかった。科学に関して問題なのは，科学的見渡しであり，非科学的問題に関してグループが出す結論ではない。

Adam Smithが自由貿易の適当な方法を支持したという事実は，その科学的重要性とはなんら関係がない。彼が航海の自由(3)を支持したように，もしも彼が保護主義(4)に賛成したならば，それはちょうど同じことであっただろう。Richardoが自由貿易の考えを持ったという事実は，彼の科学的偉大さを増すことでもなければ傷つけることでもない。科学とは，説明することと理解することとを意味し，その他は何事をも意味しないのである。

行動は知識にたよるのではなく，むしろ意志と感情にたよるのであるから，人の政治的信条と経済的理論との間には密接で説得力のある関連は決してないのであり，決してありえないのである。これこそ，重要な点である。私は，自分の意図を明らかにするために一例を挙げたい。皆さんのうちの多くは，マルクス主義者であることなしに社会主義者であることはできないと考える。実際には皆さんのうちの全ては，マルクス主義者であることが社会主義者であることであると考える。両者の見解が間違っていることを立証することは，容易である。

政治上では皆さんは，マルクス主義者であることなしに社会主義者であるかも知れない。経済学の近代理論と呼ばれるかも知れぬものの大創始者の一人Vilfred Paretoは，自分が社会主義者だと私に語った。彼は自分の科学的著作ではこの事実を利用しなかったし，彼はこの事実を持つべきではなかった。もしも皆さんが科学的問題を取り扱うならば，それを真理に対する探索者の精神で取り扱わねばならないだろう。皆さんは全て，社会主義者であることができる，が皆さんはマルクス主義者である必要はない。

しかし，別の一層興味ある問題は，皆さんが社会主義者であることなしにマルクス主義者でありうるかどうかである。それは，社会主義者がどういうことかによるものである。もしも社会主義者であることが，来るべき社会主義が社会の組織の一形態として地歩を固めてきたということを意味するならば，そうした組織形態の存在を信じるものは誰でも社会主義者でありえ，党に所属できるのである。例えば，私は自分が死ぬだろうということを知っている。しかし，そのことは私が死ぬことを好むだろうということを意味するものではない。社会が社会主義への傾向を持っているということを科学的に立証できると私が言うとしても，そのことは私が社会主義に賛成であるということを意味しない。私は愉快な事件や事情のみならず，不愉快な事件や事情をも予言できるのである。

もしも私がマルクス主義者であるならば，私は搾取の理論を保持しなければならない。そのことは私を社会主義者にするであろうか。否。私が搾取の理論を保持する，すなわち，私が搾取は人間の文明にとって必要であると信じる，と仮定してみよう。その場合には，私はマルクス主義者である。しかし，私は必ずしも社会主義者ではないであろう。というのは，私は搾取を承認するからである。それは科学的確信の証明ではなく，それ故にマルクス主義が科学的信条である限りにおいてマルクス主義か非マルクス主義かの問題でもない。Marxがそうしたように，マルクス主義が一つの科学的体系であろうとする限り，それは社会主義的共感を強く主張するものではない。それは，反社会主義的見解に結びつけるものでもない。

私は昨日親切な同僚のいく人かと共に，京都市を訪れることができた。そこで私は，古い将軍の御殿にある芸術作品を大いに賛美した。社会主義的立場からはそうした絵画は全て，決して描かれるべきでなかった。もちろん，そうした絵画が描かれるためには，Marxが搾取と呼んだであろう手段がとられた。私は，きわめて深い芸術的賛意をこめてそうした絵画を賛美した。こうした絵画が描かれるためには搾取の量が必要であったと思う。従って，搾取の理論に賛成することと搾取に賛成することとの間には何の論理的関係もないことを，皆さんはおわかりいただけるのである。

VI

「学派」という用語の別の意味は，我々が経済学を哲学的原理に分けるものである。わが母国では，MarxをHegel哲学と結びつけて考えるのが普通である。事実がそうでないことを示すのは，容易である。Marx自身は『資本論』序言で，そうした関係がないと言っている。Marxは，剰余価値論や蓄積論やその他のところでHegelの用語を用いているけれども，彼の分析は経済的論拠に基づいている。それは，全ゆる哲学と両立しうるものである。それ故，彼の哲学はHegel哲学とちょうど同じようにKant哲学とも呼ばれる。どんな哲学的傾向も彼の分析に適合できる。ある人がある哲学の存在を信じるとしても，それは彼が経済的問題についてある見解を持っているということにはならない。

実際的方針と実際的方法に関して学派を区別することもなされうる。このことは一層期待できるように見えるかも知れないが，ここでさえ私は，もはや学派が存在しない時期に我々が近づきつつあるのだと考える。一例を挙げると，ドイツや他のところに歴史学派が存在した。我々が経済分析と競合しうるように経済史に重要性をもはや付け加えないが故に，歴史学派は消滅してしまっている。我々は，この学派を科学的仕事の一般的本体に吸収してきた。自からの本分を理解する少数の経済的歴史家しか，理論家と争いそうもないのである。両者が，一つの共通の目的に向けて努力することは認められる。

実験物理学者と理論物理学者の場合をとってみよう。理論物理学者は，実験と実験的仕事についてほとんど知らない。実験物理学者が数学とうまくやってゆくやり方を知らないなら，彼は理論物理学者の助けを求める。そのことは，協同のやり方である。一方が間違いで他方が正しいと言っても無駄である。歴史学派は消滅してしまっており，人々が方法について争いをやめ，実際問題に取り掛かる時にどのようにして学派が消滅するかを，それは例証している。

私がハーバードにいた時，ハーバードの歴史家の一人Robert Blake氏が私にレバント貿易の歴史をしてくれた。〔Schumpeterは訪日前の4ヵ月をハーバード大学で過ごしていた。〕[5]その中には次のような多くの問題があった。すなわち，ローマの貿易収支はアウグスツス皇帝の時代から紀元後

300年頃まで赤字か黒字であったか。赤字なら, どんな結果が期待されうるだろうか。ビザンチンとペルシァのコインがある地区に浸透してその他のところには入り込まなかったのを, あなたはどのように説明するか。そうした問題は全て, Alfred Marshallが一つの道具, 一つの分析機関として定義づけた意味での理論を必要とする。そうした問題についてある点では, そうした分析機関を与えるのが私の特権であった。協同するのは, きわめて当然である。学派を実際的, 実験的, あるいはその他の範疇として区別しても無駄である。それ故, 私は学派について述べるつもりはない。結局その用語は, しばしば無知を隠すキャッチフレーズに過ぎないのである。学派の中のメンバーは, 才能を置き換えるのに十分であると学派の一員によって時々考えられる。学派は, 全ゆる点で有害なものである。科学が進歩するにつれて, 学派が我々から無くなるだろうと思う。

VII

いろんな国での我が科学の状態について, 一言してみよう。特にイギリスは, 幸運である。イギリスの経済学者は, ロンドンとケンブリッジに非常に集中しているので, 討論と個人的接触によって共通の基盤をうち立てるのが容易である。その用語の厳密な意味で, 経済学上の最大の教師Alfred Marshallは, まったく長い期間この共通の基盤の上に立った。イギリスの経済学者の99パーセントが, A. Marshallの学徒である。もちろん, 「ロンドン・スクール・オブ・エコノミックス」出のいく人かの反対者がいた。

独力の反対者もいたが, その中にはJohn Hobson氏がいた。彼は, 我が科学に於いて発展してきた現象の好例である。その他の諸科学では一人の人が何かを理解しないなら, 彼はそれをかまわずにほっておく。我が科学では, もし彼が了解しないなら彼は競争する権威者だと主張するのである。Hobson氏は, 限界分析が何たるかを知らない。彼は, 限界収益点を小さな増分でなく大きな増分の限界まで変化させることによって限界分析を論破する。

どんな科学に於ても全ゆる限界分析は, 当該科学が取り扱う諸量と比べて極度に小さい諸量でもってのみ作用する。皆さんが小さな量を大きな量に取り替えるなら, もちろん別の論理が当てはまる。小さな量について言えることは, 大きな量については言えないのである。Hobson氏はその事実を知らないで, 経済学者にとって小さな量についてあてはまることが, 大きな量については言えないということを立証するのは容易であると思った。そのことは, 真実である。だが, もしも誰かが物理学者の教室でそのことを同じように議論するなら, 彼は単に無視されるだろう。経済学では新しい権威が, こうした成果に基づいて立てられてきたのである。

しかし, 全体としてはイギリスに於ける経済学は, 非常に高い水準にある。共通に引き受けられた基盤から発して, イギリスの経済学者の最も著名人であるMarshallの学徒は皆んな, Marshallの仕事を発展させてきた。新しい経済学を求めて叫んでみても無駄である。我々が, 新しい経済学を作らねばならない。そしてそのことこそ, そうしたMarshall学徒達が着々と行なっているものである。しかも彼等は, かなりの進歩をなしてきた。

私は, Marshallが経済理論上でどれだけの進歩をなしたか知らない。Marshallの教義が, 彼の公表された仕事よりももっと先へ行ったという一つの伝説がある。彼は, 公表するのが非常に遅かった。彼が極端な老齢で本を出した時, 彼は自分が心に留めていることを非常に明白に提起することができなかった。私は, A. C. Pigouとその他の学徒が, 例えば貨幣についてどれだけMarshallを越えてしまったか正確には知らない。Marshallの寛大な学徒達は, 自分達の発見物を常にMarshallの手柄にした。

しかし, かかる学徒達はずいぶんたくさんの用具を発展させてきた。例えばPigouは, 統計的なやり方で供給や量や家計やのデータに基づく需要の弾力性を確定する一方法を持っている。その上, Pigouはたくさんの貴重な定理によって分析を改善してきたし, その表面や基盤を変化させずにMarshallの体系をゆっくりと再建してきた。Marshall自身は, その点で私が後ほど言及する一つの条件に熟達していた。

我が科学がフランスでは非常に貧しい状態にあるのは, 驚くべきことである。このことは特にそうである。なぜなら, フランスの天才が当該科学の歴史に於いて非常に見事に傑出しているからである。当該科学が今までに持ってきた三名の最も天賦の才ある経済学者は, 皆んなフランス人であった。すなわち, François Quesnay, Antoine A. Cournot, Léon Walrasであった。例えば, フランスでの天賦の才ある人々が教授の職を得るのは困難だと考える時に, Cournotだけが母国で成功しただけだった。

我が母国のドイツでは, 全ゆる事が過渡状態にある。歴史学派に対する反動は, 30年前に溯る。しかし, 歴史家の住居を去ってしまっていた後では, 経済学者はいろんな方法で経済的事実を分析するやり方を必ずしも知らなかった。そこで経済学者は, 私がいつも経済学上の最大の不幸の一つと考えるものを出発させた。経済学者は方法について言い争いを始めた。

方法についての何百冊もの書物が, ドイツで現われた。定期刊行物の中の100の論文のうちから, 私は方法論的性質の36論文を数えてみた。それはものすごいものである。なるほど, いくつかのよい論文もあるかも知れないが, それらはエネルギーの浪費によって帳消しにされる。皆さんが良い経済学者であるなら, 皆さんは経済問題に働きかけるべきであって, 論理学者の仕事を取り上げるべきではない。認識論が我々の必要を考慮に入れるならば, なぜ我々自身がわざわざある領域に入ろうとしないのか, そして我々がちようどうまくなしで済ませるという問題をわざわざ取り扱おうとするのか。それは偉大な国にとっては, 惨めな事態である。私は, 心からそれを恥かしく思う。私は, ドイツに於いて科学の他の部門がよりよく現われることをただうれしく思う。

驚くべきことには, 多くのことがイタリアでは為されつつある。この賞賛すべき天賦の才ある国は, 経済的環境により課された限界を克服してきた。その国には数知れぬ大学があるが, それらを支えるお金がない。多くの教授の椅子は, 用意されていない。だが, どれほど良い仕事がなされつつあるか, そしてどれだけ多くの著名な人々が常に現われつつあるか, 驚くべきことである。イタリアでの最近の経済学研究は, Maffeo Pantaleoniの時代に始まる。彼の教義を基礎として非常に大勢の若い人々が, 優れた仕事をなしつつある。

時間があれば, 私はヨーロッパの北部の国々で非常に良い仕事がどれほど為されつつあるか話すことができるだろう。オランダばかりか, ノールウエー, スウェーデン, デンマークで特に若い人々が, 経済学を先へ進めつつある。私は, 後に偉大な仕事をするずいぶん多くの北ヨーロッパの経済学者を知っている。

我が科学がそれに払われる関心の点では, アメリカでは一番幸運であるということを付け加えさせていただきたい。わが国には, Frank Taussing[(6)]やIrving Fisherという大指導者やより重要でない多くの人々がいる。人目をひく輝やかしい業績はないけれども, ものすごい量の良い実験的仕事がある。多くの見込みのある可能性が, 統計家[(7)]と理論家の間の協力に存在する。彼等の間で言い争をする時が去って, 今や協同が確立されるようになりつつある。アメリカについての重要な事実は, 彼等ができるだけ最大の成功でもって仕事を一層進めようとする正しい意図と手段とを持っているということである。

全ゆる事が，アメリカではどこでもスムースには行かない。ドイツでは誤りにより駄目にされたGustav von Schmollerの仕事の例の部分が，たいていの経済学者によって脇にやられてきているけれども，アメリカではそうした誤りが制度主義という名で復活している。制度主義は，ドイツの歴史家達の方法論的誤り以外の何ものでもなく，それは彼等が我が科学に対してなした偉大で永続的貢献を考慮に入れていない。アメリカでは，それは単に誤りに過ぎないのであって業績ではないのである。もちろん，このことはアメリカの環境では一つの暗い汚点である。

日本の経済学の様相をヨーロッパとアメリカの人々に付け加えるほど，私はずうずうしくはない。皆さんはそれについて私よりもよく知っている。しかしながら，私は事態をアメリカの状況と比較してもよいでしょう。ちょうどアメリカ人が，そのエネルギーを実際的問題に熱中した19世紀に長いひと仕事をしたように，皆さんは社会的・政治的構造を完全に再編することに努めねばならなかった。そうした時代には，我が科学のような一科学は栄えはしないのである。全世界がまもなく耳にするだろうと私の思う偉大な進化が，1890年以来なされてきている。

VIII

さて，科学的見地から統合される限りにおいて学派と呼ばれうるグループに触れてみよう。私は，Othmar Spannの名を中心とする浪漫主義学派，ベルリンのFriedrich von Gottl - Ottlilienfeldの周りの学派，Franz Oppenheimerの農業社会主義について話したいのですが，時間がありません。そうした学派の全てのうちで最も興味があり価値のある2, 3の用語は，新マルクス主義と呼ばれるものである。

Engelsが死んだ時，マルクス主義がちょうどドイツとロシアの社会主義を克服してしまっていた。フランスではマルクス主義は，社会主義を決して克服しなかったし，イタリアでもそうであった。イタリアではマルクス主義者は，非常に小さいグループを形成した。ドイツではマルクス主義は，実際には社会民主党の公的信条になった。その党の信条になることにより，通常では科学的理論の運命ではないある事態が生じた。信条の変化が，威信の失隊を意味するのだから，政党はその信条を変化できないのである。しかし，変化するのが科学の本質である。そのことこそ，科学的教えと宗教的教えとの間の相違である。

宗教的教えは，永遠の真理であると主張する。しかし，科学はそれを主張できない。科学的真理は，特殊な種類の問題に関連する。かくして，非常に長い間永遠の真理と見なされたIsaac Newton卿の力学は，もはやそうしたことを保持されえなかった。Albert Einsteinの相対性理論が，その基盤(8)を変えてしまった。こうした具合であるのだから，マルクス主義が経済学という科学の永遠の規範であると期待しても無駄である。

それにもかかわらず社会民主党は，マルクス主義を固守する。この哀れな事態が始まって以来ずっと，ヨーロッパに於ける全ゆるマルクス主義政党のうちで最良のサークルが，Marxの信条への忠義と忠誠を必要条件として保持してきている。しかし，我々は科学者としては，Marxについていくことはできない。我々は一般に受け入れられている教義から離れるのだから，我々は非難されるものの不愉快な立場にある。このことが，Eduard Bernsteinに降りかかった。彼は，Marxに一連の反対をした。私は，Bernstein論争をもてはやすものではない。その論争は，皮相的であり，Marx自身より劣っている。しかし，Bernsteinは社民党に最もてこずった。彼は，全ゆる新マルクス主義者とともに，社民党から除名された。なぜなら，彼等は信条に従わなかったからであった。

Marxは，大いに神学者たるの立場にいる。彼は，永遠の輝きを持つ人々が表明するのが普通である例の予言的意見で語るのである。きわめて不運なことに，個人へのこうした試みからは何も生れてこない。事態は，非常に多くの人間をマヒさせてしまっている。Otto Bauer や Rosa Luxemburg(9)やその他の人々は皆んな，例外的な能力の持主であった。彼等の発展は，どんな科学者も耐えることができない足かせにより窒息させられた。というのも，そうした足かせが科学の生命の鼓動を止めるからである。こうした人々全てが，もはや保持されえないものを保持しようとする自からの能力の最上のものと取っ組み合っているのを見るのは，悲劇的な事であった。

IX

学派を去って今や私は，しばらくの間Marxと争った例の新しい経済理論――限界効用――に於いてなされつつあるものに触れたい。近代経済理論――限界分析――は，マルクス主義が狭小化してくる間に拡大してきた。近代社会主義者は，実際的な政治の点で他の経済学者との共通の基盤をますます受け入れてきている。このことは当然のことであり，事実そうである。社会主義者にだけあてはまる真理なんてないのである。それは社会主義者と非社会主義者の両者にあてはまるか，両者にあわないかのいずれかである。そこで，我々は認めたくはないけれども，今日経済学を観察する我々の一般的やり方がますます一様になりつつあるのである。我々は，相違点を強調して類似点をあいまいにしたい。

例えば，ヨーロッパでの経済学の著名な指導者Gustav Cassellの体系を見ていただきたい。彼の体系は何であるか。まず第一に，それは均衡理論であり，考慮に入れられない物価安定策の名をもつ物価安定策に過ぎないのである。もしそれが新しい発展であることを証明しようと努める傾向がないとしても，その仕事は大いに役に立つであろう。我々がその名前を変えても，我々は事態を変えないであろう。経済学者の小グループがあり，そのうちのどれも「新しい」教えを得ようと苦闘しつつあり，厳しいめにあっている。

イギリスではほとんど同じ事が，生じてきている。このことは，私がAlfred Marshallという偉大な名前に表する敬意の一必要条件を意味する。William Stanley Jevonsから独立してMarshallは，Jevonsが彼以前に公表していた大効用原理を発見した。John Maynard Keynes〔Keynes卿〕(5)は，読んで楽しい本であるMarshall伝〔『Alfred Marshall回想録』，1925年〕(5)でこのことを語っている。Marshallが自分の古典的先行者に対して大いに忠実であることを見たり，彼が不明僚な名前にさえ価値をわり当てるためになした用心を見ることは，非常に興味のあることである。

皆さんが知るのに重要である偉大な真理を立証せんがために，私は次の事を述べよう。今日経済理論には学派が存在せず，表面に現われるよりも少ししか相違がないのである。もしも皆さんがMarshallの読み方を知れば，それが限界効用であり，その外のものではないことを知るでしょう。皆さんは，費用原理があると言うかも知れない。然り。だが，それも又，限界効用理論である。Marshallが費用と効用を一丁のハサミの両刃にたとえるなら，答えは両刃が同じ材料，効用の両面から作られているということである。費用を取り扱うときにMarshallは，効用が費用とは関係がないということ，費用がRichardoの明らかにしようと努めていた稀少費用であるということ，を主張しようと試みた。Marshallは失敗した。

Marshallがイギリスにとって重要であると同じように，スウェーデンにとって重要である一人の経済学者がいた。しかし，彼はMarshallの欠点の全てから免れていた。Knut Wicksellは，19世紀の末から20世紀の始めにかけての最も有能で能力ある独創的な人物の一人である。彼の成果は，Marshallのものとほとんど同じであった。アメリカでも，John Bates Clarkの学徒であるClark経済学者がいる。かくして，多くの学派があるように見えるものは，全ゆる有能な経済学者の間では同じ教えであることがわかる。経済学についてのこうした思考法は，どうなってきているか。

限界効用分析は，後でLéon WalrasやJevonsやその他の人々によって発展された。限界効用理論それ自体が消滅し，なおも効用に基づく均衡理論が現われるまで，限界効用分析は洗練された。この点ではJevonsよりはるかに優れたFriedrich von Wieserによって，限界効用分析が既に述べられていた。達成されたものは，決して完全ではないということがわかった。より洗練された体系は，晩年に経済学に取り掛かった一技師Walrasによって限界効用分析に基づいてうち立てられた。彼はその理論をあちこちで変え，それを一層エレガントにした。今や我々は実際，非常に素晴らしい分析体系を持っているのである。

多くのアメリカの経済学者が，今や理論を統計的データで充たそうと努めていることは，興味ある事実である。このことは，前の世代には不可能だと思われた。以前の経済学者は，経済学に於けるどんな理論も数字で示されるようになるのは不可能だと見なした。今や我々は，このことをうまく達成しつつあるのである。それは経済科学に於いて新しい時代を意味するであろう。というのは，もしも経済学者が結果を計算できるなら，理論がまったく違った権威を有するだろうからである。〔これを執筆した1ヵ月前にSchumpeterは，オハイオのクリーヴランドでのアメリカ経済学会の大会で大会議長を務めた。そしてこの大会は，計量経済学会を設立した。〕(5)

X

不幸にして我々は現在でもなお，数字で表わされる一経済科学の目標どころの話しではない。その理由は，次の事によるのである。すなわち，物理学者の諸事実はある既知の事情の下で生み出されうるけれども，我が科学の諸事実は同じやり方では決して繰り返されない事情の下で我々に与えられるからである。換言すれば，物理的データは確率の基本的法則に支配されている。こうしたデータは，観察の誤りに従ってのみ規準から逸れるであろう。かくして，二つの惑星間の距離を測る時には，観察の誤りから生れるわずかに異なった結果が，二人又はそれより多い観察者によって得られるかも知れないであろう。このことは，測定の数学的平均値をとることによって正されるのである。

しかしながら，我が科学ではデータ自身が変化される。測定されるデータも変化する。我々の事実を時系列に置くことは，経済学では普通のことである。一つの精密科学，すなわち数学で表わされる一科学としての経済学に於いて最高の困難のうちで大問題なのは，我々の理論的法則を充たすだろう時系列を数字から蒸留することにある。

このことは，自然諸科学では既知の一問題でもある。皆さんが大海の波を観察すれば，それが不規則であることを見い出すでしょう。例えば，月の引力――潮の満干――による大海のうねりがあり，風による小さなさざ波がある。もしも皆さんが波長を測定しようとすれば，皆さんは一種類の波以外には全てを除去しなければならないだろう。しかし，この問題は経済科学の重要な部分であるほどには自然諸科学の重要な部分ではない。時々自然科学で起こることは，常に経済学で起こるのである。

我々は今や，経済学で第一歩が見えるに過ぎない。将来の世代は，恐らく別の数学によって全力をつくさねばならないでしょう。この数学は，時系列が非常に小さな役割を演じる自然諸科学に含まれるものである。我々のケースは，別である。我々は，別の数学的技術を欲する。現在我々は，あちこちでその始まりを見ることができる。歴史や統計学や理論やの領域間にある障害は，無くなりつつあり，こうした領域は1つに併合されつつある。企業経営が，簿記と費用計算をもたらす。こうした計算は，どうなりつつあるか。進歩は，しばしば信じられるよりもはるかに大きかったのである。

銀行業の領域では, Keynes氏の書物で念入りに明瞭に述べられているように, 大きな改善が理論的道具で行われてきている。Keynesは, その考えではきわめて厳密である。彼は世界には貨幣理論を理解する者は5人といない, とかつて私に語った。彼がそれを私に言った時, 私は彼がそうした人のうちに私を含めていたと思う。他の3人が誰であるか, 私は知らない。とにかく, 彼の書物〔『貨幣論』1930年〕(5)は, 貨幣理論のMarshall型を非常に良く表したものである。そこに皆さんは, 材料の改善された集まりの手の届くところにもたらされる統計的銀行業問題と関係する問題を見い出すでしょう。

こうした問題を集めるのが, どれほど困難であるかの一例を挙げてみましょう。皆さんは、多くのいろんな貨幣理論を伝え聞いてきている。そのうちの一つは正しいにちがいないし, その他のものは間違いにちがいない。貨幣理論の重点でどこが正しくどこが間違いかを, 我々はどのようにして言うことができるでしょうか。我々が数量説に与えうる意味は, 我々の持っている統計学に依存するのである。もしも私が例えば所得統計を持てば, 理論は明確な意味を帯びるであろう。実際には, 私は所得データを持っていない。が, 私はいくつかの国々にとって法定貨幣量についての数字を必ず持っている。そこで私は, 通貨的見地から一層都合よく見られる理論を定義でき築き上げることができるのである。

しばしばデータというものは, 理論が正しいか間違いかではなく, 理論の利用と解釈を決定するポイントなのである。国際貿易論は, 最近大いに進歩してきている。成果は, 未だ公表されていない。そうでなければ捨てられてしまっている労働価値で作用する古い古典的理論に, 我々がいかに長くこの特殊な領域で固守してきたか, 驚くべきことである。このことは, スウェーデンのBertil Ohlinとヴィーンの Gottfried Haberlerのような人々の仕事によって間もなく変化させられるはずである。統計学にすがるのに適した理論概念を導入しようとするこの傾向は, とても興味のあるものである。そうした道具のうちで最も興味あるものは, Taussig学徒の交換貿易体系である。私は, 皆さんにTaussig『国際貿易』〔1927年〕(4)を強く推薦しうる。

XI

富の分配と移転の不平等に関連する限り社会問題は, Pigouの著作中に記念碑的基盤を得てきている〔『厚生経済学』1920年, 1929年。〕(5)それにしても, その科学的方法は全く新しく, それには欠点も見られるかも知れない。理想として社会問題を論議することが, いつかできるかも知れない。が, 現実にまごまごする限り社会問題は, 例えば社会主義がするように, 行動行程に任せる分析をうけつけないのである。

皆さんにお話したように, 我が科学は政治的目的と関係がないのである。経済学の道具や論争や諸事実を政治的判断にあてはめることによって諸現象を説明することは, こうした判断に対して判断自体を論議するよりもはるかに良い助けを与える。それに経済学の道具は, 進歩しつつある。私は, 我々が政治家たるべきでないとは言わない。が, 皆さんが戦うつもりなら, よく準備されねばならない。しかしながら, 皆さんが科学的仕事をしようとする限り, それを科学的精神でやっていただきたい。その時には皆さんは, 自分の理想のために努力しつつあるでしょう。というのは, いかなる理想も科学的真理との関係なしには生きられえないからです。

我々の全ゆる社会的見渡しは, 我々が所得と富の分配の諸事実を知ることによってか知らないことによって影響される。19世紀の人々が何も知らなかったように, 皆さんがこの分配について何も知らないなら, 皆さんは上流階級を測りしれない富を持っているものと見なすでしょう。富を生産した大衆は, 分配の無知な知識に応じて富を少ししかもたず極貧に苦しむのであった。こうしたことは, 事実の問題であるとともに科学的方法の問題でもある。興味ある人は誰であれ, こうした二つの武器を獲得すべきである。

最後に我々は, 専門化した理論――景気循環理論――の最も近代的なものと接触を保つべきである。景気循環理論家は, 科学的重要性の統計的事実を続々と浴びせる。こうしたデータは, 予見の試みや景気循環の説明から成るのでなく, 循環理論によって集められ示される諸事実である。循環の研究は, 循環自体の直接の問題を越えて重要である。それは経済学の全ゆる局面についてうまく考える立場にある急激な変化を引き起こすのに, 遅かれ早かれ役立つかも知れない。

それから趨勢の研究がある。もちろん, ここでは, 統計的立場からの研究は非常に困難である。我々は, 既にいくつかの進歩をとげてきた。こうした検討に対するいくつかの重要な貢献は, 我々が度外視すべきでない一人の若い科学者――ノールウェー人のRagnar Frisch――による。〔Ragnar Frischは, 1969年経済学ノーベル賞の第一回受賞者であった。〕(5)

私が進めば進むほどますます, 道が広がっていく。しかし, もちろん, 例えばこのような一つの議論上の唯一の目的は, いくつかの関心点をあちこちと暗示し, その他のことを皆さんに任せることに過ぎないのである。(「法経論叢」第8巻第1号, 1990年12月20日. pp.11-34より転載)

注

(1) Joseph Schumpeter, Recent Developments of Political Economy (1931) Note by Loring Allen. Kobe University Economic Review. No. 28, 1982. pp.2-15.

(2) 原文はsister scienceである。これは社会学等を指す。

(3) Joseph Schumpeter, op.cit. , p.6. ここではshippingとなっている。

(4) Ibid. , p.6. ここではprotectionとある。

(5) 〔〕内はL. アレンの編注。

(6) Ibid. , p.14. ここではTaussingとある。正しくは, シュンペーターがアメリカのMarshallと呼んだFrank William Taussig (1859―1940) である。

(7) Ibid. , p.10. ここではstatiaticiansとあり, statisticiansの誤り。

(8) Ibid. , p.11ここでのgoundは, groundの誤り。

(9) Ibid. , p.11. ここではLuxembourgとある。

「『利子の理論』で蘊蓄を吐露す　十日、第三日の講演」

次いで十日はシユムペーターの最も得意とする「利子の理論」と題する最後の講演が三時より五時まであり、ボエームバヴエルクに至るまでの利子学説をべつ見し、利子現実の現象を詳細に観察して後、博士自身の理論を次の如く展開した

利子は投下資本の再生産以上の余剰として、賃金所得や地代所得の成立とは全然異つた根拠を持たねばならない。労働者や地主にありて純粋所得として現れる所のものは企業者にあつて直に生産費として現れるものであるから、従つて賃銀や地代の成立は生産要素の側から説明すべきものである。だが資本にあつては之れと異なる。使用された資本も亦生産費の埒内に現れるけれども、それは資本家にとつて未だ決して純粋所得を意味するものではない。それであるから利子所得は生産要素たる資本の側から説明すべきものではなくて、吾々は利子の独自の成立原因をば、しかも反対の側から、即ち利子現物の考察から探求しなければならない。利子はプレミアムであり、従つて投下資本の価値以上に生ずる所の余剰でなければならない。併し費用価値以上の持続的な価値余剰は一方には競争に依り、他方には一般的価値原則即ち主として生産的寄与の帰属の原則によつて、不可能にされる。それ故に投下資本の価値以上の余剰は偏へにこの価値余剰の消失を惹起す所の右の二つの条件の成立が妨げられる所に於いて生じなければならない。かゝる原理は経済的発展のうちに見出すことが出来る。経済的発履は生産過程の改革新しき結合に依つてプレミアムを生ぜしめ、このプレミアムを消失し得るためには競争がこれを捉へようと努めねばならず、且つ新しい収益基礎に基く生産財の価値変更が行はれるためには事実を必要とするそれ故にこのプレミアムは時日と経済的発展の二要素の結合に帰せらるべきのである(「神戸商大新聞」第12号, 昭和6年2月15日号 第1面より転載)

B.　年譜

1883年　毛織物工場主の父（Josef Alois Karl Schumpeter）とイグラウの有名な医者の出の母（Johanna Margürite Grüner）の長男として、オーストリア・ハンガリー帝国のメーレン州トリーシュで生まれる（2月8日）。

1889年　父の死（狩猟事故）から2年余りして、母とグラーツに移り住む（10月8日）。Klosterwiesgasse21の賃貸アパート、その後Mozartgasse8の4階建アパート最上階から、フォルクスシューレに通う。初めてオペラを見、シンフォニーを聴く。

1893年　フォルクスシューレを4年して母とヴィーンに移り、Doblhofgasse3のアパートに住む（9月6日）。
母が、陸軍中将Sigismund von Kelerと結婚し（9月9日）、ヴィーンの貴族のためのテレジアヌムに通う。そのモットーは、「ほんの少しばかりおばかさんであることが、高尚である」。

1901年　テレジアヌムを優等卒業。ヴィーン大学法・国家学部に入学。法学、政治学の必修科目、統計学、数学の講義・演習に出る。マイアーの財政学ゼミ、その後フィリポヴィッヒ、ボェーム、ヴィーザーのゼミに参加する。

1906年　経済学における数学の貢献を論ずる「理論経済学における数学的方法に関して」の論文発表。
ヴィーン大学法学士（2月16日）、同法学博士を授与される（12月20日）。
両親離婚（7月3日）
夏学期にはベルリン大学のシュモラーの国家学ゼミに加わり、秋にはイギリスのロンドン・スクール・オブ・エコノミックスの研究生となり、大英博物館で読書ノートをとる。マーシャルやエッジワースに会う。

1907年　Gladys Ricarde Seaver（英国教会の娘ですてきな美人）と結婚（11月5日）。
カイロのイタリア人法律事務所で法律実習する。エジプトの国際混合裁判所で働く。

1908年　処女作『理論的国民経済学の本質と主要内容』を刊行する。
ヴィーン大学の政治経済学の講師資格請求、ハビリタチオン論文が承認される（12月）。

1909年　最初の英語論文「社会的価値の概念に関して」を発表する。
ヴィーン大学の政治経済学の私講師となる(3月16日）。オーストリア・ハンガリー帝国の最年少経済学者。
チェルノヴィッツ大学の政治経済学の員外教授（10月4日）となり、アラビアンナイトと見まがうばかりの法外な活躍をする。

1911年　『理論的国民経済学の本質と主要内容』の続編又は反駁としての第2作『経済発展の理論』を出版する。
グラーツ大学の政治経済学の正教授となる（11月13日）。オーストリア・ハンガリー帝国の最年少正教授としてグラーツのParkstraße17に住む。

1912年　グラーツ大学で学生による講義ボイコット（10月14日～11月15日）が生じる。

1913年　第1回オーストリア交換教授として、秋から翌年春までニュー・ヨークのコロンビア大学で講義する。
タウシング、フィッシャー、ミッチェル等の経済学者と会う。
コロンビア大学名誉文学博士を授与される（12月1日）。

1914年　経済学の歴史に関する論稿「学説史と方法史の諸段階」を出す。

1916—17年　グラーツ大学法学部長となる。
政治的文書で、オーストリア・ハンガリー帝国の維持、戦争と講和について画策する。

1918年　「租税国家の危機」を講演する（5月）
「社会主義の時が未だ来ていない。それにもかかわらず、その時は来るだろう」。

前年からヴィーンの帝国商務省の戦時・過渡経済のための総委員会の共同研究者となる。

1919年 ドイツ社会化委員会に参加する(1-2月)。

カール・レナー内閣の大蔵大臣に就任する(3月15日)が、インフレの阻止と健全予算を目ざす財政安定のための財政プランが挫折して蔵相を辞任する(10月15日)。

1920年 グラーツ大学で講義を再開する(夏学期)。

Gladysと正式離婚する。

1921年 グラーツ大学の講座解任にサインし(10月)、グラーツ大学の教授を辞任し、ヴィーン9区のStrudelhofgasse17に移り住む。大部分の時間は母とDoblhofgasseの大きなアパートで過ごす。母は暗やみの中でショパンのポロネーズをピアノで弾いている。

ビーダーマン銀行の頭取(7月23日)となる。

1924年 オーストリアの経済危機で、ビーダーマン銀行も倒産し、多額の負債をかかえて同銀行頭取を辞任する(9月11日)。

退職手当10万シリングを受け取るも、人生最悪の年となる。

1925年 ボン大学の経済社会科学の正教授として(10月15日)、財政学を担当する。ライン川を見渡す大学近くのCoblenzerstraße39の大きな家に住む。

「教授職で生活を立てるや否や、科学にもどることが、常に私の意図でした」。

アニー・ライジンガー(母の住むアパートの管理人で雑貨商の娘)と結婚式をあげ(11月5日)、シュンピー、ヨシと呼ばれ、カトリックからルター派に改宗する。

1926年 マミーと呼んだ母が、午後4時に65才で動脈硬化で死亡する。最大の悲劇となる。

アニーが、産褥で長男「ヨーゼフ・シュンペーター」とともに死亡し(8月3日)、妻・子・母の三重の災難に会う。「妻よ、母よ、私の上にあらせ給え」と私的日記に記す。アニーの日記を発見し、模写し始める。

「グスタフ・フォン・シュモラーと今日の諸問題」を書き、広範な基盤に立つ社会経済学を展開する。

1927年 “Geld und Währung”に関する本に植民地奴隷のごとく取り組む。

ミアと呼ばれる秘書兼家政婦Mia Stöckelと知り合う。

秋から翌年春にかけてハーヴァード大学経済学部の客員教授となる。

1928年 「資本主義の不安定性」という雑誌論文で、資本主義は長期間にわたって生き残れず、社会主義にとってかわられると主張する。

1929年 ベルリンのプロイセン文部省法律研究改革委員会会議の共同研究者として、「法律家の国民経済的研究に関する報告」をする(4月29日)

1930年 9月から年末までハーヴァード大学経済学部の客員教授となり、タウシッグ邸宅のScott Street2に住む。

ケインズの「貨幣論」を「リカードの力業」とし、「新しいものは何もない」とみなす。

クリーヴランドのアメリカ経済学会に出席し、フリッシュやフィッシャーとともに計量経済学会を設立する(12月29日)。

1931年 サンフランシスコを立って(1月10日)、ドイツへの帰国途中に日本を訪れ、3週間滞在する。日本をエンジョイする。

1932年 ボン大学の国家科学学部で、「わが科学はどこから来てどこへ行こうとしているのか」という訣別講演をする(6月20日)。

秋にドイツを去って、ハーヴァード大学へ移る。「ドイツを去って、ハーヴァードへの招聘を受け入れた個人的動機は、ヒトラーの権力掌握を切迫したものと考えなかったからである。科学の仕事という動機が、それ以上に重要であった。」

1933年 不況の終了に役立つ経済プログラムの作成にかかわる。

ドイツのユダヤ人亡命者の救済組織作りに尽力する。
3ヵ月の間ヨーロッパに滞在し、ミアと過ごす(5月29日から9月末まで)

1934年 『経済発展の理論』(1926年)の改訂英訳版を出版する。
6月から9月にかけてミアといっしょにレンタカーで、フランスの大聖堂を見物し、ニースなどのフランス各地とイタリアを旅し、ドイツの温泉につかり、テニスやピクニックをして過ごす。
ヘンリーを主人公とする小説「霧の中の船」を執筆する。

1935年 コロンビア特別区のワシントンで「資本主義は、生き延びうるか」を講演する。
タウシッグが75才で退職したのを受けて、ハーヴァード大学で経済理論の大学院講義(EC-11)をする。
夏休暇は、ヨーロッパに滞在して過ごす。

1936年 ケインズ・ゼミに参加したロバート・ブライスが、ハーヴァードを訪れ、ケインズの『一般理論』を紹介したのに対し激論を闘わす(3月7日)。
現代経済学の量的方法を徹底点検し改善するために、「経済学の理論的用具」という題でN. Georgescu-Roegenと共同研究するプランを立てる。
毎年の何か月にわたるヨーロッパ旅行を取り止める。
2、3の演劇と小説が頭にわく(10月19日)。

1937年 『経済発展の理論』日本語訳が出版される。
春にはウィルソンの数理経済学の講義にクラス出席する。
エリザベス・ブーディ・フィルスキー(中背で細身の、茶色の毛と薄茶の目)と結婚する(8月6日)。ケンブリッジのAsh Street15に住む。

1938年 計量経済学会の副会長となる。
6月にケンブリッジのAcacia Street7に移り、そこが終の住処となる。
ソフィア大学名誉哲学博士(12月28日)を授与される。

1939年 『景気循環』全2巻を出版する。その副題は、「資本主義的過程の理論的、歴史的、統計的分析」となっていて、『経済発展の理論』の続編を意図したものである。
アメリカ合衆国の国籍を得る(4月3日)。
社会諸科学における合理性に関するセミナー(10月から翌年4月)を10回程開く。

1940年 計量経済学会会長につく(12月31日)。
亡き母とアニーを「ハーゼン」と呼んで私的神へと昇華させる。自らも死に取りつかれつつある。

1941年 ボストンのローウエル研究所で全8回の公開講義をする。この講義をもとにエリザベスと共著で「わが時代の経済的解釈」という本を出版する計画であった。

1942年 『資本主義・社会主義・民主主義』の刊行。これは、『景気循環』を補完し、その続編となる最も有名なベストセラーとなる。
人生における主要な関心は、「女性—芸術—スポーツ—科学—政治—旅行—お金」である、と私的日記に記す(6月10日)。

1943年 経済思想の歴史ではなく、科学としての経済学の歴史、経済理論の歴史を書きつつある。
「生きることは愛することであり、悩むことである。生きることは闘うことであり、死ぬことでもある」というアフォリズムを残す。

1944年 子供がいないので、アイリッシュ=セッターの愛犬ペーターを飼う(夏)。
ハーヴァードで社会主義の経済学と呼ばれる新たなコースを教える。

1945年 戦時期と同様に、上級経済理論、景気循環、社会主義の経済学、経済思想史を講義する。

1946年 ハーヴァード大学経済学部で、資本主義と社会主義に関する討論会を開く。

「資本主義が死にたえている」のは、「ガン」(スウィージー)ではなく、「精神病」からだと主張する。
「経済学はますます良くなってきているが、経済学者はますます悪くなってきている。」

1947年 ほとんど毎日、夕食前に1~3杯のアルコールを飲み、就眠前に探偵小説や歴史や自伝物や軽い読み物を読む。

1948年 メキシコ・シティの大学で、2つの英語講演と10の講義を行なう(1月)。
「理論的構成を手がかりとして、現実を記述するよりも現実を理解する」ことが必要だと強調する。
アーサー・H・コールと企業者史研究調査センターを設立する。
オハイオのクリーヴランドのアメリカ経済学会で会長に選ばれる(12月30日)。
経済学におけるイデオロギーの役割について、「科学とイデオロギー」という有名な会長講演をする。

1949年 体重の増加と高血圧に悩む。
創設の国際経済学会の初代会長に選出される(7月)。
ニュー・ヨークのアメリカ経済学会の年次大会に、「社会主義への前進」というペーパーを提出する。

1950年 コネティカット州のタコニックの別荘ウィンディー・ヒルで睡眠中に、重い発作を起こし、脳出血で早朝死亡する(1月8日)。

1954年 エリザベスの編集による遺稿の『経済分析の歴史』が出版される。アメリカ合衆国時代の第3の記念碑的労作で、全1巻1260ページに達する。

Ⅳ　執筆者名索引

執筆者名索引

【あ】

【い】

【う】

【え】

【お】

【か】

【き】

【く】

【け】

【こ】

【さ】

【し】

【す】

【せ】

【そ】

【た】

【ち】

【つ】

【て】

【と】

【ひ】

【ふ】

【へ】

【ほ】

【ま】

【 み 】

【 む 】

【 め 】

【 も 】

【 や 】

【ゆ】

【よ】

【ら】

【り】

【れ】

【ろ】

【わ】

【 ABC 】

あとがき

シュンペーター生誕100年の余燼が覚めやらぬ1991年に私は、わが国で初めて本格的なシュンペーターに関する関係文献目録を、アルファベットの著者名順にして公表した（「Josef Alois Julius Schumpeter 関係文献目録」(1991年))。1993年頃にそれに基づく新たな文献目録の作成を約束していたが、それ以後シュンペーター手書き草稿類の整理と解読に時間をとられ、その作業は遅々として進展せず今日に至った。その間シュンペーターへの関心もその研究も、多面的に飛躍的に向上した。そこで、取り敢えず生誕110年間にわが国でシュンペーターに関して書かれたり、言及されたり、発行された諸資料を収集し、整理し、目録化した。

この目録作成作業は、東畑文庫の資料を利用することから始まった。それに関して東畑精一の家族（隆介、朝子)、古谷友子、東畑家の遠縁の浦城晋一から大量の関係資料を提供していただいた。

シュンペーターを直接知る安井琢磨、板垣與一、都留重人からは、エレガントで勢力的なシュンペーター像を拝聴できた。特に都留からは、本目録の内容と進展を絶えず温かく見守っていただいた。

柏祐賢、吉田昇三、熊谷尚夫、大野忠男、水田洋、杉山忠平、岩崎秀二、辻村江太郎、福岡正夫、浜崎正規、永友育雄、早坂忠、岩野茂道、塩野谷祐一、蓑谷千凰彦、保住敏彦、金指基、東條隆進、八木紀一郎、賀村進一、吉尾博和からは、自らの関係資料の教示をいただいた。

日本におけるシュンペーター写真の所在については、伊東光晴のアドヴァイスを得た。

関連資料の検索・収集については、主に以下の関係機関を利用し協力を得た。

愛知学院大学図書館、名古屋大学中央図書館、名古屋大学経済学部図書室、東京大学総合図書館、東京大学経済学部図書室、国会図書館、一橋大学附属図書館、京都大学経済学部図書室、三重大学附属図書館、三重県立図書館、東畑記念館。

本目録の性質上、遺漏なしとしないので関係各位の教示を期待する。

最後に、厳しい時間的制約の下で、このような書誌の形に巧みに編集していただいた編集局の比良雅治に、心から謝意を表します。

米川　紀生（よねかわ・のりお）
1940年　三重県に生まれる
1970年　一橋大学大学院博士課程修了
1974年　新潟大学助教授
1986年～2004年　三重大学教授
現在、三重大学名誉教授　国際シュンペーター研究家
論文：「協調会の成立過程」1979年
「協調会の労働組合論」1979年
「Joseph Alois Schumpeter経済学の基盤」1986年
「新たに発見されたJ.A.Schumpeter自筆草稿『資本主義・社会主義・民主主義』」1987年
「大蔵大臣としてのJoseph A.Schumpeterの理論と行動」1989年
「J.A.Schumpeter『資本主義・社会主義・民主主義』の準備的考察」1990年
「増補　Joseph Alois Schumpeter関係文献目録」1997年
その他、シュンペーター関係多数。

人物書誌大系39
シュンペーター

2008年7月25日　第1刷発行

編　者／米川紀生
発行者／大高利夫
発行所／日外アソシエーツ株式会社
〒143-8550 東京都大田区大森北1-23-8 第3下川ビル
電話(03)3763-5241(代表)　FAX(03)3764-0845
URL http://www.nichigai.co.jp/
発売元／株式会社紀伊國屋書店
〒163-8636 東京都新宿区新宿3-17-7
電話(03)3354-0131(代表)
ホールセール部(営業)　電話(03)6910-0519

電算漢字処理／日外アソシエーツ株式会社
印刷・製本／株式会社平河工業社

《中性紙H-三菱書籍用紙イエロー使用》
ISBN978-4-8169-2121-6
Printed in Japan, 2008

『人物書誌大系』

刊行のことば

歴史を動かし変革する原動力としての人間、その個々の問題を抜きにしては、真の歴史はあり得ない。そこに、伝記・評伝という人物研究の方法が一つの分野をなし、多くの人々の関心をよぶ所以がある。

われわれが、特定の人物についての研究に着手しようとする際の手がかりは、対象人物の詳細な年譜・著作目録であり、次に参考文献であろう。この基礎資料によって、その生涯をたどることにより、はじめてその人物の輪郭を把握することが可能になる。

しかし、これら個人書誌といわれる資料は、研究者の地道な努力・調査によりまとめられてはいるものの、単行書として刊行されているものはごく一部である。多くは図書の巻末、雑誌・紀要の中、あるいは私家版などさまざまな形で発表されており、それらを包括的に把え探索することが困難な状況にある。

本シリーズ刊行の目的は、人文科学・社会科学・自然科学のあらゆる分野における個人書誌編纂の成果を公にすることであり、それをつうじ、より多様な人物研究の発展をうながすことにある。この計画の遂行は長期間にわたるであろうが、個人単位にまとめ逐次発行し集大成することにより、多くの人々にとって、有用なツールとして利用されることを念願する次第である。

1981年4月

日外アソシエーツ